CENTER STAGE 2

Express Yourself in English

Lynn Bonesteel   Samuela Eckstut-Didier

Series Consultants

MaryAnn Florez

Sharon Seymour

PEARSON
Longman

D0139238

Center Stage 2: Express Yourself in English

Pearson Education, 10 Bank Street, White Plains, NY 10606

Staff credits: The people who made up the *Center Stage 2* team, representing editorial, production, design, and manufacturing, are Elizabeth Carlson, Tracey Cataldo, Dave Dickey, Laura Le Dréan, Gabriela Moya, Robert Ruvo, Julie Schmidt, and Kim Steiner

Photo Credits: p. 5 (top left) Leland Bobbe/Corbis; (top right) LWA-Dann Tardif/zefa/Corbis; (bottom left) Medio Images/Getty Images; (bottom right) Royalty-Free/Corbis; **p. 7** Royalty-Free/Corbis; **p. 10** Royalty-Free/Corbis; **p.11** Masterfile/Digital Vision/Fotosearch; **p. 12** Alamy Limited; **p. 17** (left) Anwar Hussein/Contributor/Getty Images; (middle) Lynn Goldsmith/Corbis; (right) 2000 Twentieth Century Fox Film Corporation-All Rights Reserved © 2000 Fox Broadcasting/FotofestNYC; **p. 21** Michael Prince/Corbis; **p. 22** Rufus F. Folkks/Corbis; **p. 33** Stone/David Sacks/Getty Images; **p. 35** Will & Deni McIntyre/Corbis; **p. 36** Royalty-Free/Corbis; **p. 42** (left) Alaska Stock LLC/Alamy; (middle) Free Agents Limited/Corbis; (right) Sylvain Grandadam/Getty Images; **p. 43** Ed Kashi/Corbis; **p. 44** (top left) Royalty-Free/Corbis/Fotosearch; (top right) Royalty-Free/Corbis; (bottom left) Kelly-Mooney Photography/Corbis; (bottom right) Macduff Everton/Corbis; p. 45 Design Pics Royalty Free/Fotosearch; **p. 46** Royalty-Free/Corbis; **p.47** (left) Chad Slattery/Getty Images; (right) image 100/Alamy; **p. 54** Royalty-Free/Corbis; **p. 57** Index Stock Imagery, Inc.; **p. 61** Photodisc Red/Ryan McVay/Getty Images; **p. 62** (top) Robert Holmes/Corbis; (bottom) Richard Cummins/Corbis; **p. 71** Getty Images-Stockbyte; **p. 72** Grace/zefa/Corbis; **p. 73** (top left) AFP/Staff/Getty Images; (top middle) Nicklaham/Staff/Getty Images; (top right) AFP/Staff/Getty Images; (bottom left) Chris Trotman/NewSport/Corbis; (bottom middle) Paul Hanna/Reuters/Corbis; (bottom right) Alessandro Bianchi/Reuters/Corbis; **p. 83** Tom Stewart/Corbis; **p. 86** (first) Sean Justice/Getty Images; (second) Stock Image Pixland/Alamy; (third) Comstock Images/Alamy; (fourth) Ron Chapple/Getty Images; **p. 87** bildagentur-online.com/th-foto/Alamy; **p. 91** Royalty-Free/Corbis; **p. 96** Artiga Photo/Corbis; **p. 97** (top left) Penny Tweedie/Getty Images; (top right) Jeff Greenberg/Alamy; (bottom left) Sylvain Grandadam/Getty Images; (bottom right) Ryan McVay/Getty Images; **p. 104** Photo Edit, Inc.; **p. 105** Digital Vision/Getty Images; **p. 107** Stephanie Maze/Corbis; **p. 109** Andersen Ross/Photodisc Red/Getty Images; **p. 111** Jim Arbogast/Getty Images; **p. 117** Royalty-Free Corbis; **p. 121** Thomas Northcut/Getty Images; **p. 123** (top left) Royalty-Free/Corbis; (top right) Creatas ESD/Fotosearch; (bottom left) Randy Faris/Corbis; (bottom right) Getty Images-Stockbyte; **p. 124** David Young Wolff/Photo Edit; **p. 128** Ray Kachatorian/Getty Images; **p. 129** Royalty-Free/Corbis; **p. 130** Mitch Hrdlicka/Getty Images; **p. 131** (left) Albeiro Lopera Reuters/Corbis; (right) Royalty-Free/Corbis; **p. 132** Peter Dazeley/The Image Bank/Getty Images; **p. 133** Royalty-Free/Corbis; **p. 134** Zubin Shroff/Stone/Getty Images; **p. 136** Stephen Oliver/Dorling Kindersley Media Library; **p. 140** Adam Crowley/Getty Images; **p. 146** ColorBlind Images/Getty Images; **p. 147** Dynamic Graphics Group/Alamy; **p. 148** Reed Kaestner/Corbis; **p. 155** (first) George Doyle/Getty Images; (second) Royalty-Free/Corbis; **p. 160** Royalty-Free/Corbis; **p. 171** Robert Harding Picture Library Ltd./Alamy; **p. 179** Digital Vision/Getty Images; **p. 181** Holly Harris/Getty Images; **p. 182** Steve Klaver/Star Ledger/Corbis; **p. 183** Brooks Kraft Corbis; **p. 184** (top) Robert Landau/Corbis; (bottom) Bettmann/Corbis; **p. 185** San Francisco Museum of Modern Art/Pearson Asset Library; **p. 186** Courtesy of Lynn Bonesteel; **p. 192** Ariel Skelley/Corbis; **p. 194** Don Mason/Corbis; **p. 195** (top) Royalty-Free Corbis; (bottom) Royalty-Free/Corbis; **p. 196** Charles & Josette Lenars/Corbis; **p. 197** BrandX Pictures/Alamy; **p. 198** (second) George Hall/Corbis; (fourth) Jennie Woodcock/ Reflections Photolibrary/Corbis; **p. 199** Catherine Karnow/Corbis; **p. 210** Royalty Free/Corbis; **p.220** Stuart Dee/Getty Images; **p. 221** Anthony Bolante/Reuters/Corbis; **p. 222** (top) Sam Sargent/Getty Images; (bottom) Bob Rowan/Progressive Image/Corbis; **p. 223** Annie Belt/Corbis; **p. 229** (top) David Vintiner/zefa/Corbis; (bottom) LWA Stephen Welstead/Corbis; **p. 233** Denis Scott/Corbis; **p. 235** Kevin Cooley/Getty Images; **p. 236** Fabio Cardoso/zefa/Corbis; **p. 240** Royalty-Free/Corbis; **p. 247** Royalty-Free/Corbis.

Text composition: 101 Studio / Aphik

Text font: 12.5 Minion

Illustrations: A Corazón Abierto (Marcela Gómez), Steve Attoe, Kenneth Batelman, Keith Batcheller, Precision Graphics, Marty Harris, Alan King, Luis Montiel, Francisco Morales, Mari Rodríguez, Roberto Sadí, John Schreiner, Gary Torrisi, Cam Wilson

Library of Congress Cataloging-in-Publication Data

Frankel, Irene.
Center Stage.—1st ed.
    p. cm.
    Contents: 1. Beginning / Irene Frankel — 2. High beginning / Lynn
Bonesteel and Samuela Eckstut — 3. Intermediate / Lynn Bonesteel and
Samuela Eckstut — 4. High imtermediate / Lynn Bonesteel and Samuela Eckstut.
    ISBN 0-13-170881-3 (student book : bk. 1 : alk. paper) — ISBN
0-13-187490-X (student book : bk. 2 : alk. paper) — ISBN 0-13-194778-8 (student book : bk. 3 : alk. paper) —
ISBN 0-13-194784-2 (student book : bk. 4 : alk. paper) 1. English language--Textbooks for foreign speakers. 2. English
language—Grammar—Problems, exercises, etc. 3. Vocabulary
—Problems, exercises, etc. 4. Life skills—United States.   I. Bonesteel,
Lynn. II. Eckstut-Didier, Samuela. III. Title. PE1128.F67425 2007
428.2'4—dc22

2006014957

ISBN: 0-13-187490-X

Printed in the United States of America
1 2 3 4 5 6 7 8 9 10-QWD-11 10 09 08 07 06

Acknowledgments

We would like to thank everyone at Pearson Longman for the time and effort they have put into seeing this project through. Specifically, we would like to thank our editors, Andrea Bryant, Julie Schmidt, and Kim Steiner, for their attention to detail and their insights; to Rhea Banker, for her considerable contributions to the design and visual appeal of the series, and to Laura Le Dréan, for her commitment to every phase of this complex project. Most importantly, we are grateful to Claudia and Robert for their support and encouragement and for always reminding us of the other worlds out there.

**Lynn Bonesteel and Sammi Eckstut-Didier,
authors of Student Books 2, 3, and 4**

The publisher would like to extend special thanks to MaryAnn Florez and Sharon Seymour, our Series Consultants, and to the following individuals who reviewed the *Center Stage* program and whose comments were instrumental in shaping this series.

Ruth Afifi, Fresno Adult School, Fresno, CA; **Janet L. Barker**, Tarrant Community College, Fort Worth, TX; **Sarah Barnhardt**, Community College of Baltimore County, Baltimore, MD; **Janet Bryant**, Truman College, Chicago, IL; **Rachel Burns**, New England School of English, Cambridge, MA; **Debby Cargill**, Prince William County Public Schools, Manassas, VA; **Veronique Colas**, Los Angeles Technology Center, Los Angeles, CA; **Dave Coleman,** Belmont Community Adult School, Los Angeles, CA; **Eleanor Comegys**, Los Angeles Community Adult School, Los Angeles, CA; **Ludmila Ellis**, Dutchess Community College, Poughkeepsie, NY; **MaryAnn Florez**, Arlington Education & Employment Program, Arlington, VA; **Liz Flynn**, Centers for Education and Technology, San Diego, CA; **Gayle Forgey**, Garden Grove Unified School District, Lincoln Education Center, Garden Grove, CA; **Stephanie Garcia,** Gwinnett Technical College, Lawrenceville, GA; **Jennifer Gaudet**, Santa Ana College, Santa Ana, CA; **Sally Gearhart**, Santa Rosa Junior College, Santa Rosa, CA; **Jeanne Gibson**, Colorado State University, Pueblo, CO; **Anthony Halderman**, Cuesta College, San Luis Obispo, CA; **Cam Tu Huynh**, Banning Adult Learning Center, Los Angeles Unified School District, Los Angeles, CA; **Iordana Iordanova**, Triton College, River Grove, IL; **Mary Jane Jerde**, Price George's County Adult Education and Howard Community College, Bladensburg, MD; **Britt Johnson**, Albany Park Community Center, Chicago, IL; **Kathleen Krokar**, Truman College, Chicago, IL; **Xay Lee**, Fresno Adult School, Fresno, CA; **Sarah Lynn**, Somerville Community Adult Learning Experiences, Somerville, MA; **Ronna Magy**, Division of Adult and Career Education, LAUSD, Los Angeles, CA; **Dr. Suzanne Medina**, California State University, Carson, CA; **Dr.; Diana Mora**, Fresno Adult School, Fresno, CA; **Jenny Moreno**, LAUSD, Los Angeles, CA; **Meg Morris**, Los Altos Adult Education, Mount View, CA; **John Nelson, Ph.D.**, Co-Director ESOL MA Program, University of Maryland, Baltimore County, MD; **Robert Osgood**, Westchester Community College, Valhalla, NY; **Judie Plumb**, Gwinnett Technical College, Lawrenceville, GA; **Barbara Pongsrikul**, Cesar Chavez Campus, San Diego, CA; **Dr. Yilin Sun**, Seattle Central Community College, Seattle, WA; **Alisa Takeuchi**, Garden Grove Adult Education, Chapman Education Center, Garden Grove, CA; **Garnet Templin-Imel**, Bellevue Community College, Bellevue, WA; **Lay Kuan Toh**, Westchester Community College, Valhalla, NY; **Marcos Valle**, Edmonds Community College, Edmonds, WA; **Carol van Duzer,** Center for Adult English Language Acquisition, Center for Applied Linguistics, Washington, DC; **Michele Volz,** Centennial Education Center, Santa Ana, CA; **Merari Weber**, Glendale Community College, Los Angeles, CA.

Scope and Sequence

Writing	CASAS	LAUSD	FL. Adult ESOL High Beginning	Life Skills and Test Prep 2
Solve simple math problems Prewriting: Complete a school registration form Write a paragraph about yourself Writing Tip: Use capital letters for nationalities	0.2.1, 0.2.2, 0.2.3, 0.2.4 0.1.2, 0.2.2	Competencies: 1, 3, 4, 5 Grammar: 1a, 16a, 16b, 16d, 20a, 27, 28a Competencies: 3, 6, 63	3.05.01, 3.14.02, 3.15.11, 3.16.01, 3.16.02, 3.16.03, 3.16.05, 3.16.09, 3.17.01, 3.17.02, 3.17.03, 3.17.05 3.05.01, 3.16.01, 3.16.03	Unit 1, Lesson 1 • Fill out a registration form Unit 2, Lesson 3 • Describe physical characteristics of family and friends; use pronouns
Complete a family tree Prewriting: Write personal information questions Write a paragraph about a classmate Writing Tip: Use full forms in formal writing	0.2.1, 0.2.2, 0.2.3, 0.2.4, 4.1.6 0.1.2, 0.1.4, 0.2.1, 0.2.2, 1.1.4, 4.1.2, 6.6.4	Competencies: 3, 4, 6, 63 Grammar: 1a, 16b, 16c, 17c, 27, 28a, 28c Competencies: 1, 3, 4, 5, 10, 31, 52	3.14.01, 3.15.01, 3.15.02, 3.15.05, 3.16.01, 3.16.02, 3.16.03, 3.16.07 3.01.03, 3.05.01, 3.05.03, 3.14.01, 3.16.03	Unit 1, Lesson 2 • Ask and answer questions about personal information Unit 2, Lessons 1-4 • Learn words for family relationships; give basic information about family members; describe physical characteristics; give and receive compliments Unit 7, Lesson 2 • Understand the American system of measuring dimensions Unit 11, Lesson 2 • Fill out a simple job application
Prewriting: Read an employee evaluation form Complete an evaluation form Summarize an employee's job performance Understand the qualities needed to be a good worker Writing Tip: Write the main ideas in a summary	0.2.3, 0.2.4, 4.1.1, 4.1.7, 4.1.8, 4.4.1, 4.4.2, 4.4.4 0.1.2, 0.2.1, 4.1.3, 4.1.5, 4.1.6, 4.1.7	Competencies: 51, 52, 54 Grammar: 1a, 17c, 20a, 20b, 27, 28a, 28c Competencies: 3, 12, 51, 53, 54	3.01.01, 3.01.02, 3.03.01, 3.15.01, 3.15.02, 3.15.04, 3.15.05, 3.15.06, 3.16.01, 3.16.02, 3.16.03, 3.16.05 3.01.01, 3.01.06, 3.05.01, 3.16.03	Unit 1, Lesson 4 • Learn names for school employees Unit 2, Lesson 3 • Describe physical characteristics Unit 11, Lessons 1-4 • Read help wanted ads that include common abbreviations; respond appropriately to job interview questions; practice appropriate job interview behavior
Draw a map Prewriting: Complete a chart Write a postcard Writing Tip: Begin letters with Dear Address letters	2.2.1, 2.2.5, 2.3.3, 2.6.1 2.2.1, 2.5.4	Competencies: 23a, 23b, 23c Grammar: 17e, 18, 21b, 27, 28a, 28c Competencies: 23	3.09.03, 3.15.01, 3.15.06, 3.15.08, 3.16.01 3.09.03	Unit 4, Lesson 3 • Locate places on a map

All information printed in red pertains to *Life Skills and Test Prep 2*

Scope and Sequence

Unit	Grammar	Listening	Speaking	Reading
5 **Food and Drink** Page 52	Count and Noncount Nouns Quantifiers: *Some / A little / A lot of / A few / Any* Count and Noncount Nouns: Questions	Listen to supermarket staff assisting customers Listen to a comparison of supermarkets Listen for main topics Listen for details	Identify common foods and their containers Ask about and compare prices Compare quantities of foods Describe favorite dishes Ask about availability of food / drinks Evaluate quality of products and stores	Read a recipe Read a receipt Read an ad Read a menu Read a newsletter about U.S. food / culture Understand how to prepare meals Understand measurements Read for details Guess meaning from context
6 **Physical Exercise** Page 64	Present Progressive: Statements Present Progressive: *Yes / No* Questions Present Progressive: Information Questions	Listen to a telephone conversation about peoples' activities Listen to a news report about sports events Listen for main topics Listen for details	Ask about and describe people's activities Ask about and describe people appearance/ clothing Talk about sports	Read descriptions of sports events Draw conclusions Read for the main idea Guess meaning from context
7 **Do's and Don'ts** Page 76	Imperatives Prepositions Object Pronouns	Listen to a mother giving instructions to her son Listen to instructions and warnings Understand requests from a police officer Understand child rearing practices and parenting skills Make inferences Identify speakers and locations	Give orders Give instructions Give warnings Explain where objects are located Talk about appropriate classroom behavior Talk about rules in the community Talk about safety and emergency procedures	Read about safety procedures Read instructions for hospital patients Read about evacuation plans in case of fire Draw conclusions Understand common signs
8 **Possessions** Page 88	*This / That / These / Those* Possessive Adjectives and Possessive Pronouns Simple Present: *Have*	Listen to a salesperson assisting customers Listen to a customer ordering food in a restaurant Listen to a conversation between a police officer and a driver Understand ways to thank and apologize Understand requests for clarification Identify locations Draw conclusions	Identify and describe objects Compliment people Talk about possessions Talk about things you want to buy Translate words for everyday objects from English to other languages Request clarification	Read a home insurance form Read for details Guess meaning from context Understand how to insure property Understand parts of electronic goods

Writing	CASAS	LAUSD	FL. Adult ESOL High Beginning	Life Skills and Test Prep 2
Prewriting: Make a list of traditional food Write a paragraph about a traditional dish Writing Tip: Use *for example*	0.2.3, 1.1.7, 1.2.1, 1.2.2, 1.2.5, 1.3.8, 1.6.1, 3.5.1, 3.5.2, 3.5.9, 7.2.1, 7.2.4 0.1.2, 0.1.3, 0.1.6, 1.1.7, 1.2.1, 1.2.2, 1.3.8, 1.3.9, 2.6.4, 8.1.4	Competencies: 27, 31a, 32, 34, 35, 36 Grammar: 16d, 16e, 17a, 17e, 18, 27, 28a, 28c Competencies: 11, 27, 30, 32, 34, 36	3.07.05, 3.11.01, 3.11.03, 3.15.05, 3.15.08, 3.16.01, 3.16.02, 3.16.03, 3.16.04, 3.16.07 3.05.03, 3.07.05, 3.08.01, 3.11.01, 3.11.03, 3.12.03	Unit 5, Lessons 1-2, 4-6 • Identify common foods and their containers; identify and ask for common quantities of food; read and compare information in advertisements; read and order from a simple menu; ask for clarification using different strategies Unit 6, Lessons 2, 4 • Read and compute a receipt; make a simple request about availability of items in a store
Prewriting: Make a list of action verbs to describe an event Write about an event in progress Writing Tip: Use *and* with verbs in a series	0.1.3, 0.2.3, 3.5.5, 3.5.8, 3.5.9, 7.2.1, 7.2.2, 7.2.4 0.1.4, 2.1.8	Competencies: 62, 63 Grammar: 2a, 27, 28a, 28c Competencies: 17	3.05.03, 3.15.01, 3.15.02, 3.15.03, 3.16.01, 3.16.02, 3.16.03, 3.16.07 3.06.02	Unit 3, Lesson 1 • Begin and end telephone conversations
Prewriting: Read advice from a travel guide Write advice for a travel guide Writing Tip: Use adjectives in a series	0.1.3, 3.4.1, 3.5.5, 3.5.7, 3.5.8, 4.3.1, 4.6.1, 4.8.1, 4.8.3 5.5.6	Competencies: 8a, 15, 48 Grammar: 8, 19a, 27a, 27b Competencies: 42	3.09.01, 3.09.03, 3.09.04, 3.15.01, 3.15.02, 3.15.03, 3.16.01, 3.16.02, 3.16.03, 3.16.04, 3.16.07	Unit 10, Lesson 3 • Learn how to respond to requests from a police officer
Prewriting: Complete a form Write a paragraph about your property Writing Tip: Use pronouns	0.2.3, 1.2.5, 1.3.4, 7.2.1, 7.2.2, 7.2.4 0.1.4, 0.1.6	Competencies: 62, 63 Grammar: 17a, 17b, 17c, 19b, 20a, 20b Competencies: 10, 11	3.05.03, 3.15.01, 3.15.02, 3.15.03, 3.16.01, 3.16.02, 3.16.03 3.05.03	Unit 2, Lesson 4 • Give and receive compliments Unit 5, Lesson 6 • Ask for clarification using different strategies

All information printed in red pertains to *Life Skills and Test Prep 2*

CORRELATIONS TO STANDARDS

Writing	CASAS	LAUSD	FL. Adult ESOL High Beginning	Life Skills and Test Prep 2
Prewriting: Complete a daily planner Write an answer to a survey question about daily routines Writing Tip: Use *or*	0.1.2, 0.2.1, 0.2.2, 0.2.3, 0.2.4 0.1.2, 4.4.1, 4.4.3, 4.6.5	Competencies: 7a, 59, 62, 63 Grammar: 1c, 27, 30a Competencies: 4, 55	3.15.01, 3.15.02, 3.15.03, 3.15.04, 3.15.05, 3.15.06, 3.16.01, 3.16.02, 3.17.01, 3.17.02 3.05.01, 3.14.01	Unit 2, Lesson 2 • Give basic information about family members Unit 12, Lesson 3 • Read and talk about a work schedule
Prewriting: Read a paragraph about outdoor markets Write a paragraph about shopping customs Writing Tip: Use *because*	0.2.3, 1.2.1, 1.2.2, 1.2.3, 1.2.5, 1.3.1, 1.6.4, 7.2.1, 7.2.2, 7.2.3, 7.2.4 0.1.3, 1.3.3, 1.3.9, 1.6.3, 1.8.1, 1.8.2, 8.1.4	Competencies: 27, 32 Grammar: 1c, 23f, 24, 28a, 28c, 30a Competencies: 28, 29, 30, 33, 59	3.05.03, 3.11.03, 3.15.01, 3.15.02, 3.15.03, 3.15.04, 3.16.01, 3.16.02, 3.16.03, 3.16.04, 3.16.05, 3.16.07, 3.16.08 3.08.06	Unit 6, Lessons 1, 3, 4-5 • Use an ATM; read and fill out a check; make a simple request about availability of items in a store; give reasons for returning or exchanging an item
Prewriting: Answer questions about a holiday in your country Write a newsletter paragraph about a holiday Writing Tip: Place adverbs correctly in sentences	0.2.3, 2.7.1, 2.7.2 0.1.4	Competencies: 5, 7, 62 Grammar: 1a, 1c, 19a, 28c Competencies: 9 Grammar: 28c	3.15.01, 3.15.02, 3.15.05, 3.16.01, 3.16.02, 3.16.03, 3.16.07, 3.16.08 3.05.03, 3.16.02, 3.16.07	Unit 1, Lesson 3 • Ask questions with *When* and *Where* Unit 4, Lesson 2 • Make and respond to invitations
Prewriting: Complete a career counseling form Write about educational and career goals Writing Tip: Use paragraphs	2.7.3, 4.1.2, 4.1.3, 4.1.5, 4.1.6, 4.1.7, 4.1.8, 4.2.1, 4.4.1, 4.4.4, 4.4.5 0.2.1, 0.2.2, 4.1.2, 4.1.5, 4.1.6, 4.1.7, 4.2.1, 4.4.1, 4.4.3, 4.6.5	Competencies: 52, 54, 55, 59, 62, 63 Grammar: 1a, 1b, 1c, 2a, 3, 27, 28a, 28b, 28c Competencies: 52, 53, 54, 55, 56, 59	3.01.02, 3.01.06, 3.02.03, 3.05.03, 3.15.01, 3.15.02, 3.15.03, 3.15.06, 3.16.01, 3.16.02, 3.16.03, 3.16.07 3.01.03, 3.01.06, 3.02.04, 3.15.07	Unit 11, Lessons 2-4 • Fill out a simple job application; put events in chronological order; respond appropriately to job interview questions; practice appropriate job interview behavior Unit 12, Lessons 1, 3 • Read a simple paycheck stub; read and talk about a work schedule

All information printed in red pertains to *Life Skills and Test Prep 2*

Unit	Grammar	Listening	Speaking	Reading
13 **Feelings and Opinions** Page 152	Simple Past of *Be*: Statements Simple Past of *Be*: *Yes / No* Questions Simple Past of *Be*: Information Questions	Listen to descriptions of past events / experiences Listen for details Listen for topics	Describe a memorable event Describe recent travels Make inferences Complain	Read a letter of complaint Read an ad Understand a calendar Understand dates and times Read for the main idea Recognize tone Understand details
14 **Fact or Fiction** Page 164	Simple Past: Regular Verbs Simple Past: Irregular Verbs Simple Past: Negative Statements	Listen to descriptions of unusual events Listen for the main topic Listen for gist Make inferences Distinguish *–ed* endings	Talk about recent activities Tell a story Pronounce final *–ed*	Read a police report Read newspaper headlines Understand the order of events in a narrative Understand U.S. laws Understand the American system of measuring dimensions Understand how to report a crime Understand how to interact with law enforcement
15 **Life Stages** Page 176	Simple Past: *Yes / No* Questions Simple Past: Information Questions Information Questions with *Who* and *What* as Subject *How long ago* and *How long*	Listen to a conversation about life experiences Listen to a report about the life of an artist Listen for details Listen for main ideas	Talk about childhood experiences Talk about first-time experiences Talk about important life events Understand how to become a U.S. resident or citizen Talk about the life stories of famous people	Read timelines Read about a café worker's daily routine Read a biography Read for the main idea Identify topics
16 **Looking Ahead** Page 188	*Be going to*: Statements *Be going to*: *Yes / No* Questions *Be going to*: Information Questions	Listen to a conversation about short-term plans Listen to a weather report Listen for the main idea Listen for details	Talk about the weather Talk about everyday activities Talk about home-care skills Talk about long-term and short-term goals Talk about travel plans	Read a community calendar Read a personal note Read for details Make inferences Understand a weather chart Understand temperatures

Writing	CASAS	LAUSD	FL. Adult ESOL High Beginning	Life Skills and Test Prep 2
Write a formal letter of complaint Writing Tip: Use business letter format Address letters	0.2.3, 1.6.3, 2.3.2, 2.3.3, 2.7.1 1.2.1, 1.2.2, 2.3.2	Competencies: 5, 7, 30 Grammar: 5a, 20a, 20b, 21a, 22c, 27 Competencies: 25, 32	3.15.01, 3.15.02, 3.15.03, 3.15.04, 3.15.05, 3.15.06, 3.15.12, 3.16.01, 3.16.02, 3.16.03, 3.16.07 3.08.03, 3.11.03	Unit 4, Lesson 1 • Read calendars Unit 5, Lesson 4 • Read and compare basic information in simple advertisements
Prewriting: Discuss and take notes on crimes Complete a police report Write a paragraph about a crime Describe a person Writing Tip: Use *when*	0.1.2, 0.1.4, 0.2.3, 0.2.4, 7.2.1, 7.2.2, 8.2.2 1.1.4, 2.1.2, 6.6.4	Competencies: 7, 64 Grammar: 5b, 5c, 24, 27, 28a, 28b, 28c Competencies: 20, 31	3.10.01, 3.15.01, 3.15.02, 3.15.03, 3.15.04, 3.15.05, 3.15.06, 3.16.01, 3.16.02, 3.16.03, 3.16.07, 3.17.01, 3.17.02 3.06.01, 3.10.01	Unit 7, Lesson 2 • Understand the American system of measuring dimensions Unit 10, Lesson 2 • Learn how to call 911 to report an emergency
Draw timelines Prewriting: Write interview questions Organize information into paragraphs Write a short biography Writing Tip: Use time expressions	0.1.2, 0.2.1, 0.2.3, 0.2.4, 2.7.6 0.1.4	Competencies: 4, 5, 7, 59 Grammar: 28a, 28b, 28c, 29 Competencies: 10	3.15.01, 3.15.02, 3.15.03, 3.15.04, 3.15.05, 3.15.06, 3.16.01, 3.16.02, 3.16.03, 3.16.07 3.05.03	Unit 2, Lesson 5 • Give and receive sympathy and congratulations
Prewriting: Make weekend plans Write a note about weekend plans Writing Tip: Use contractions	0.1.2, 0.1.6, 0.2.1, 0.2.2, 0.2.3, 2.3.2, 2.3.3, 5.2.4, 5.2.5 1.1.5, 2.3.2	Competencies: 3, 5, 7, 59 Grammar: 3, 28a, 28b, 28c Competencies: 25, 26	3.09.01, 3.13.01, 3.15.01, 3.15.02, 3.15.03, 3.15.07, 3.16.01, 3.16.02, 3.16.03, 3.16.04, 3.16.07, 3.16.08 3.08.03	Unit 4, Lesson 1 • Read calendars Unit 7, Lesson 1 • Understand temperatures in Celsius and Fahrenheit

All information printed in red pertains to *Life Skills and Test Prep 2*

Writing	CASAS	LAUSD	FL. Adult ESOL High Beginning	*Life Skills and Test Prep 2*
Write an email to a medical professional Writing Tip: Use *Sincerely* in formal letters / e-mails	0.2.1, 0.2.3, 0.2.4, 3.1.1, 3.3.2, 3.3.3, 3.4.1, 3.5.4, 3.5.7, 3.5.8, 3.5.9 0.1.2, 1.1.7, 1.2.1, 1.3.8, 1.6.1, 2.5.5, 3.1.1, 3.1.2, 3.2.1, 3.3.1, 3.3.2, 3.3.3, 3.5.1	Competencies: 5, 45, 46, 47 Grammar: 15, 28a, 28b, 28c Competencies: 16, 34, 35, 43, 44, 45, 46, 47	3.07.02, 3.07.03, 3.15.01, 3.15.02, 3.15.03, 3.15.05, 3.15.06, 3.16.01, 3.16.02, 3.16.03 3.07.01, 3.07.03, 3.07.04, 3.07.05, 3.08.01, 3.11.01, 3.14.04	**Unit 1, Lesson 6 •** Write an absence note to your child's teacher **Unit 5, Lessons 1-3 •** Identify common foods and their containers; identify common quantities of food; read information on food packaging and labels **Unit 9, Lessons 1-7 •** Identify parts of the body and face; talk about injuries; identify common symptoms; make a doctor's appointment; identify common diseases and conditions; identify common medicines; read medicine labels
Prewriting: Find the main idea in an e-mail Write an e-mail Writing Tip: Use expressions of opinion	0.2.3, 1.4.1, 1.4.2, 5.2.4, 5.2.5 0.1.2, 1.1.4, 1.2.1, 1.2.2, 1.4.2, 1.4.7, 4.5.1, 6.6.4	Competencies: 37, 38 Grammar: 20c, 20d, 28a, 28b, 28c Competencies: 31, 32, 37, 38, 39, 60	3.11.04, 3.11.05, 3.15.01, 3.15.02, 3.15.03, 3.15.05, 3.15.06, 3.16.01, 3.16.02, 3.16.03 3.04.01, 3.11.03, 3.11.04	**Unit 5, Lesson 4 •** Read and compare information in advertisements **Unit 7, Lesson 3 •** Understand the American system of measuring distance **Unit 8, Lessons 1-3 •** Read ads for apartments; ask about an apartment for rent; describe common problems in an apartment **Unit 12, Lesson 4 •** Identify the parts of a computer
Prewriting: Make a list of new year resolutions Write a paragraph about future goals Writing Tip: Use *instead*	0.2.1, 0.2.3, 2.7.3, 3.5.7, 3.5.9, 4.4.1, 7.2.3 0.1.4	Competencies: 7, 59, 63 Grammar: 4, 28a, 28b, 28c Competencies: 10	3.15.01, 3.15.02, 3.15.03, 3.15.05, 3.15.06, 3.16.01, 3.16.02, 3.16.03 3.05.03	**Unit 2, Lesson 5 •** Give and receive sympathy and congratulations
Prewriting: Make a list of problems in your town Write a letter of complaint Identify community needs Understand social issues Writing Tip: Indent paragraphs Address letters	0.1.2, 0.1.3, 0.1.4, 0.2.3, 2.2.3, 2.2.4, 7.2.1, 7.2.2, 7.2.4 0.1.2, 0.1.3, 0.1.4, 1.3.8, 2.1.1, 2.2.1, 2.5.4, 7.4.5	Competencies: 8, 9 Grammar: 9, 11a, 12, 14, 28a, 28b, 28c Competencies: 8, 9, 19, 23, 36, 58	3.09.01, 3.09.02, 3.15.01, 3.15.02, 3.15.03, 3.15.05, 3.15.06, 3.16.01, 3.16.02, 3.16.03 3.05.03, 3.06.05, 3.09.03, 3.11.01, 3.12.03	**Unit 1, Lesson 7 •** Use *Could I* and *Could you* to make requests and ask for permission **Unit 3, Lessons 4-5 •** Use the yellow, blue, and white pages of a phone directory **Unit 4, Lessons 2-3 •** Make and respond to invitations; ask for and give directions **Unit 5, Lesson 5 •** Read a menu

All information printed in red pertains to *Life Skills and Test Prep 2*

To the Teacher

Center Stage is a four-level, four-skills course that balances grammar instruction and successful communication. Practical language and timely topics motivate adult students to master speaking, listening, reading, and writing skills.

Features

- *Grammar to Communicate* presents key grammar points with concise charts and abundant practice in real-life situations.

- **Communicative activities** such as *Time to Talk*, promote opportunities for students to express themselves and engage in active learning.

- Extensive **listening** practice, in addition to **reading** and **writing** activities, help students to master the English they need in their daily lives.

- *Review and Challenge* helps teachers to assess students' progress and meet the needs of multi-level classrooms.

- Clear, easy-to-follow **two-page lessons** give students a sense of accomplishment.

Additional Components

- A **companion student book**, *Life Skills and Test Prep 2*, provides thorough practice of life skills and is linked to the unit themes and vocabulary of *Center Stage*.

- The **Teacher's Edition** includes unit tests, multi-level strategies, learner persistence tips, expansion activities, culture, grammar and language notes, and answer keys.

- A **Teacher's Resource Disk**, bound in the Teacher's Edition, offers numerous worksheets for supplementary grammar practice, supplementary vocabulary practice, and learner persistence.

- **Color transparencies** provide an ideal resource for introducing, practicing, and reviewing vocabulary.

- The **Audio Program** contains recordings for all listening activities in the Student Book.

- The *ExamView® Assessment Suite* includes hundreds of test items, providing flexible, comprehensive assessment.

Unit Description

Each of the twenty units centers on a practical theme for the adult learner. A unit consists of 12 pages and is divided into the following lessons: *Vocabulary and Listening, Grammar to Communicate 1, Grammar to Communicate 2, Grammar to Communicate 3, Review and Challenge*, and *Reading and Writing*.

Each lesson is presented on two facing pages and provides clear, self-contained instruction taking approximately 45 to 60 minutes of class time.

Vocabulary and Listening

Each unit opens with an eye-catching illustration that sets the context and presents high frequency, leveled vocabulary that is recycled in the unit and throughout the course. After hearing the new words, students listen to a dialogue related to the unit theme. In the dialogue, students hear the grammar for the unit before it is formally presented. Students listen for meaning and check their comprehension in follow-up exercises.

Grammar to Communicate

Each unit has three *Grammar to Communicate* lessons that present target structures in concise charts. Students practice each language point through a variety of exercises that build from controlled to open-ended. Extensive meaningful practice leads students toward mastery.

> **Look Boxes.** *Grammar to Communicate* is often expanded with tips in *Look Boxes*. These tips provide information on usage, common errors, and vocabulary.

> **Time to Talk.** *Grammar to Communicate* culminates with a *Time to Talk* activity. This highly communicative activity gives students the chance to personalize what they have learned.

Review and Challenge

Review and Challenge helps students review the unit material, consolidate their knowledge, and extend their learning with a variety of expansion activities. *Review and Challenge* includes:

> **Grammar.** Students check their understanding of the three grammar lessons of the unit.

> **Dictation.** Students listen to and write five sentences that recycle the language of the unit, giving them the opportunity to check their aural comprehension.

> **Speaking.** Students engage in a speaking activity related to the unit theme. This allows for lively practice as well as reinforcement of instructional material.

> **Listening.** Students listen to authentic material, such as radio interviews and reports. Comprehension exercises check students' understanding of the main idea and details, as well as their ability to make inferences. The listening section ends with a *Time to Talk* activity that calls for students to demonstrate what they have learned as they actively apply the material to their own lives.

Reading and Writing

A reading and writing lesson close the unit. Both lessons mirror the unit theme and offer further opportunities to work with the language in natural contexts.

> **Reading.** The reading selections include practical documents as well as informational texts, such as newspaper articles. Students read for general meaning. Comprehension questions build reading skills such as recognizing the main idea, guessing meaning from context, and scanning for details. The reading selections also encourage students to read for life skills, for example, interpreting a college registration form.

Writing. The writing lesson begins with a prewriting activity that prepares students for the main writing task. These tasks range from filling out forms, to writing letters, to writing paragraphs. For each assignment, students are given a model to guide their writing. In addition, each lesson contains a Writing Tip, which highlights a grammar or an editing point.

Games

Colorfully illustrated games are a unique feature of *Center Stage 2*. The *Games* appear after every four units and review the language presented in the units in a light and communicative context. The Games motivate students to practice the language in a relaxed situation.

Standards and Assessments

Standards. Meeting national and state standards is critical to successful adult instruction. *Center Stage 2*, together with the companion text, *Life Skills and Test Prep 2*, clearly integrates material from key grammar and life skills standards. The scope and sequence on pages iv - xiii links the two books with the corresponding standards.

Assessment. *Center Stage* also includes several assessment tools. Teachers have multiple opportunities for performance-based assessment on productive tasks using the 80 *Time to Talk* communicative activities. In addition, teachers can test student performance in the *Review and Challenge* section. Students have many opportunities for self-assessment with both the *Games* and the *Review and Challenge* section.

The testing material for *Center Stage* includes end-of-unit tests found in the *Teacher's Edition*. In addition, the *ExamView® Assessment Suite* includes hundreds of test items for each Student Book. The *Life Skills and Test Prep 2* companion book features CASAS-style tests.

Life Skills and Test Prep 2

Life Skills and Test Prep 2 gives teachers the flexibility to teach additional life skills topics and test-taking tips and practice based on student needs. The 58 lessons, correlated to CASAS competencies, allow teachers and students to choose among many topics—from Family and School and Finding a Job, to Giving Personal Information and Health. This competency-based, multiple skills student book prepares students for any standards-based test. *Life Skills and Test Prep 2* has a separate audio program. The *Center Stage Teacher's Edition* provides specific point-of-use cross references to the lessons in *Life Skills and Test Prep 2*.

About the Authors

Lynn Bonesteel has been teaching ESL since 1988. She is currently a full-time senior lecturer at the Center for English Language and Orientation Programs at Boston University Center for English Language and Orientation Programs (CELOP). Ms. Bonesteel is also the author of *Password 3: A Reading and Vocabulary Text*.

Samuela Eckstut-Didier has taught ESL and EFL for over twenty-five years in the United States, Greece, Italy, and England. She currently teaches at Boston University, Center for English Language and Orientation Programs (CELOP). She has authored or co-authored numerous texts for the teaching of English, notably *Strategic Reading 1, 2 and 3*; *What's in a Word? Reading and Vocabulary Building*; *Focus on Grammar Workbook*; *In the Real World*; *First Impressions*; *Beneath the Surface*; *Widely Read*; and *Finishing Touches*.

About the Series Consultants

MaryAnn Florez is the lead ESL Specialist for the Arlington Education and Employment Program (REEP) in Arlington, Virginia where she has program management, curriculum development, and teacher training responsibilities. She has worked with Fairfax County (VA) Adult ESOL and the National Center for ESL Literacy Education (NCLE), and has coordinated a volunteer adult ESL program Northern Virginia. Ms. Florez has offered workshops throughout the U.S. in areas such as teaching beginning level English language learners, incorporating technology in instruction, strategies for a multi-level classroom, and assessment. Her publications include a variety of research-to-practice briefs and articles on adult ESL education. Ms. Florez holds an M.Ed in Adult Education from George Mason University.

Sharon Seymour is an ESL instructor at City College of San Francisco where she has extensive experience teaching both noncredit adult ESL and credit ESL. She recently completed ten years as chair of the ESL Department at CCSF. She is also currently a co-researcher for a Center for Advancement of Adult Literacy Project on Exemplary Noncredit Community College ESL Programs. Ms. Seymour has been president of CATESOL and a member of the TESOL board of directors and has served both organizations in a variety of capacities. She has served on California Community College Chancellor's Office and California State Department of Education committees relating to ESL curriculum and assessment. Ms. Seymour holds an M.A. in TESOL from San Francisco State University.

Tour of a Unit

Welcome to *Center Stage*

Center Stage is a four-level program that balances grammar instruction and successful communication. Practical language and timely topics motivate adult students to master vocabulary, speaking, listening, reading, and writing skills.

Target grammar is clearly defined at the start of the unit.

Students **listen** for general comprehension and details in real life contexts.

Unit 5
Food and Drink

Grammar
● Count and Noncount Nouns
● Quantifiers: *Some / A little / A lot of / A few / Any*
● Count and Noncount Nouns: Questions

Vocabulary

🔊 33 Read and listen. Then circle the things that are good for you.

1. fruit
2. apples
3. bananas
4. oranges
5. vegetables
6. carrots
7. tomatoes
8. spinach
9. ice cream
10. mayonnaise
11. eggs
12. bread
13. meat
14. beef
15. chicken
16. fish
17. a box of rice
18. a carton of juice
19. a can of soup
20. a box of tea
21. a carton of milk
22. a bag of candy
23. a package of cookies

Listening

A 🔊 34 Listen. A man and a woman talk about food shopping. Check (✓) the statements that the man agrees with.

☐ 1. The oranges in the store are cheap.
☐ 2. Fruit is expensive in the U.S.
☐ 3. Vegetables are cheap in the U.S.
☐ 4. Rice is cheap in Haiti.
☐ 5. Meat isn't expensive in Haiti.
☐ 6. Tomatoes are cheap in Haiti.

B 🔊 35 Read and listen again. Write the missing words. Use the words in the box.

A few	a little	How many	~~How much~~

René: And fruit is really cheap. Hmm . . . There aren't any tomatoes.

Worker: There are a few tomatoes over there, next to the bananas.

René: Oh, great. Thanks. Hmm, is there any spinach?

Worker: It's right here. _How much_ do you need?
1.

René: Just _____ . One package is fine.
2.

Lynn: Wow, these tomatoes are expensive— $5.00 a pound!

René: $5.00 a pound? _____ are there in a pound?
3.

Worker: _____—about 3 or 4.
4.

52 Unit 5

Food and Drink 53

Theme-based vocabulary is illustrated with dynamic art. These high-frequency words are recycled in unit exercises.

Students **see and listen** to an excerpt of a conversation which models the unit grammar.

Each unit has three **Grammar to Communicate** lessons that present the target grammar in a clear and concise chart followed by practice exercises.

Look Boxes expand on the *Grammar to Communicate* charts and include usage information, common errors, and vocabulary notes.

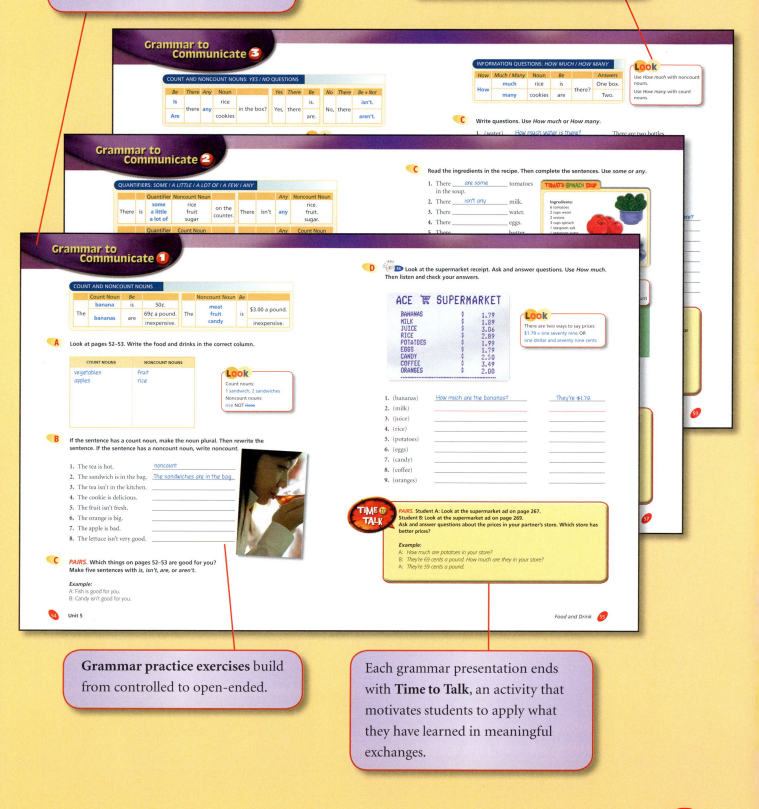

Grammar practice exercises build from controlled to open-ended.

Each grammar presentation ends with **Time to Talk**, an activity that motivates students to apply what they have learned in meaningful exchanges.

Review and Challenge reviews, consolidates, and extends the *Grammar to Communicate* lessons.

Challenging **listening exercises** give students practice with more advanced listening skills.

Prewriting activities prepare students for the writing task.

Reading features high-interest texts and practices essential reading skills.

Writing guides students to complete the writing task with clear, controlled models.

Writing Tips give editing and grammar guidelines.

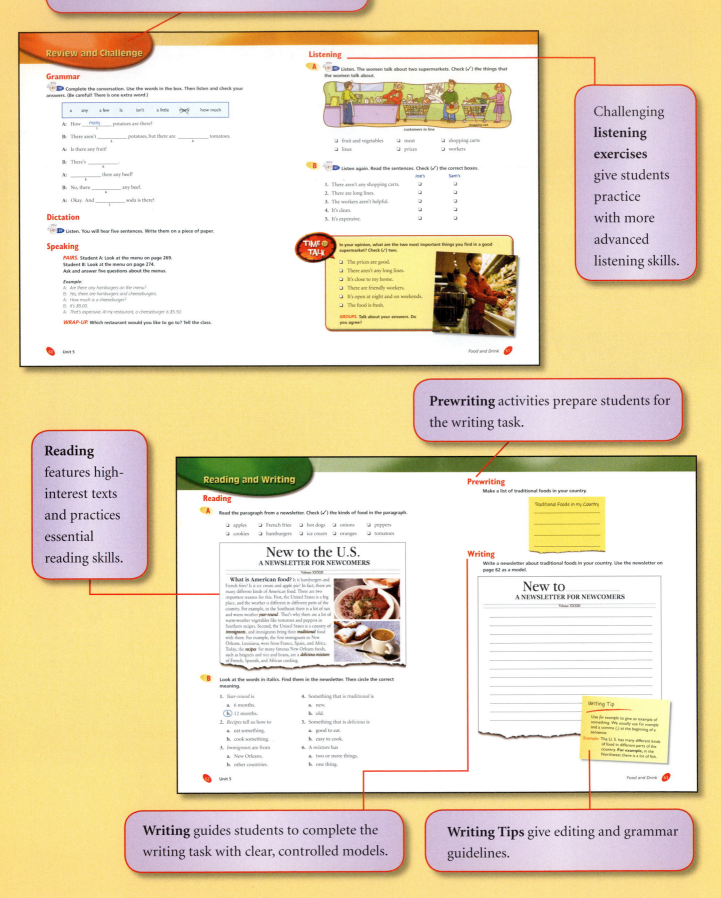

Beyond the Unit

Colorful, fun **Games** after every four units provide opportunities for self-assessment as well as language review.

Grammar Summaries review and expand on the *Grammar to Communicate* presentations.

A variety of **Charts** provide additional support.

Teaching Support

The *Center Stage* **Teacher's Edition** features learning goals, learner persistence tips, step-by-step teaching notes, expansion activities, multi-level strategies, unit tests, and answer keys. The accompanying **Teacher's Resource Disk** includes supplementary grammar and vocabulary exercises and learner persistence worksheets.

Learner persistence tips introduce techniques to engage and retain students and help teachers adapt to a variety of student needs.

Clear links to the *Life Skills and Test Prep 2* companion book are provided.

Multi-level strategies maximize flexibility for every classroom.

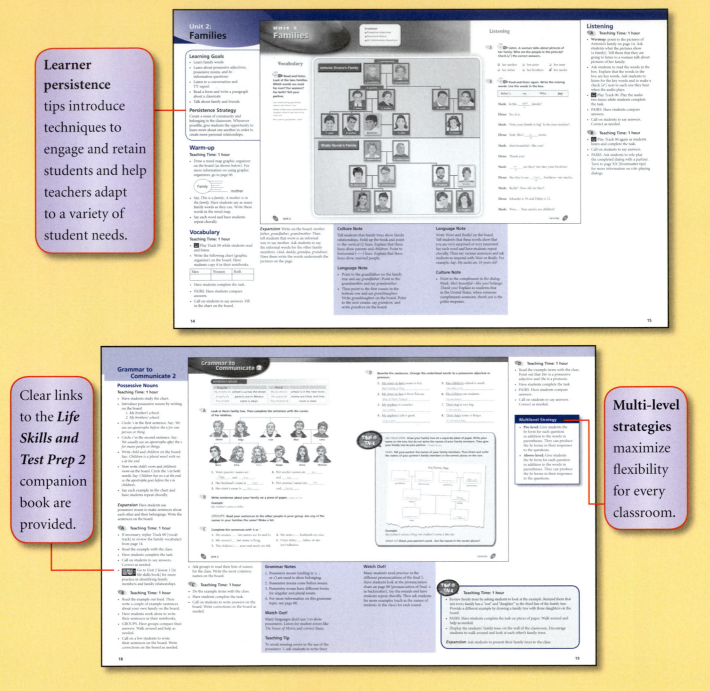

The complete *Center Stage* program
- Audio program
- *ExamView®* Assessment Suite
- Transparencies
- Companion Website

Life Skills and Test Prep 2

Life Skills and Test Prep 2, a companion book, provides instruction in the life skills competencies that adult students need at home, at work, and in their communities.

Each lesson features extensive practice in **listening, speaking, reading, and writing.**

A total of **58 life skills** lessons are correlated to key CASAS competencies.

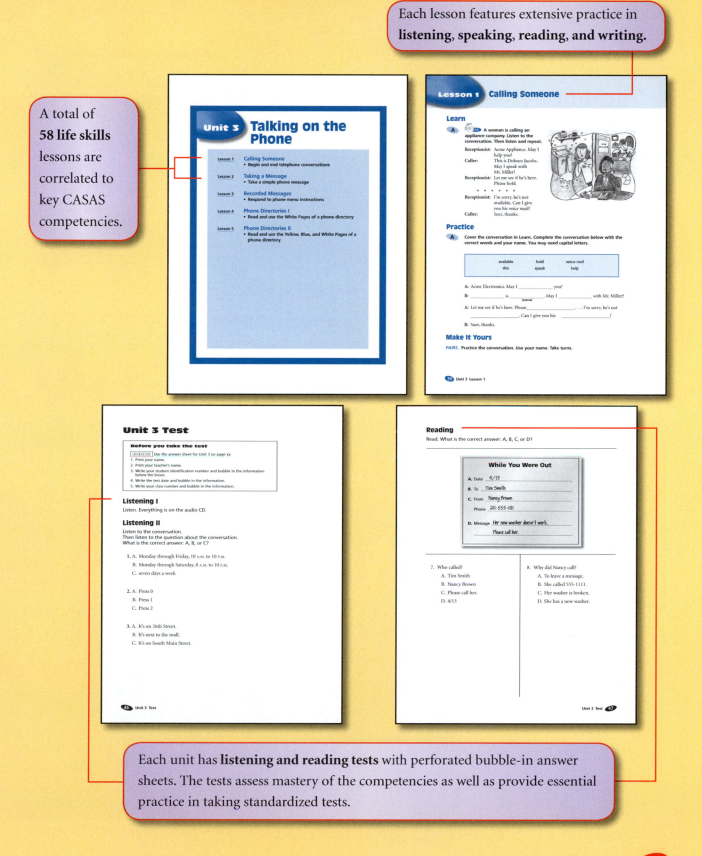

Each unit has **listening and reading tests** with perforated bubble-in answer sheets. The tests assess mastery of the competencies as well as provide essential practice in taking standardized tests.

Unit 1
People

Grammar
- *Be*: Affirmative and Negative Statements
- *Be*: Yes / No Questions and Short Answers
- Regular Count Nouns and Irregular Nouns

Vocabulary

CD 1 TRACK 2 **Read and listen. Then circle the words that describe you.**

1. beautiful
2. average height
3. tall
4. short
5. heavy
6. serious
7. talkative
8. quiet
9. good-looking
10. young
11. thin
12. average weight
13. funny
14. middle-aged
15. old

Listening

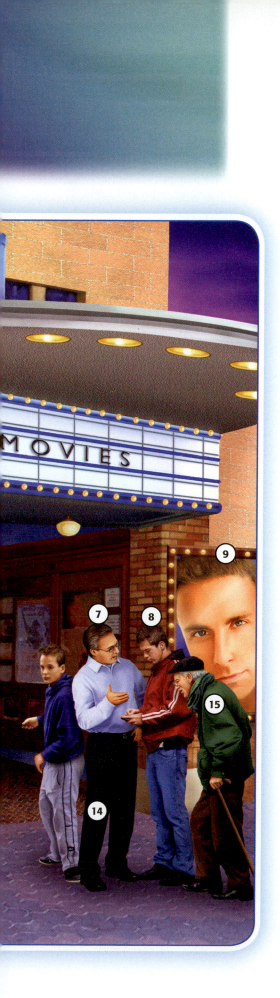

A CD 1 TRACK **3** Listen. Two women talk about Patty and Alvaro. Complete the sentences. Write *P* (Patty) or *A* (Alvaro).

1. _____ is not American.
2. _____ isn't heavy.
3. _____ is a student.
4. _____ is a doctor.
5. _____ is 35.
6. _____ is 22.

B CD 1 TRACK **4** Read and listen again. Write the missing words. Use the words in the box.

Are	~~he's~~	isn't	not	They're

Ava: Alvaro? Is he American?

Mia: No, ____*he's*____ not. He's Mexican.
    1.

Ava: Is he good-looking?

Mia: He's OK. He's tall. He _____ thin, but
    2.

he isn't heavy. He's average weight.

Ava: _____ he and Patty students in the same
    3.

class?

Mia: No, they're not. _____ neighbors. And
    4.

he's a doctor, not a student.

Ava: A doctor? Is he old?

Mia: No, he's _____ old. He's about 35.
    5.

Ava: 35? But Patty's only 22.

Mia: So? 35 isn't old!

People **3**

Grammar to Communicate 1

BE: AFFIRMATIVE STATEMENTS

Subject	Be	Adjective	Contractions	
I	am		I + am →	I'm
He She It	is	quiet.	He + is → She + is → It + is →	He's She's It's
We You They	are		We + are → You + are → They + are →	We're You're They're

You are quiet, **John**.
(*You* = 1 person)
You are quiet, **John and Anna**.
(*You* = 2 or more people)

A Complete the sentences. Use *is* or *are*.

1. Martha __is__ smart.
2. The dog _____ friendly.

3. David and Laura _____ married.
4. Jack _____ single.

5. Jen and Ed _____ noisy.
6. Sam _____ hardworking.

B Rewrite the sentences in Exercise A. Use *He's*, *She's*, *It's*, or *They're*.

1. _She's smart._____   3. _____   5. _____
2. _____   4. _____   6. _____

PAIRS. Write three sentences about yourself on a piece of paper. Use *I'm* and the adjectives above. Tell your sentences to your partner.

BE: NEGATIVE STATEMENTS

Subject	Be	Not	Adjective	Contractions		
I	am			I'm		
He She It	is	not	quiet.	He's She's It's	not	quiet.
We You They	are			We're You're They're		

Look

We also say:
Isn't and **aren't**

C Write sentences about the ages of the people. Use contractions.

1.

(25, 65)

They're not 25. They're 65.

2.

(18, 8)

3.

(45, 22)

4.

(30, 55)

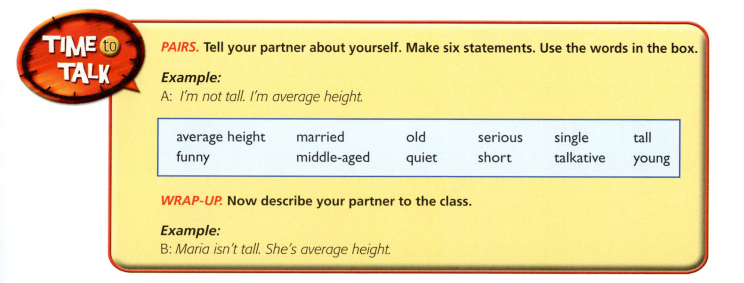

TIME to TALK

PAIRS. Tell your partner about yourself. Make six statements. Use the words in the box.

Example:
A: *I'm not tall. I'm average height.*

average height	married	old	serious	single	tall
funny	middle-aged	quiet	short	talkative	young

WRAP-UP. Now describe your partner to the class.

Example:
B: *Maria isn't tall. She's average height.*

Grammar to Communicate 2

BE: YES/NO QUESTIONS AND SHORT ANSWERS

Be	Subject	Adjective			Affirmative				Negative	
Am	I				I	**am.**			**I'm**	
Is	he she it	quiet?	**Yes,**		he she it	**is.**	**No,**		**he's she's it's**	**not.**
Are	we you they				we you they	**are.**			**we're you're they're**	

 A   Answer the questions about you and people you know. Use short answers.

1. Is your class quiet?   _Yes, it is._ OR _No, it's not._

2. Are you friendly?   _____

3. Are your classmates hardworking?   _____

4. Is your best friend married?   _____

5. Are you and the people in your family tall?   _____

6. Are your neighbors noisy?   _____

Look

Statements:
You are old.   She is old.

Questions:
Are you old?   Is she old?

B   Write questions. Put the words in the correct order. Then complete the answers.

1. _____Is Carla from Canada?_____   Yes, ___she is.___
   (Carla / from / Canada / is)

2. _____   Yes, _____
   (are / married / Ken and Lori)

3. _____   Yes, _____
   (the teacher / is / friendly)

4. _____   Yes, _____
   (are / hardworking / you and your friend)

5. _____   No, _____
   (20 / is / Tom)

6. _____   No, _____
   (you / late / are)

7. _____   No, _____
   (Brazilian / she / is)

8. _____   No, _____
   (are / here /they)

 Unit 1

C CD 1 TRACK **5** **Complete the conversation. Use _am_ or _are_. Then listen and check your answers.**

Lara: ___Are you___ a student in this class?
　　　　1. (you)

Bob: No, _____ the teacher.
　　　　　　2. (I)

Lara: Oh, _____ Professor Michaelson?
　　　　　　　3. (you)

Bob: Yes, _____. _____ in English 101?
　　　　　　　4. (I)　　　　5. (you)

Lara: Yes, _____.
　　　　　　　6. (I)

Bob: Then _____ in my class. Welcome.
　　　　　　　　7. (you)

D **Write questions. Use _am, is,_ or _are_. Then answer the questions about you and people you know. Use short answers.**

1. ___Are you tall?___ 　　　　　___No, I'm not._ OR _Yes, I am.___
　　　(you / tall)

2. _____ 　　　　_____
　　　(you / 35)

3. _____ 　　　　_____
　　　(you and your family / from New York)

4. _____ 　　　　_____
　　　(your classmates / friendly)

5. _____ 　　　　_____
　　　(your best friend / talkative)

6. _____ 　　　　_____
　　　(your neighbors / noisy)

PAIRS. **Ask and answer the questions above.**

TIME to TALK

ON YOUR OWN. **Write the names of four classmates on a piece of paper.**

PAIRS. **Try to guess the names of the classmates on your partner's list. Ask questions. Then change roles and answer your partner's questions.**

Example:
A: _Is this classmate tall?_
B: _No, he isn't._
A: _Is he friendly?_
B: _Yes, he is._
A: _Is the classmate Marco?_
B: _Yes!_

Grammar to Communicate 3

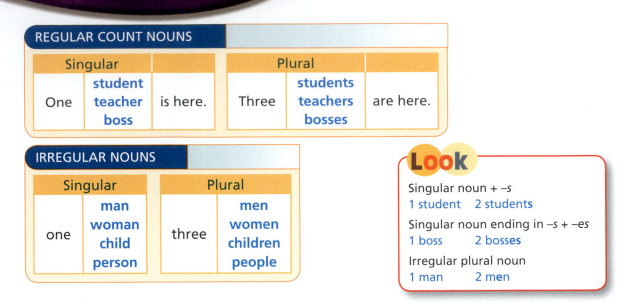

REGULAR COUNT NOUNS					
Singular			**Plural**		
One	student teacher boss	is here.	Three	students teachers bosses	are here.

IRREGULAR NOUNS			
Singular		**Plural**	
one	man woman child person	three	men women children people

Look

Singular noun + –s
1 student   2 students

Singular noun ending in –s + –es
1 boss   2 bosses

Irregular plural noun
1 man   2 men

A Do the math. Write the missing singular or plural nouns.

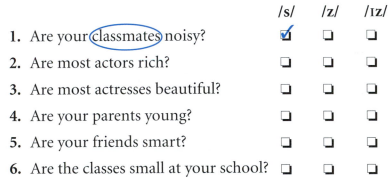

1. three students
   + one **student**
   four students

2. one friend
   + seven ▨
   ▨

3. five ▨
   + one class
   ▨

4. one woman
   + ▨
   five women

5. nine people
   + one ▨
   ▨

6. one ▨
   + ▨
   four children

B 🎵 CD 1 TRACK 6 Circle the plural noun in each sentence. Then listen. What is the sound of each noun ending? Check (✓) the correct column.

	/s/	/z/	/ɪz/
1. Are your (classmates) noisy?	✓	❑	❑
2. Are most actors rich?	❑	❑	❑
3. Are most actresses beautiful?	❑	❑	❑
4. Are your parents young?	❑	❑	❑
5. Are your friends smart?	❑	❑	❑
6. Are the classes small at your school?	❑	❑	❑

Look

Pronunciation of final –s

students   /s/
teachers   /z/
bosses   /ɪz/

PAIRS. Ask and answer the questions above.

C Rewrite the sentences. Make the nouns plural.

1. My friend is smart.   <u>My friends are smart.</u>
2. My classmate is talkative.   _____
3. My neighbor is middle-aged.   _____
4. My boss is hardworking.   _____
5. My child is quiet.   _____

D Look at the pictures. Write sentences about the people. Use *is*, *isn't*, *are*, or *aren't*.

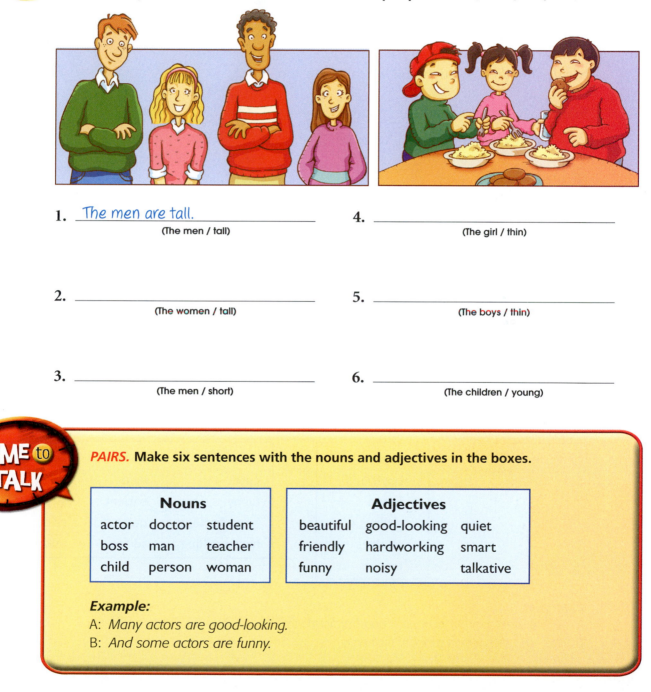

1. <u>The men are tall.</u>
       (The men / tall)

2. _____
       (The women / tall)

3. _____
       (The men / short)

4. _____
       (The girl / thin)

5. _____
       (The boys / thin)

6. _____
       (The children / young)

TIME to TALK

PAIRS. Make six sentences with the nouns and adjectives in the boxes.

Nouns		
actor	doctor	student
boss	man	teacher
child	person	woman

Adjectives		
beautiful	good-looking	quiet
friendly	hardworking	smart
funny	noisy	talkative

Example:
A: *Many actors are good-looking.*
B: *And some actors are funny.*

Review and Challenge

Grammar

 TRACK 7 Correct the conversation. There are seven mistakes. The first mistake is corrected for you. Then listen and check your answers.

Juan: Hello. ~~I~~ *I'm* Juan Montero.

Nicole: Hi. My name is Nicole Summers.

Juan: Are you from Miami?

Nicole: Yes, I'm. My boyfriend he from here, too.

Juan: My girlfriend and I are no from here. They're from Caracas, Venezuela.

Nicole: Caracas is nice?

Juan: Very nice. The persons are friendly.

Dictation

 TRACK 8 Listen. You will hear five sentences. Write them on a piece of paper.

Speaking

PAIRS. Make sentences with the words in the boxes and your own ideas.

The perfect . . .

boss
boyfriend
friend
girlfriend
student
teacher

beautiful	honest	smart
cute	nice	strict
funny	patient	strong
good-looking	quiet	sweet
hardworking	serious	talkative

Example:
A: *The perfect teacher is patient and hardworking.*
B: *Yes, and the perfect teacher isn't strict.*

10   Unit 1

Listening

A 🔊 **9** **Listen. A TV reporter talks about the secrets to a happy life. Write the percentages (%).**

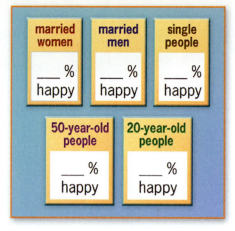

married women	married men	single people
____ % happy	____ % happy	____ % happy

50-year-old people	20-year-old people
____ % happy	____ % happy

B 🔊 **10** **Listen again. Circle the correct answers. There may be more than one correct answer.**

1. The first man thinks that the secrets to a happy life are
   a. good health.
   b. marriage.
   c. love.
   d. fun.

2. The second man thinks the secret to a happy life is
   a. good health.
   b. marriage.
   c. love.
   d. fun.

3. The woman is
   a. happy.
   b. late.
   c. at work.
   d. married.

TIME to TALK

ON YOUR OWN. In your opinion, what are the secrets to a happy life? Write *1* for very important, *2* for important, and *3* for not important.

_____ a big family	_____ fun	_____ hard work	_____ money
_____ children	_____ good food	_____ love	_____ music
_____ education	_____ good health	_____ luck	_____ a nice car
_____ friends	_____ a good job	_____ marriage	_____ a nice house

GROUPS. Compare your answers.

Example:
A: *A big family is very important.*
B: *A big family is not important for me. Education is very important.*

Reading and Writing

Reading

Jacques Chaumin wants to study at Centerville Community College. Read the paragraph and the registration form. Then read the questions. Circle the correct answers.

My name is Jacques Georges Chaumin. I am married. My birthday is in December. I am 25 and my wife, Jeanette, is 22. We are from Port au Prince, Haiti. We are Haitian.

Centerville Community College

Jacques Chaumin
10 Monitor Street
Centerville, NY
11111

9 780 131 947080

cCc

CENTERVILLE COMMUNITY COLLEGE REGISTRATION FORM

PLEASE PRINT.   DATE _May 25, 2007_

NAME ___Chaumin_____Jacques_____G._____
                LAST   FIRST   MIDDLE INITIAL

ADDRESS __10 Monitor Street____Centerville,_____NY_____11111____
                    STREET   CITY   STATE   ZIP CODE

TELEPHONE NUMBER _(917) 111-4570_

SEX   (MALE)   FEMALE   DATE OF BIRTH _December 15, 1980_

                                        NATIONALITY _Haitian_____

1. What is Jacques Georges Chaumin's last name?

    a. Jacques
    b. Georges
    c. Chaumin

2. What is Jacques's middle initial?

    a. Georges
    b. G.
    c. C.

3. What is Jacques's street address?

    a. 10 Monitor Street
    b. Centerville, NY
    c. 11111

4. Where is Centerville?

    a. New York
    b. New Mexico
    c. New Jersey

5. What is Jacques's nationality?

    a. New York
    b. Haitian
    c. Haiti

Prewriting

You want to study at the college, too. Fill in the form with information about yourself.

CENTERVILLE COMMUNITY COLLEGE REGISTRATION FORM

PLEASE PRINT.   DATE _____

NAME _____
              LAST   FIRST   MIDDLE INITIAL

ADDRESS _____
              STREET   CITY   STATE   ZIP CODE

TELEPHONE NUMBER _____

SEX   MALE   FEMALE   DATE OF BIRTH _____

                                     NATIONALITY _____

Writing

Now write several sentences about yourself.
Use the paragraph on page 12 as a model.

Writing Tip

Use a capital letter for nationalities.

Example: I am **D**ominican.

_____

_____

_____

_____

_____

_____

_____

_____

_____

_____

Unit 2
Families

Grammar
- Possessive Adjectives
- Possessive Nouns
- *Be:* Information Questions

Vocabulary

CD 1 TRACK

11 Read and listen. Look at the two families. Which words are used for men? For women? For both? Tell your partner.

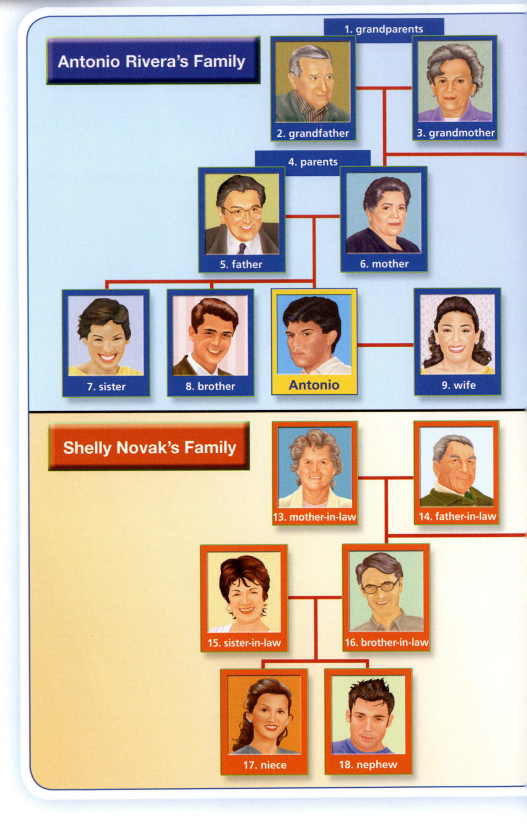

Antonio Rivera's Family

1. grandparents
2. grandfather
3. grandmother
4. parents
5. father
6. mother
7. sister
8. brother
Antonio
9. wife

Shelly Novak's Family

13. mother-in-law
14. father-in-law
15. sister-in-law
16. brother-in-law
17. niece
18. nephew

Listening

CD 1 TRACK 12 **A** Listen. A woman talks about pictures of her family. Who are the people in the pictures? Check (✓) the correct answers.

- ☑ her mother
- ☐ her father
- ☐ her sister
- ☐ her brothers
- ☐ her aunt
- ☐ her uncles

CD 1 TRACK 13 **B** Read and listen again. Write the missing words. Use the words in the box.

father's	my	Who	~~your~~

Mark: Is this ___your___ family?
1.

Elena: Yes, it is.

Mark: Wow, your family is big! Is she your mother?

Elena: Yeah. She's _____ mom.
2.

Mark: She's beautiful—like you!

Elena: Thank you!

Mark: _____ are they? Are they your brothers?
3.

Elena: No, they're my _____ brothers—my uncles.
4.

Mark: Really? How old are they?

Elena: Eduardo is 10, and Felipe is 12.

Mark: Wow . . . Your uncles are children!

Families 15

10. uncle
11. aunt
12. cousin

19. husband
Shelly
20. son
21. daughter

Grammar to Communicate 1

POSSESSIVE ADJECTIVES

Subject Pronoun	Possessive Adjective	Example Sentence
I	**my**	My husband is from Colombia.
you	**your**	Your cousin is tall.
he	**his**	His wife is friendly.
she	**her**	Her brother is good-looking.
it	**its**	Its name is Spot.
we	**our**	Our children are young.
they	**their**	Their grandmother is 90.

A Complete the sentences. Use the words in the box.

children	daughter	grandson
cousin	grandfather	parents

1. I'm their mother.
   They are my ____children.____

2. We're her parents.
   She is our _____

3. He's our son.
   We are his _____

4. She is my grandmother.
   I'm her _____

5. They are your cousins.
   You are their _____

6. She is my granddaughter.
   I'm her _____

B Complete the sentences. Use *my, his, her, its, our,* or *their*.

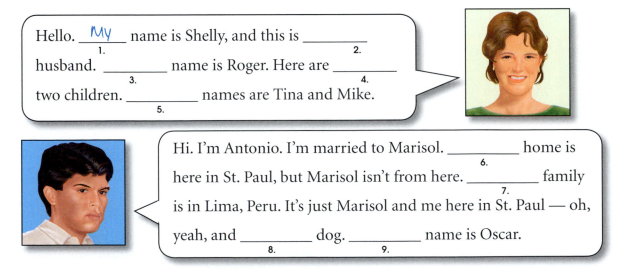

Hello. ___My___ name is Shelly, and this is _____
1.   2.
husband. _____ name is Roger. Here are _____
         3.   4.
two children. _____ names are Tina and Mike.
              5.

Hi. I'm Antonio. I'm married to Marisol. _____ home is
                                         6.
here in St. Paul, but Marisol isn't from here. _____ family
                                               7.
is in Lima, Peru. It's just Marisol and me here in St. Paul — oh,
yeah, and _____ dog. _____ name is Oscar.
          8.   9.

C  **Complete the conversation. Then listen and check your answers.**

Stan: Hi. I'm _____*your*_____ new neighbor. _____ name is Stan Sims.
1. (you / your)   2. (I / My)

Betty: It's nice to meet you, Stan. _____ Betty.
3. (I'm / My)

Stan: Nice to meet you, too. Um . . . are _____ Josh's mother?
4. (you / your)

Betty: No, Ann and Jim Parr are _____ parents. _____ apartment is next door.
5. (he / his)   6. (They / Their)

Stan: Oh. Well, _____ very noisy! _____ music is always so loud.
7. (he's / his)   8. (He / His)

Betty: Um . . . that's _____ daughter's music. Is _____ loud? Sorry!
9. (we / our)   10. (it / its)

Stan: Oh! Um . . . that's OK . . . It *is* nice music. Is _____ a music student?
11. (she / her)

Betty: Yes, she is. _____ very proud of her.
12. (We're / Our)

TIME to TALK

PAIRS. **Look at the pictures of three famous families. Point ☞ at the people and make sentences about the family relationships.**

Example:
A: *Queen Elizabeth is his mother. Prince Charles is her son.*

a. Prince Charles, Prince William, Queen Elizabeth

b. Ellis Marsalis, Wynton Marsalis

c. Homer, Marge, Lisa, Bart, Maggie

Families 17

Grammar to Communicate 2

POSSESSIVE NOUNS			
Singular		**Plural**	
My brother**'s**	school is across the street.	My brothers**'**	school is in the next town.
Angelica**'s**	parents are in Mexico.	Her parents**'**	names are César and Inez.
The child**'s**	room is clean.	The children**'s**	room is clean.

A Look at Vera's family tree. Then complete the sentences with the names of her relatives.

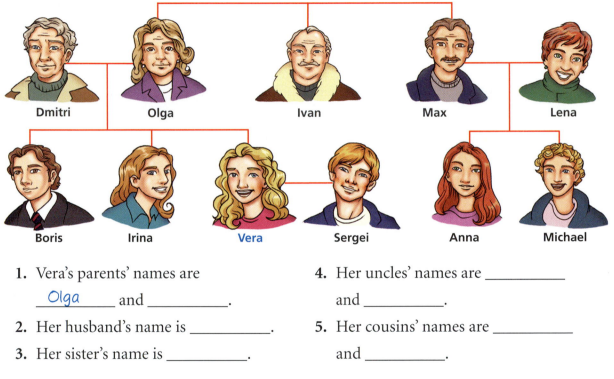

Dmitri   Olga   Ivan   Max   Lena

Boris   Irina   Vera   Sergei   Anna   Michael

1. Vera's parents' names are
   ____Olga____ and _____.

2. Her husband's name is _____.

3. Her sister's name is _____.

4. Her uncles' names are _____
   and _____.

5. Her cousins' names are _____
   and _____.

B Write sentences about your family on a piece of paper.

Example:

My mother's name is Celia.

GROUPS. Read your sentences to the other people in your group. Are any of the names in your families the same? Make a list.

C Complete the sentences with **'s** or **'**.

1. My cousins__'__ last names are Yu and Li.

2. My cousin__'s__ last name is Pang.

3. The children____ aunt and uncle are old.

4. My sister____ husbands are nice.

5. Uncle John____ father-in-law isn't talkative.

D **Rewrite the sentences. Change the underlined words to a possessive adjective or pronoun.**

1. <u>My sister-in-law's</u> name is Fay.
   Her name is Fay.

2. <u>My sister-in-law</u> is from Taiwan.
   She is from Taiwan.

3. <u>My nephew</u> is a teacher.
   _____

4. <u>My nephew's</u> job is good.
   _____

5. <u>His children's</u> school is small.
   _____

6. <u>His children</u> are students.
   _____

7. <u>Their dog</u> is very big.
   _____

8. <u>Their dog's</u> name is Bingo.
   _____

TIME to TALK

ON YOUR OWN. Draw your family tree on a separate piece of paper. Write your name on the tree, but do not write the names of your family members. Then give your family tree to your partner.

PAIRS. Tell your partner the names of your family members. Then listen and write the names of your partner's family members in the correct places on the tree.

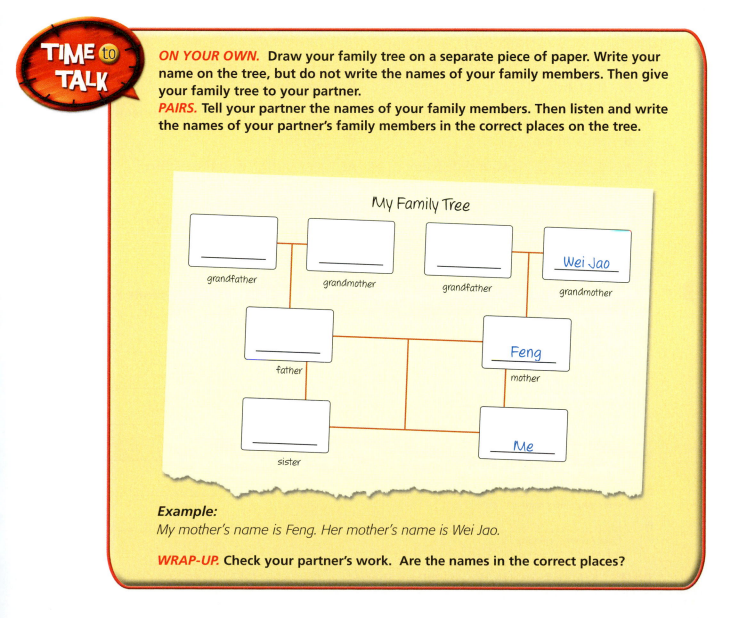

My Family Tree

grandfather   grandmother   grandfather   *Wei Jao* grandmother

father   *Feng* mother

sister   *Me*

Example:
My mother's name is Feng. Her mother's name is Wei Jao.

WRAP-UP. Check your partner's work. Are the names in the correct places?

Grammar to Communicate 3

BE: INFORMATION QUESTIONS

Wh-word	Be	Subject	Answers
Where	am	I?	In Atlanta.
Who	is	she?	My sister.
		he?	My brother.
When		it?	At 3:00 P.M.
Where		we?	In Cleveland.
How	are	you?	Fine.
What		they?	Pictures of my family.

Look

Use *how* + adjective to ask questions:
How old are you? 18.
How tall are you? 5 feet, 3 inches.

A Complete the questions. Use *Who, What, Where, How, How old,* or *How tall*.

1. A: ___What___ is your name?

   B: It's Chris.

2. A: _____ are your children?

   B: Six and ten.

3. A: _____ is your wife from?

   B: South Africa.

4. A: _____ is your son?

   B: He's 4 feet 6 inches tall.

5. A: _____ is your family?

   B: Fine, thanks.

6. A: _____ is your telephone number?

   B: 555-3639.

7. A: _____ is in the picture?

   B: My wife's brother.

8. A: _____ is your daughter?

   B: She's at school.

B Write questions. Put the words in the correct order. Then answer the questions with true information.

1. ___What is your last name?___   _____

   (last / is / your / what / name)

2. _____   _____

   (friend / old / your / how / is)

3. _____   _____

   (is / your / from / teacher / where)

4. _____   _____

   (where / family's / is / your / home)

5. _____   _____

   (tall / you / are / how)

6. _____   _____

   (your / when / birthday / is)

PAIRS. Ask and answer the questions above.

C  **15** **Read the answers. Then write questions. Use *Who, What, Where, How, How old*, or *How tall*. Then listen and check your answers.**

1. **A:** _Where are your parents from?_

    B: My parents are from South Korea.

2. **A:** _____

    B: My family's fine, thanks.

3. **A:** _____

    B: I'm 19.

4. **A:** _____

    B: Nina is my aunt—my mother's sister.

5. **A:** _____

    B: The children are at my mother's house.

6. **A:** _____

    B: My brother is 6 feet tall.

7. **A:** _____

    B: My uncles' names are Greg and Norman.

TIME to TALK

GROUPS. Bring photographs of your family and friends to class. Ask and answer questions about the pictures.

Example:
A: *Who is she?*
B: *She's my sister.*
A: *What's her name?*
B: *Lisa.*
A: *Is she married?*
B: *No, she's single.*

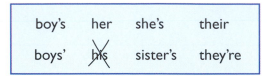

Review and Challenge

Grammar

 16 Complete the conversation. Use the words in the box. Then listen and check your answers. (Be careful! There are two extra words.)

boy's	her	she's	their
boys'	~~his~~	sister's	they're

Andrea: This is a nice picture. Who's in it?

Leona: Oh, that's my son, Paul. And here's a picture of ____his____ children—my two
1.
grandsons and my granddaughter.

Andrea: What are _____ names?
2.

Leona: The _____ names are Bill and Tommy. Their _____ name is Alicia.
3.   4.

Andrea: They're cute! How old is Alicia?

Leona: Oh, _____ seven years old. And here she is in a picture with _____ mother.
5.   6.

Andrea: Oh, so that's your daughter-in-law. She's pretty.

Leona: Yes, she is.

Dictation

 17 Listen. You will hear five sentences.
Write them on a piece of paper.

Speaking

GROUPS. Bring in magazines or newspapers
with photos of famous people. Ask your
classmates questions about the people.

Example:
A: *Who is he?*
B: *He's Will Smith. He's an American actor.*
A: *He's handsome! Is he married?*
B: *I think so.*

Listening

CD 1 TRACK

A 🔘 **18** Listen. A TV reporter talks about families in Italy and Saudi Arabia. For each sentence, write *T* (true) or *F* (false).

__F__ 1. Silvia's parents are the same age.

_____ 2. The age of marriage for most Italian women is 20.

_____ 3. Silvia's family is small.

_____ 4. Saleh's family is very different from other Saudi families.

_____ 5. There are many people in Saleh's house.

_____ 6. All of Saleh's sisters are married.

CD 1 TRACK

B 🔘 **19** Listen again. Check (✓) all of the people that live in Saleh's house.

☑ his mother and father   ❑ his married brothers   ❑ his married sisters

❑ his grandparents   ❑ his sisters-in-law   ❑ his brothers-in-law

❑ his single sisters   ❑ his brothers' children   ❑ his sisters' children

TIME to TALK

ON YOUR OWN. In your opinion, are the sentences true or false? Write *T* (true) or *F* (false).

_____ 1. Small families are very common.

_____ 2. Girls are close to their mothers.

_____ 3. Boys are close to their fathers.

_____ 4. Good friends are the same as family.

_____ 5. For women, it is good to get married at 35.

_____ 6. For men, it is good to get married at 35.

_____ 7. Mothers-in-law and daughters-in-law are usually not friends.

GROUPS. Talk about the sentences. Explain your answers to the people in your group.

Reading and Writing

Reading

Look at the form. Then answer the questions.

Section I—Contact Information

NAME   LAST: _Guerrero_   FIRST: _Adriana_   MIDDLE: _____

ADDRESS   STREET: _75 Pleasant St._   APT. NO.: _222_
CITY: _Alameda_   STATE: _CA_   ZIP CODE: _92262_

TELEPHONE   DAYTIME: _333-555-1810_   EVENING: _333-635-2345_
CELL PHONE: _927-333-4444_

Section II—Employment Information

EMPLOYMENT STATUS   ☐ Full time   ☑ Part-time   ☐ Unemployed

EMPLOYER	EMPLOYER'S ADDRESS	JOB TITLE/POSITION
College Dining Services	600 College Row, Room 223 Alameda, CA	Cashier

---

Section III—Household Information

NAME	RELATIONSHIP TO YOU	DATE OF BIRTH (MM/DD/YY)	SEX
Adriana Guerrero	self	03/12/75	F
John Ryder	spouse	09/08/70	M
Cecilia Ryder	daughter	08/07/02	F
Juan Ryder	son	10/01/99	M

SIGNATURE _____   TODAY'S DATE _09/09/2006_

---

1. You need to talk to Adriana. It's 7:00 P.M. What number do you call?

    a. 333-555-1810   **b.** 333-927-4444   **c.** 333-635-2345

2. What does *unemployed* mean?

    a. not working   **b.** working full time   **c.** working part-time

3. What is Adriana's position?

    a. College Dining Services   **b.** part-time   **c.** cashier

4. In this form, who is *self*?

    a. Adriana   **b.** Adriana's son   **c.** Adriana's brother

5. What does *spouse* mean?

    a. man or woman   **b.** brother or sister   **c.** husband or wife

6. What is Adriana's son's date of birth?

    a. January 10, 1999   **b.** August 7, 2002   **c.** October 1, 1999

Prewriting

Make a list of questions to ask a classmate. Use the words in the box.

what / last name	what / job	are / you married
what / address	how / tall	what / husband's (or wife's) name
what / phone number	what color / your eyes	

QUESTIONS	ANSWERS
1. What is your last name?	
2.	
3.	
4.	
5.	

PAIRS. **Ask and answer the questions above. Write your classmate's answers.**

Writing

Read the paragraph. Then write about your classmate. Use the information from your list above.

My classmate's name is Adriana Guerrero. Her address is 75 Pleasant Street. Her phone number is 333-327-1810. Adriana is a part-time cashier at College Dining Services on College Row. She is 5 feet 4 inches tall. Her eyes are green. She is married, and she is a mother. Her husband's name is John Ryder. Their children's names are Cecilia and Juan.

> **Writing Tip**
>
> For formal writing, use the full form of the verb, not the contracted form.
> Example: I am a part-time cashier.
> NOT ~~I'm~~ a part-time cashier.

Vocabulary

🔊 CD 1 TRACK **20** **Read and listen. Is your job in one of the pictures? Circle the job title. If your job is not in the pictures, write your job here:**

_____

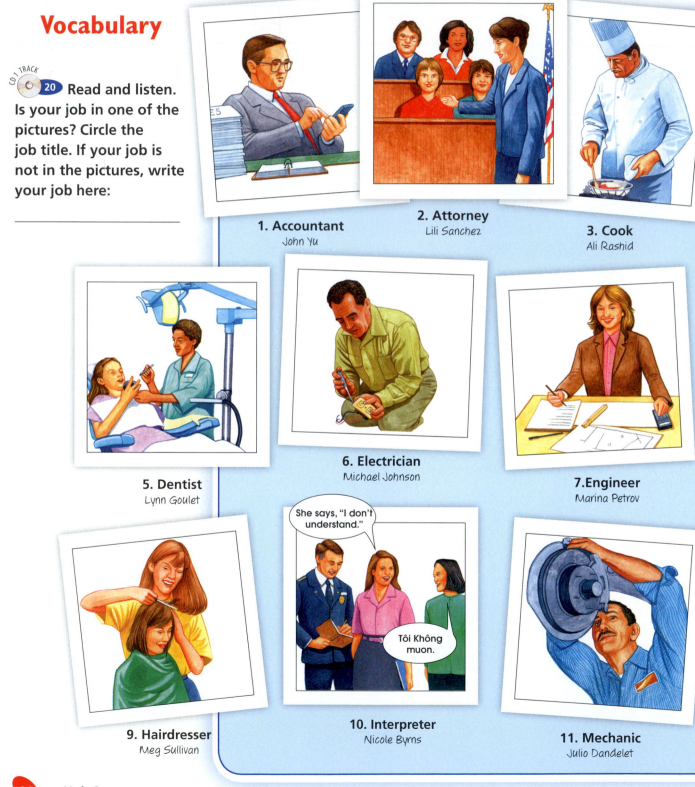

1. Accountant
John Yu

2. Attorney
Lili Sanchez

3. Cook
Ali Rashid

5. Dentist
Lynn Goulet

6. Electrician
Michael Johnson

7. Engineer
Marina Petrov

9. Hairdresser
Meg Sullivan

She says, "I don't understand."

Tôi Không muon.

10. Interpreter
Nicole Byrns

11. Mechanic
Julio Dandelet

Listening

A 🔘 21 **Listen. Bill and Nick are talking about their jobs. Write their jobs.**

Nick is a _____.   Bill is an _____.

B 🔘 22 **Read and listen again. Write the missing words. Use the words in the box.**

a	nice	an	~~new~~	the

Bill: Hey, Nick, what's up? How are you?

Nick: I'm great. I have a ___new___ job.
                                    1.

Bill: Really?

Nick: Yeah, I'm _____ cook at Rico's on First
                              2.
Street.

Bill: Oh, my friend Andy is a cook there too.

Nick: Oh yeah, Andy . . . he's _____ breakfast
                                          3.
cook. I'm the lunch cook.

Bill: So, how is it?

Nick: Well, it isn't _____ easy job, but it's
                                  4.
interesting. The restaurant is always busy.

Bill: Is the pay good?

Nick: It's not bad. And the boss is a _____ guy.
                                                    5.

4. Nurse
Mónica Gómez

8. Plumber
Pete Murphy

12. Waiter
Mario Tecce

13. Waitress
Maria Recine

Grammar to Communicate 1

A AND *AN* WITH SINGULAR COUNT NOUNS

A	Noun
a	**w**aiter **d**octor **n**urse **t**eacher **m**echanic
She's **a d**octor.	

An	Noun
an	**e**ngineer **i**nterpreter
He's **an e**ngineer.	

> **Look**
> Consonants = *b, c, d, f, g, . . .*
> Vowels = *a, e, i, o, u*

A Look at the pictures. Complete the sentences with *a* or *an*.

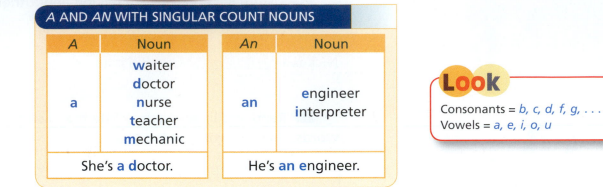

Ali   Pete   Maria   Meg   Marina

1. Ali Rashid is __*a*__ cook.
2. Pete Murphy is _____ plumber.
3. Maria Recine is _____ waitress.

4. Meg Sullivan is _____ hairdresser.
5. Marina Petrov is _____ engineer.

Now make sentences about the people's jobs on pages 26–27.

6. Lynn Goulet ___*is a dentist.*___
7. John Yu _____
8. Nicole Byrns _____

9. Michael Johnson _____
10. Mónica Gómez _____
11. Mario Tecce _____

> **Look**
> Do not use *a / an* with plural nouns.
> They are **nurses.**
> NOT They are ~~a~~ **nurses.**

B Unscramble the words. Then write sentences with the words.

1. ratheec   ___*teacher*___   You ___*are a teacher.*___
2. nudetts   _____   I _____
3. suern   _____   She _____
4. yettrano   _____   He _____
5. oock   _____   You _____

C **Make the sentences in Exercise B plural.**

1. _You are teachers._
2. _____
3. _____
4. _____
5. _____

D **Write sentences about the jobs of people you know.**

1. _My friend Danny is an accountant._
2. _My brothers are mechanics._
3. _____
4. _____
5. _____
6. _____
7. _____
8. _____

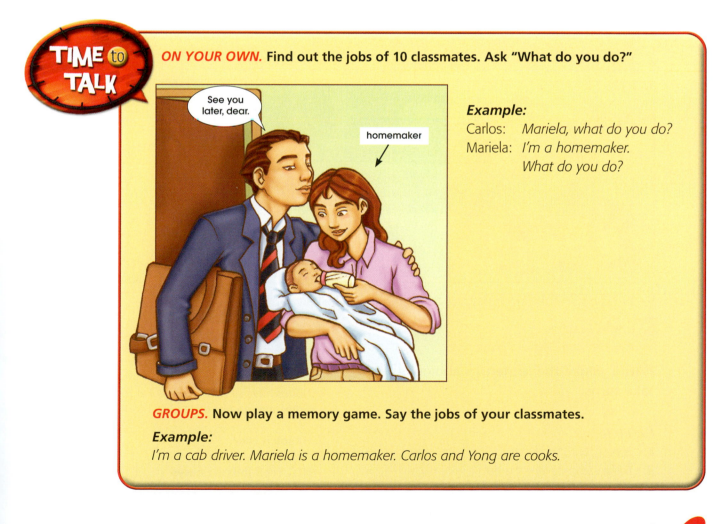

ON YOUR OWN. Find out the jobs of 10 classmates. Ask "What do you do?"

See you later, dear.

homemaker

Example:
Carlos: *Mariela, what do you do?*
Mariela: *I'm a homemaker.*
What do you do?

GROUPS. Now play a memory game. Say the jobs of your classmates.

Example:
I'm a cab driver. Mariela is a homemaker. Carlos and Yong are cooks.

Grammar to Communicate 2

ADJECTIVES AND NOUN WORD ORDER					
	Adjective	Singular Noun		Adjective	Plural Noun
He is a	**good**	**engineer.**	They are	**good**	**engineers.**

 A **Underline the adjectives in the sentences. Circle the nouns.**

1. His taxi cab is neat.

2. Her taxi cab is messy.

3. Her job is difficult.

4. His job is easy.

5. He is a careful hairdresser.

6. She is careless.

7. Her job is boring.

8. His job is interesting.

**PAIRS. Make the sentences above plural.
Take turns.**

Example:
A: *Their taxi cabs are neat.*
B: *Their taxi cabs are messy.*

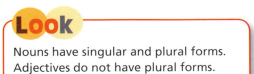

Look

Nouns have singular and plural forms.
Adjectives do not have plural forms.

His **job** is **easy.**
Their **jobs** are **easy.**
NOT Their **jobs** are ~~easys.~~

B **Read the questions. Write _a_, _an_, or leave the sentence blank.**

1. Are you ___a___ neat worker?

2. Are you _____ messy?

3. Is your job _____ boring?

4. Is your boss _____ interesting person?

5. Are you _____ happy at your job?

6. Are you _____ fast worker?

> **Look**
>
> Use _a / an_ + adjective + singular count noun.
> You are **a good worker**.
>
> Do not use _a / an_ when there is no noun after the adjective.
> You are **good**.
> NOT **You are ~~a~~ good.**

Find classmates with jobs. Ask and answer the questions above.

C **Write sentences. Put the words in the correct order.**

1. _My job is interesting._
   (job / interesting / my / is)

2. _____
   (am / student / a / good / I)

3. _____
   (teacher's / our / is / job / difficult)

4. _____
   (classmates / my / are / students / serious)

5. _____
   (hardworking / my / friends / are)

6. _____
   (I / slow / worker / am / a / not)

PAIRS. Which sentences are true about you and people you know? Tell your partner.

ON YOUR OWN. Which qualities are important for the jobs below? Check (✓) the boxes.

	CAREFUL	FAST	FRIENDLY	HONEST	KIND	PATIENT	SMART	STRONG
accountant	✓							
attorney								
dentist								
interpreter								
mechanic								

GROUPS. Now talk about your opinions.

Example:
A: _In my opinion, good accountants are careful and neat._
B: _In my opinion, good accountants are honest._

Grammar to Communicate 3

A / AN / Ø

	A / An	Singular Noun
Veronica is	**a**	cook.

	Ø	Plural Noun
Yoko and Lisa are	**(Ø)**	waitresses.

THE

	The	Singular Noun	
Veronica is	**the**	tall woman	in the picture.

	The	Plural Noun	
Yoko and Lisa are	**the**	young women	in the picture.

Look

Use *a*, *an*, or Ø to make a general statement about someone or something.

Use *the* to identify someone or something.

A Look at the picture and read the sentences. Then label the people in the picture.

1. Keith is the little boy in the picture.
2. The short guy is Tom.
3. Joe is the heavy guy.
4. Mary is the woman with long hair.
5. The woman with black hair is Lucy.
6. Jim is the tall, thin guy.

B Look again at the picture in Exercise A. Sam is showing it to his friend. Read what he says and fill in the blanks with *a*, *the*, or Ø.

Tom and Jim are ___Ø___ cooks. They are _____ funny guys. Joe's our boss. He's _____
1.   2.   3.

nice guy, and he's _____ good cook. Mary is _____ waitress. Lucy is _____ cook.
4.   5.   6.

_____ little boy is Mary's son, Keith. He's _____ good kid. Mary's husband is not in
7.   8.

_____ picture, but he's _____ waiter.
9.   10.

C Look at the business cards. Write sentences. Put the words in the correct order.

1.   The attorney's first name is Lili.
     (is / Lili / attorney's first name / the)

2.   _____
     (young / is / the / attorney)

3.   _____
     (the / 702-452-1215 / is / plumber's phone number)

4.   _____
     (the / plumber's email address / atorres@yoohoo.com / is)

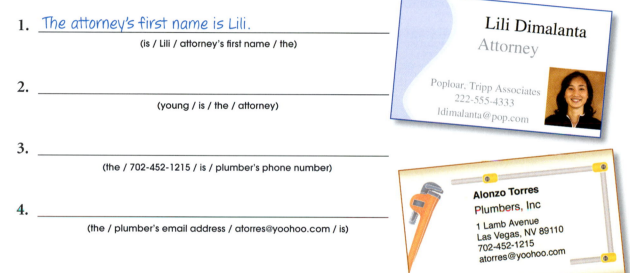

Lili Dimalanta
Attorney

Poploar, Tripp Associates
222-555-4333
ldimalanta@pop.com

Alonzo Torres
Plumbers, Inc

1 Lamb Avenue
Las Vegas, NV 89110
702-452-1215
atorres@yoohoo.com

Now write sentences in your notebook about other information in the business cards.

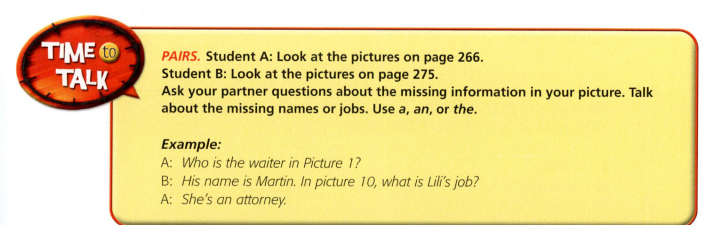

TIME to TALK

PAIRS. Student A: Look at the pictures on page 266.
Student B: Look at the pictures on page 275.
Ask your partner questions about the missing information in your picture. Talk about the missing names or jobs. Use *a*, *an*, or *the*.

Example:
A: *Who is the waiter in Picture 1?*
B: *His name is Martin. In picture 10, what is Lili's job?*
A: *She's an attorney.*

Review and Challenge

Grammar

Find the mistake in each sentence. Circle the letter and correct the mistake.

1. <u>She</u> is <u>a</u> <u>hairdresser careful</u>.
    A   B   Ⓒ
       Correct: *She is a careful hairdresser.*

2. <u>Waiter's</u> <u>name</u> <u>is</u> Henry.
      A   B   C
       Correct: _____

3. <u>The</u> attorneys <u>are</u> <u>youngs</u>.
    A   B   C
       Correct: _____

4. <u>My</u> <u>neighbor</u> is <u>a</u> accountant.
    A   B   C
       Correct: _____

5. <u>It</u> <u>isn't</u> interesting <u>job</u>.
    A   B   C
       Correct: _____

6. <u>The</u> <u>waiters</u> are <u>people nice</u>.
    A   B   C
       Correct: _____

Dictation

 Listen. You will hear five sentences. Write them on a piece of paper.

Speaking

PAIRS. **Read the information about Minh Tran. Look at page 267. Which job is good for him? Explain your choice to the class.**

> **Look**
>
> Experience = the kind of work you have done and the amount of time you have done it

---

MINH TRAN
Wilson Avenue
Bronx NY 10469
(718) 898-3075
email: Mtran@yoo.com

Work experience:
Eric's Auto Shop, Bronx, NY 2005–2006

Education:
Automotive Career and Technical Education High School
Brooklyn, NY, diploma 2006

Listening

A 🔘 **24** Listen. Who is Gabriella talking to? Check (✓) the correct answer.

❏ a customer

❏ a waiter at Stage
     Restaurant

❏ the manager at Stage
     Restaurant

B 🔘 **25** Listen again. Check (✓) the sentences that are true about Gabriella.

❏ **1.** She's the morning waitress at the
            Stage Restaurant

❏ **2.** She's an experienced waitress.

❏ **3.** She's fast.

❏ **4.** She's a messy worker.

❏ **5.** She's available on Sundays.

TIME to TALK

ON YOUR OWN. In your opinion, what is important in a job? Write *1* for very
important, *2* for important, and *3* for not important.

_____ a lot of money   _____ easy work

_____ nice people to work with _____ a hardworking manager

_____ interesting work   _____ a clean workplace

_____ a nice manager   _____ no work on weekends

_____ an organized workplace   _____ benefits (health insurance, vacation, etc.)

GROUPS. Compare your answers.

Example:
A: *A lot of money is important in a job.*
B: *A lot of money isn't important. I think interesting work is more important.*

Reading and Writing

Reading

A   Read the evaluation form. Is Maria a good waitress? Write *yes* or *no*. _____

EMPLOYEE EVALUATION			
Name: Maria Recine		**Position:** Waitress	
Date of Hire: 1/15/05		**Date of Review:** 1/15/06	

Please evaluate the employee. Circle one number for each item.

Rating System: 1 = poor 2 = fair 3 = good

Relationship with kitchen staff	1	2	③
Relationship with customers	1	2	③
Organization	1	2	③

Summary

Maria is an excellent waitress. She is hardworking and serious. She is friendly and kind to the customers. The cooks and other kitchen staff are happy with her work. They say that she is an organized worker. She is never late. Her work area is always neat. She is never careless.

Manager (please sign): _Lisa Sheinheite_

B   Find the italic words in the form. Circle the correct answers.

1. An *employee* is
   a. a worker.   b. a job.
2. *Position* is the same thing as
   a. name.   b. job.
3. On a job evaluation, *poor* is
   a. very good.   b. bad.
4. *Fair* is
   a. okay.   b. very bad.
5. The *staff* are
   a. customers.   b. workers.
6. A *manager* is
   a. a customer.   b. a boss.

customers

Prewriting

Look at the picture of Doug Malone and read his evaluation form.

EMPLOYEE EVALUATION

Name: Doug Malone   Position: Waiter

Date of Hire: 12/10/05   Date of Review: 1/10/07

Please evaluate the employee. Circle one number for each item.

Rating System: 1 = poor 2 = fair 3 = good

Relationship with kitchen staff	①	2	3
Relationship with customers	①	2	3
Organization	①	2	3

Writing

Complete the summary part of the form for Doug Malone. Use the summary on page 36 as a model.

Use the summary on page 36 as a model.

Writing Tip

In a summary, write the main ideas or most important information.

Summary

Manager (please sign): _Lisa Sheinheite_

Unit 4
Places

Grammar

- *There is / There are:* Statements
- *Some / A lot of / Any*
- *Is there / Are there*

Vocabulary

CD 1 TRACK **26** Read and listen. Then circle the places in your neighborhood.

1. airport
2. office building
3. café
4. supermarket
5. apartment building
6. buildings
7. outdoor market
8. hotel
9. movie theater
10. hospital
11. restaurant
12. museum
13. store
14. shopping mall

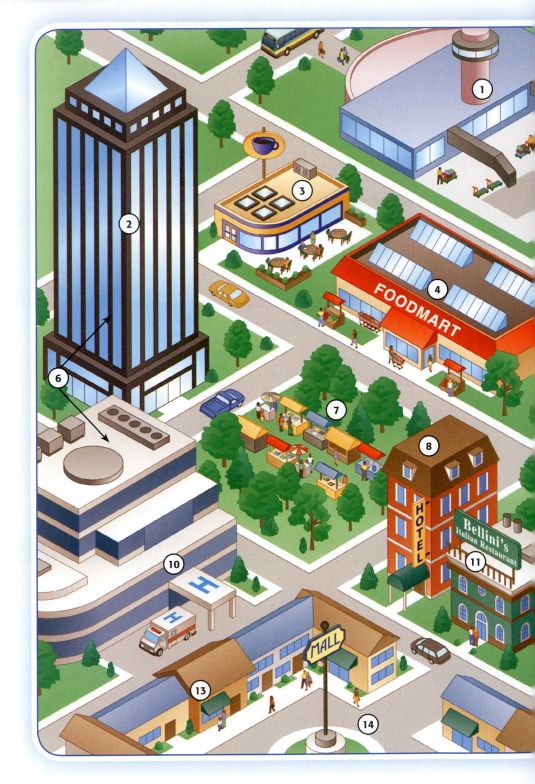

Listening

A CD 1 TRACK **27** **Listen. Check (✓) the places in the woman's neighborhood.**

❏ a shopping mall

❏ an old movie theater

❏ a supermarket

❏ an expensive restaurant

❏ some cheap restaurants

❏ some stores

❏ some cafés

❏ a park

❏ a beach

B CD 1 TRACK **28** **Read and listen again. Write the missing words. Use the words in the box.**

~~any~~	aren't	isn't	some	There's

Natasha: There are some nice stores and cafés, and there's a new movie theater on the next street.

Pedro: It sounds nice. Are there ___any___ good
1.
restaurants?

Natasha: Yes. _____ a good restaurant near
2.
my apartment building. It's expensive, but the food is excellent. There are also

_____ cheap restaurants in the
3.
neighborhood.

Pedro: Is there a supermarket near your apartment?

Natasha: No, there _____ a supermarket, but
4.
there's a big outdoor market.

Pedro: And is there a nice park?

Natasha: There _____ any parks, but there's a
5.
beautiful beach.

Grammar to Communicate 1

THERE IS / THERE ARE: STATEMENTS

There	Be	Subject		There	Be + Not	Subject	
There	is	a restaurant an airport	here.	There	isn't	a restaurant an airport	here.
There	are	restaurants big airports		There	aren't	restaurants big airports	

Contractions
there + is ⟶ there's

A Look at the map of River City. Complete the sentences with *is, isn't, are,* or *aren't.*

Look

The subject comes after *There is* or *There are. There* is not the subject.
There **is a restaurant**. (Singular subject)
There **are restaurants**. (Plural subject)

1. There ____is____ an outdoor market.

2. There _____ two supermarkets on River Street.

3. There _____ a movie theater.

4. There _____ a bank on Center Street.

5. There _____ any restaurants on Center Street.

6. There _____ a big park on Center Street.

7. There _____ a dog in the park.

8. There _____ students at the college.

9. There _____ a hotel on Center Street.

B Look at the pictures. Then look back at the map of River City in Exercise A. Complete the sentences. Use *There is* or *There are* and the places in the box.

| ~~bank~~ | buildings | movie theater | outdoor market | shopping mall |

1. _____There is_____ a hospital between the _____bank_____ and the park.

2. _____ an _____ in the park.

3. _____ some _____ on River Street.

4. _____ a _____ across from the supermarket.

5. _____ a _____ next to the shopping mall.

C Complete the sentences. Use *There's* or *There are*.

1. _____There are restaurants_____ next to the shopping mall.
   (restaurants)

2. _____ across from the college.
   (an old museum)

3. _____ between the shopping mall and the hotel.
   (a movie theater)

4. _____ in the shopping mall.
   (stores)

5. _____ on Elm Street.
   (an apartment building)

PAIRS. Talk about the map in Exercise A. Where are the places in the box? Tell a partner.

| apartment building | movie theater | museum | restaurants | stores |

ON YOUR OWN. Draw a map of your neighborhood on a separate piece of paper. Write in the street names, but do not write the names of the buildings.

PAIRS. Give your map to your partner. Tell your partner the names and locations of the places in your neighborhood. Use *in, on, next to, between,* and *across from.* Your partner will write the places on your map. Then change roles and write the places on your partner's map.

WRAP-UP. Check your partner's map. Is everything in the correct place?

Grammar to Communicate 2

SOME / A LOT OF / ANY

There	Be	Some / A lot of	Subject		There	Be + Not	Any	Subject	
There	are	some a lot of	stores	here.	There	aren't	any	stores	here.

A Look at the picture on pages 38–39. Check (✓) the sentences that are true about the city.

☑ 1. There is a park.

❑ 2. There aren't any colleges.

❑ 3. There are a lot of banks.

❑ 4. There isn't an airport.

❑ 5. There are some restaurants.

❑ 6. There is a hospital.

❑ 7. There are some stores.

❑ 8. There aren't a lot of big hotels.

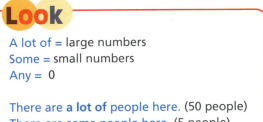

Look

A lot of = large numbers
Some = small numbers
Any = 0

There are **a lot of** people here. (50 people)
There are **some** people here. (5 people)
There aren't **any** people here. (0 people)

B Look at the pictures. Complete the sentences. Use *is, isn't, are,* or *aren't*.

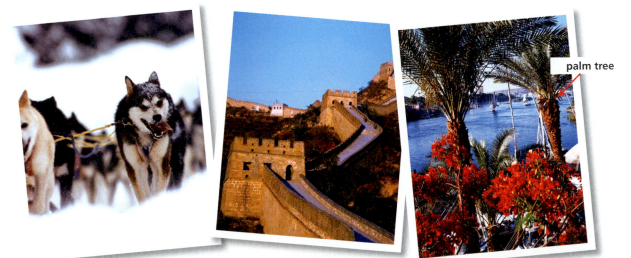

palm tree

sled dogs in Alaska

The Great Wall of China

The Nile River, Egypt

1. There ___isn't___ a very big city in Alaska.

2. There _____ sled dogs in Alaska.

3. There _____ palm trees in Alaska.

4. There _____ a famous wall in China.

5. There _____ a lot of mountains in China.

6. There _____ some palm trees in Egypt.

7. There _____ any sled dogs in Egypt.

8. There _____ a famous river in Egypt.

C **PAIRS.** Look at pages 38–39. Use the vocabulary to tell your partner about your hometown.

Example:

A: *There's a shopping mall in Lahore.*

B: *There isn't a shopping mall in Cap Haïtien.*

shopping mall in Lahore, Pakistan

D Write sentences about good and bad things in your hometown. Use the words in the box and *There is / are / isn't / aren't*, and *a, an, some, any,* or *a lot of.*

beautiful parks	expensive supermarkets	good schools
beautiful rivers	famous museums	interesting stores
big shopping malls	good hospitals	movie theaters
cheap apartments	good jobs	nice people
excellent colleges	good restaurants	young people

Good Things	Bad Things
1. *There are some good schools.*	1. *There aren't a lot of cheap apartments.*
2. _____	2. _____
3. _____	3. _____
4. _____	4. _____
5. _____	5. _____
6. _____	6. _____

TIME to TALK

GROUPS. Talk about five good and bad things in the city or town you are in now.

Example:

A: *There are some famous museums in this city. That's a good thing.*

B: *But there aren't a lot of cheap apartments. That's a bad thing.*

Grammar to Communicate 3

Be	There	Quantifier	Subject		Short Answers						
Is	there	a an	college art museum	here?	Yes,	there	is.	No,	there	isn't.	
Are		any a lot of	schools museums				are.			aren't.	

 A   **Look at the postcards. Circle the correct answers.**

Québec City, Québec — Canada

The Rocky Mountains, Alberta — Canada

Niagara Falls, Ontario — Canada

Lake Huron, British Columbia — Canada

1. Is there a beach in the postcards?
   a. No, there isn't.   **b.** Yes, there is.

2. Are there any buildings?
   a. Yes, there is.   **b.** Yes, there are.

3. Are there any mountains?
   a. Yes, there is.   **b.** Yes, there are.

4. Is there a waterfall?
   a. No, there isn't.   **b.** Yes, there is.

5. Are there a lot of people?
   a. No, there isn't.   **b.** No, there aren't.

6. Is there a lake?
   a. Yes, there is.   **b.** No, there isn't.

B   Write questions about the pictures in Exercise A. Put the words in the correct order.

1. Are there any tall mountains in Canada?
    (any / Canada/ are / there / tall / in / mountains)

2. _____
    (there / is / nice / a / in / Canada / lake)

3. _____
    (beautiful / is / waterfall / a / in / there / Canada)

4. _____
    (Canada / there/ old / in / cities / are)

5. _____
    (beautiful / there / buildings / are / in / Canada /any)

PAIRS. Ask and answer the questions above.

Example:

A: *Are there any tall mountains in Canada?*
B: *Yes, there are. They're in Alberta.*

Look

Use *There is* or *There are* to talk about something the first time. Use *It* or *They* the second time.

There is a famous waterfall in Canada. **It's** in Ontario.

There are some old cities in Canada. **They're** in Quebec.

C   Write questions about your country with *Is there* or *Are there*. Use *a, an,* or *any.*

1. Is there a desert in your country?
    (desert)

2. _____
    (famous waterfall)

3. _____
    (beautiful lakes)

4. _____
    (tall mountains)

5. _____
    (island)

desert

PAIRS. Ask and answer five questions about your country. Use the questions in Exercise C and your own ideas.

Example:

A: *Are there any nice beaches in your country?*
B: *Yes, there are. Copacabana and Ipanema Beaches are beautiful. They're in Rio de Janeiro.*

Places 45

Review and Challenge

Grammar

CD 1 TRACK **29** Correct the conversation. There are seven mistakes. The first one is corrected for you. Then listen and check your answers.

A: I'm from Pittsburgh. It's ~~great~~ *a great* city. There are a lot of stores and beautiful houses.

B: Are there any goods restaurants?

A: Oh, yes. There are any Italian and Chinese restaurants in my neighborhood. And they're cheap, too.

B: Is an art museum in Pittsburgh?

A: Yes. They are three.

B: Is there a new airport?

A: No, it isn't. But our airport is nice.

B: So Pittsburgh is small city.

A: Yes, it is. But it's really nice.

Dictation

CD 1 TRACK **30** Listen. You will hear five sentences. Write them on a piece of paper.

Speaking

PAIRS. Look at the map on page 268. Ask and answer questions about places in the U.S. Use the words in the box. Make the words plural where necessary.

big city	desert	island	old building
big lake	famous waterfall	nice beach	tall mountain

Example:
A: *Are there any tall mountains in the U.S.?*
B: *Yes, there are.*
A: *Where are they?*
B: *There are some tall mountains in Arizona, California, and Colorado. And there's also a tall mountain in Alaska. It's Mount McKinley.*

Listening

A CD 1 TRACK **31** Listen. Two women talk about food shopping in their countries. Check (✓) the correct sentence.

❏ **1.** Food shopping is expensive in the two countries.

❏ **2.** Food shopping is different in the two countries.

❏ **3.** Food shopping is the same in the two countries.

B CD 1 TRACK **32** Listen again. Read the sentences below. Write **C** (Colombia), *U.S.* (the United States), or **B** (both Colombia and the United States).

bakery   supermarket

_____ **1.** There are big supermarkets.

_____ **2.** There are a lot of small food stores.

_____ **3.** Small stores and outdoor markets are popular.

_____ **4.** Small food stores are expensive.

_____ **5.** Supermarkets are expensive.

TIME to TALK

GROUPS. Compare neighborhoods in the U.S. and neighborhoods in your home country. Make five sentences. Use the words from page 38 and your own ideas.

Example:
A: *In Los Angeles, there are a lot of big supermarkets. In my city, Dalian, China, there are a lot of outdoor markets.*
B: *I'm from Berlin, Germany. There are a lot of big supermarkets in Berlin.*

Reading and Writing

Reading

Look at the chart. Then read the postcards. Where is each postcard from? Write the correct city below each postcard.

CITY	👫	❄	☀	🏛	📖
Boston	590,192	* * *	*	* *	* * *
Orlando	201,389	*	* * *	*	*
Chicago	2,898,025	* * *	*	* * *	* * *
KEY:	👫 = population	❄ = cold days	☀ = warm days	🏛 = museums	📖 = libraries
	* = not many	* * = some	* * * = a lot of / many		

Dear Mom and Dad:

How are you? My new neighborhood is great. There are museums and libraries everywhere! There are a lot of people too—more than 2 million! But there is one big problem. It's very cold! Take care. I'll call you soon.

Love,
Tommy

Mr. and Mrs. Grant
105 Hogan St.
Houston, TX 77009

1.

Dear Susie:

I'm here in my hotel. The city is small, and there aren't many museums, but that's OK. The weather is beautiful, and the lakes are wonderful. The shopping is great, too. There are a lot of nice stores. Is there anything you want? Call me at the hotel.

See you soon,
Jimmy

Susie Tan
207 7th Ave.
San Diego, CA 92103

2. _____

Prewriting

Complete the chart with information about a city you know.

CITY	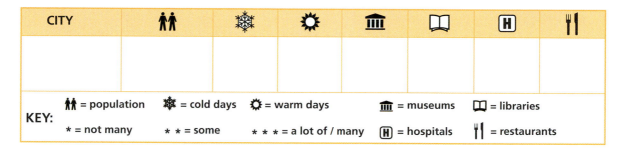						

KEY:

= population   = cold days   = warm days   = museums   = libraries
* = not many   * * = some   * * * = a lot of / many   H = hospitals   = restaurants

Writing

Write a postcard to a friend about the city in your chart above. Use the postcards on page 48 as a model.

page 48

Writing Tip

Begin letters and postcards with *Dear* + name + comma (,).

Example: Dear Sasha,

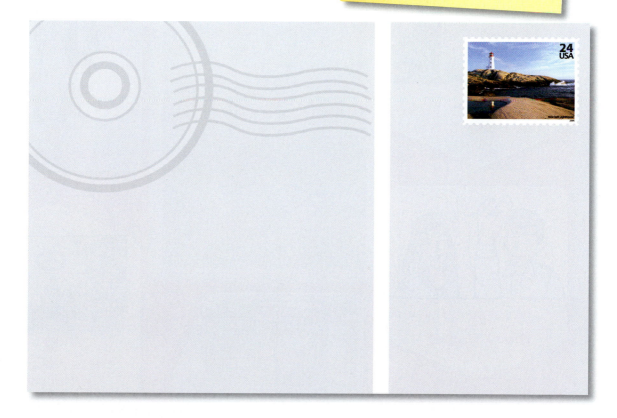

Game 1
Units 1–4

PLAYERS	2 pairs of students
MATERIALS	1 book
	1 coin
	2 markers (1 marker for each pair of students)

INSTRUCTIONS

▶ Put your markers on the START box. Pair 1 goes first.

▶ EACH PAIR: Toss the coin. Heads = Move 1 box. Tails = Move 2 boxes. Read the words in the box and look at the pictures. Complete the conversations.

Example: she / engineer?

Student A: Is she an engineer?
Student B: Yes, she is.

▶ Make sure the other pair's conversation is correct.

▶ If your conversation is *not* correct, put your marker on the box from your last turn. If you land on the box that has the other pair's marker, move to the next box.

▶ Continue taking turns. The first pair to get to the FINISH box wins.

START

1. she / engineer?

2. they / single?

3. there / museum on the street?

4. there / waitress in the cafe?

5. they / thin?

\>\>

8 how old / they?

9 how tall / Arthur / mother?

6 feet

5 feet 1 inch

3 feet

10 there / waterfall?

7 there / outdoor market in the park?

FINISH

16 what / Li / last name?

Li Pang

11 Molly / job / interesting?

Yawn

Luisa Jorge Isabel

Pablo

6 Pablo / aunt / dentist?

12 Jeff / children / quiet?

15 there / buildings on the island?

14 they / hardworking / mechanics?

13 where / beach?

Greetings from Mexico!

Food and Drink

Grammar
● Count and Noncount Nouns
● Quantifiers: *Some / A little / A lot of / A few / Any*
● Count and Noncount Nouns: Questions

Vocabulary

CD 1 TRACK **33** **Read and listen. Then circle the things that are good for you.**

1. fruit
2. apples
3. bananas
4. oranges
5. vegetables
6. carrots
7. tomatoes
8. spinach
9. ice cream
10. mayonnaise
11. eggs
12. bread
13. meat
14. beef
15. chicken
16. fish
17. a box of rice
18. a carton of juice
19. a can of soup
20. a box of tea
21. a carton of milk
22. a bag of candy
23. a package of cookies

Listening

A CD 1 TRACK **34** Listen. A man and a woman talk about food shopping. Check (✓) the statements that the man agrees with.

❏ **1.** The oranges in the store are cheap.
❏ **2.** Fruit is expensive in the U.S.
❏ **3.** Vegetables are cheap in the U.S.
❏ **4.** Rice is cheap in Haiti.
❏ **5.** Meat isn't expensive in Haiti.
❏ **6.** Tomatoes are cheap in Haiti.

B CD 1 TRACK **35** Read and listen again. Write the missing words. Use the words in the box.

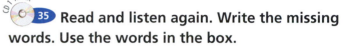

A few	a little	How many	~~How much~~

René: And fruit is really cheap. Hmm . . . There aren't any tomatoes.

Worker: There are a few tomatoes over there, next to the bananas.

René: Oh, great. Thanks. Hmm, is there any spinach?

Worker: It's right here. _How much_ do you need?
1.

René: Just _____ . One package is fine.
2.

Lynn: Wow, these tomatoes are expensive—$5.00 a pound!

René: $5.00 a pound? _____ are there in a
3.
pound?

Worker: _____—about 3 or 4.
4.

Food and Drink **53**

Grammar to Communicate 1

COUNT AND NONCOUNT NOUNS

	Count Noun	Be			Noncount Noun	Be	
The	**banana**	is	50¢.	The	**meat** **fruit** **candy**	is	$3.00 a pound.
	bananas	are	69¢ a pound.				inexpensive.
			inexpensive.				

A Look at pages 52–53. Write the food and drinks in the correct column.

COUNT NOUNS	NONCOUNT NOUNS
vegetables apples	fruit rice

Look

Count nouns:
1 sandwich, 2 sandwiches
Noncount nouns:
rice NOT ~~rices~~

B If the sentence has a count noun, make the noun plural. Then rewrite the sentence. If the sentence has a noncount noun, write *noncount*.

1. The tea is hot. _____noncount_____
2. The sandwich is in the bag. _The sandwiches are in the bag._
3. The tea isn't in the kitchen. _____
4. The cookie is delicious. _____
5. The fruit isn't fresh. _____
6. The orange is big. _____
7. The apple is bad. _____
8. The lettuce isn't very good. _____

C **PAIRS.** Which things on pages 52–53 are good for you? Make five sentences with *is, isn't, are,* or *aren't*.

Example:
A: Fish is good for you.
B: Candy isn't good for you.

D CD 1 TRACK **36** Look at the supermarket receipt. Ask and answer questions. Use *How much*. Then listen and check your answers.

```
ACE 🛒 SUPERMARKET
   BANANAS          $    1.79
   MILK             $    1.89
   JUICE            $    3.06
   RICE             $    2.89
   POTATOES         $    1.99
   EGGS             $    1.79
   CANDY            $    2.50
   COFFEE           $    3.49
   ORANGES          $    2.00
   ......................................
```

Look

There are two ways to say prices:

$1.79 = one seventy nine OR

one dollar and seventy nine cents

1. (bananas)   How much are the bananas?   They're $1.79.

2. (milk)   _____   _____

3. (juice)   _____   _____

4. (rice)   _____   _____

5. (potatoes)   _____   _____

6. (eggs)   _____   _____

7. (candy)   _____   _____

8. (coffee)   _____   _____

9. (oranges)   _____   _____

TIME to TALK

PAIRS. Student A: Look at the supermarket ad on page 267.
Student B: Look at the supermarket ad on page 269.
Ask and answer questions about the prices in your partner's store. Which store has better prices?

Example:
A: *How much are potatoes in your store?*
B: *They're 69 cents a pound. How much are they in your store?*
A: *They're 59 cents a pound.*

Grammar to Communicate 2

QUANTIFIERS: SOME / A LITTLE / A LOT OF / A FEW / ANY

		Quantifier	Noncount Noun				Any	Noncount Noun
There	is	some a little a lot of	rice fruit sugar	on the counter.	There	isn't	any	rice. fruit. sugar.

		Quantifier	Count Noun				Any	Count Noun
There	are	some a few a lot of	eggs bananas vegetables	on the counter.	There	aren't	any	eggs.

A Look at the pictures. Write *a, an, some, a few, a little,* or *a lot of.*

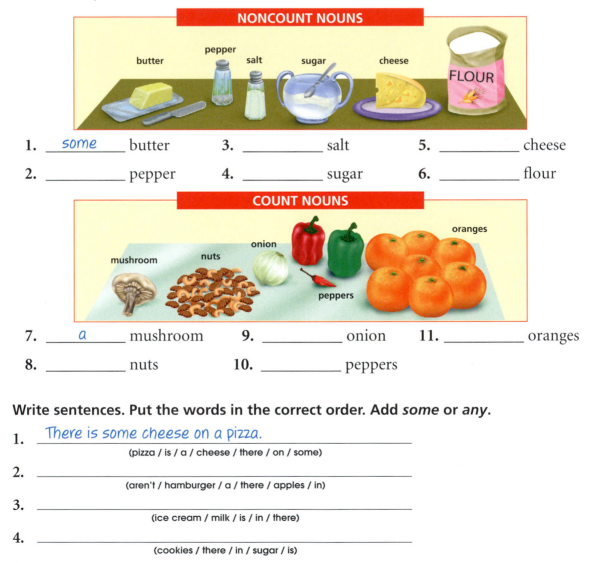

NONCOUNT NOUNS

butter pepper salt sugar cheese FLOUR

1. __some__ butter   3. _____ salt   5. _____ cheese
2. _____ pepper   4. _____ sugar   6. _____ flour

COUNT NOUNS

mushroom nuts onion peppers oranges

7. ___a___ mushroom   9. _____ onion   11. _____ oranges
8. _____ nuts   10. _____ peppers

B Write sentences. Put the words in the correct order. Add *some* or *any.*

1. _There is some cheese on a pizza._
   (pizza / is / a / cheese / there / on / some)

2. _____
   (aren't / hamburger / a / there / apples / in)

3. _____
   (ice cream / milk / is / in / there)

4. _____
   (cookies / there / in / sugar / is)

5. _____
   (a / on / there / pizza / nuts / aren't)

C   Read the ingredients in the recipe. Then complete the sentences. Use *some* or *any*.

1. There ____are some____ tomatoes in the soup.
2. There ____isn't any____ milk.
3. There _____ water.
4. There _____ eggs.
5. There _____ butter.
6. There _____ flour.
7. There _____ pepper.
8. There _____ onions.

TOMATO-SPINACH SOUP

Ingredients:
6 tomatoes
2 cups water
2 onions
3 cups spinach
1 teaspoon salt
1 teaspoon sugar
1 teaspoon pepper
1 tablespoon butter

Instructions on the back

 D   Look at the picture. Complete the sentences. Use the words in the box and *a little* or *a few*.

Look

a few eggs = 3 to 5
a little water = a small amount

1. __There's a little butter.__
2. _____
3. _____

4. _____
5. _____
6. _____

 **TIME to TALK**

GROUPS. Talk about typical dishes in your country. What are your favorite dishes? What are the ingredients?

Example:
My favorite dish is shish kebab. There is a lot of meat in shish kebab, and there are some onions and peppers in it, too.

WRAP-UP. Now tell the class about the most interesting dish in your group.

shish kebab

Grammar to Communicate 3

COUNT AND NONCOUNT NOUNS: YES / NO QUESTIONS

Be	There	Any	Noun		Yes	There	Be		No	There	Be + Not
Is	there	**any**	rice	in the box?	Yes,	there	is.		No,	there	**isn't.**
Are			cookies				are.				**aren't.**

A 🔘 **37** Look at the supermarket sign. Answer the questions about Aisle 4. Then listen and check your answers.

> **Look**
>
> Use *Is there any . . .* with noncount nouns.
>
> Use *Are there any . . .* with count nouns.

AISLE 4

Coffee
Tea
Sugar
Flour
Cookies

1. Is there any coffee? ___Yes, there is.___
2. Are there any eggs? ___No, there aren't.___
3. Is there any tea? _____
4. Are there any cookies? _____
5. Are there any nuts? _____
6. Is there any sugar? _____
7. Is there any candy? _____
8. Is there any juice? _____

B Write questions about the food in your home today. Then answer the questions.

1. (potatoes) ___Are there any potatoes?___ Yes, there are. OR No, there aren't.
2. (rice) ___Is there any rice?___ Yes, there is. OR No, there isn't.
3. (fruit) _____ _____
4. (carrots) _____ _____
5. (milk) _____ _____
6. (vegetables) _____ _____
7. (beef) _____ _____
8. (apples) _____ _____

INFORMATION QUESTIONS: *HOW MUCH / HOW MANY*

How	Much / Many	Noun	Be		Answers
How	**much**	rice	is	there?	One box.
	many	cookies	are		Two.

C   **Write questions. Use *How much* or *How many*.**

1. (water)   <u>How much water is there?</u>   There are two bottles.

2. (rice)   _____   There's one box.

3. (milk)   _____   There's one carton.

4. (potatoes) _____   There's one bag.

5. (coffee)   _____   There are two cans.

6. (cookies) _____   There are two packages.

D   **Rewrite the questions. Use *How much* or *How many*.**

1. How much water is there? (bottles)   <u>How many bottles of water are there?</u>

2. How much rice is there? (boxes)   _____

3. How much candy is there? (bags)   _____

4. How much spinach is there? (packages)   _____

5. How much milk is there? (cartons)   _____

6. How much tea is there? (boxes)   _____

7. How much soda is there? (bottles)   _____

8. How much soup is there? (cans)   _____

TIME to TALK

PAIRS. Student A: Study the picture on pages 52-53. Then close your book. Student B: Ask Student A questions about the picture on pages 52-53. Use *Is there* and *Are there*. If Student A answers *yes*, ask a question with *How much* or *How many*. After a few minutes, change roles.

Example:
A: *Are there any tomatoes?*
B: *Yes, there are.*
A: *That's correct. How many tomatoes are there?*
B: *There are four.*
A: *That's wrong. There are two.*

Review and Challenge

Grammar

CD 1 TRACK 38 Complete the conversation. Use the words in the box. Then listen and check your answers. (Be careful! There is one extra word.)

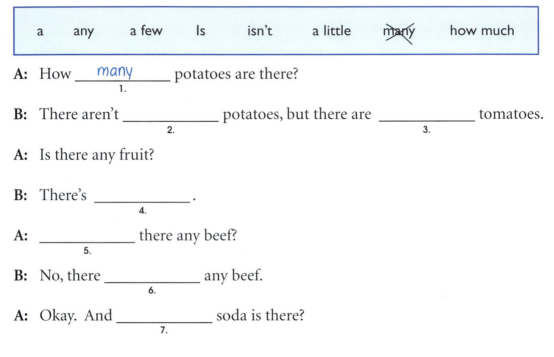

| a | any | a few | Is | isn't | a little | ~~many~~ | how much |

A: How ___many___ potatoes are there?
     1.

B: There aren't _____ potatoes, but there are _____ tomatoes.
                  2.   3.

A: Is there any fruit?

B: There's _____ .
            4.

A: _____ there any beef?
   5.

B: No, there _____ any beef.
              6.

A: Okay. And _____ soda is there?
              7.

Dictation

CD 1 TRACK 39 Listen. You will hear five sentences. Write them on a piece of paper.

Speaking

PAIRS. Student A: Look at the menu on page 269.
Student B: Look at the menu on page 274.
Ask and answer five questions about the menus.

Example:
A: *Are there any hamburgers on the menu?*
B: *Yes, there are hamburgers and cheeseburgers.*
A: *How much is a cheeseburger?*
B: *It's $8.00.*
A: *That's expensive. At my restaurant, a cheeseburger is $5.50.*

WRAP-UP. Which restaurant would you like to go to? Tell the class.

Listening

A **CD 1 TRACK 40** **Listen. The women talk about two supermarkets. Check (✓) the things that the women talk about.**

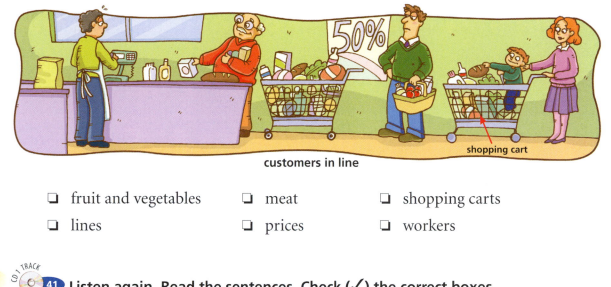

customers in line   shopping cart

❏ fruit and vegetables   ❏ meat   ❏ shopping carts

❏ lines   ❏ prices   ❏ workers

B **CD 1 TRACK 41** **Listen again. Read the sentences. Check (✓) the correct boxes.**

	Joe's	Sam's
1. There aren't any shopping carts.	❏	❏
2. There are long lines.	❏	❏
3. The workers aren't helpful.	❏	❏
4. It's clean.	❏	❏
5. It's expensive.	❏	❏

TIME to TALK

In your opinion, what are the two most important things you find in a good supermarket? Check (✓) two.

❏ The prices are good.

❏ There aren't any long lines.

❏ It's close to my home.

❏ There are friendly workers.

❏ It's open at night and on weekends.

❏ The food is fresh.

GROUPS. Talk about your answers. Do you agree?

Reading and Writing

Reading

A Read the paragraph from a newsletter. Check (✓) the kinds of food in the paragraph.

❏ apples   ❏ French fries   ❏ hot dogs   ❏ onions   ❏ peppers
❏ cookies   ❏ hamburgers   ❏ ice cream   ❏ oranges   ❏ tomatoes

New to the U.S.
A NEWSLETTER FOR NEWCOMERS

Volume XXXIII

What is American food? Is it hamburgers and French fries? Is it ice cream and apple pie? In fact, there are many different kinds of American food. There are two important reasons for this. First, the United States is a big place, and the weather is different in different parts of the country. For example, in the Southeast there is a lot of sun and warm weather *year-round*. That's why there are a lot of warm-weather vegetables like tomatoes and peppers in Southern *recipes*. Second, the United States is a country of *immigrants*, and immigrants bring their *traditional* food with them. For example, the first immigrants to New Orleans, Louisiana, were from France, Spain, and Africa. Today, the recipes for many famous New Orleans foods, such as beignets and rice and beans, are a *delicious mixture* of French, Spanish, and African cooking.

B Look at the words in italics. Find them in the newsletter. Then circle the correct meaning.

1. *Year-round* is
   a. 6 months.
   (b.) 12 months.

2. *Recipes* tell us how to
   a. eat something.
   b. cook something.

3. *Immigrants* are from
   a. New Orleans.
   b. other countries.

4. Something that is *traditional* is
   a. new.
   b. old.

5. Something that is *delicious* is
   a. good to eat.
   b. easy to cook.

6. A *mixture* has
   a. two or more things.
   b. one thing.

Prewriting

Make a list of the different kinds of traditional food in your country.

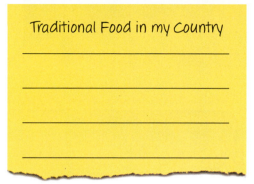

Traditional Food in my Country

_____

_____

_____

_____

Writing

Write about the traditional food of your country for the newsletter. Use the newsletter on page 62 as a model.

New to _____
A NEWSLETTER FOR NEWCOMERS
Volume XXXIII

_____

_____

_____

_____

_____

_____

_____

_____

_____

_____

_____

_____

Writing Tip

Use *for example* to give an example of something. We usually use *For example* and a comma (,) at the beginning of a sentence.

Example: The U. S. has many different kinds of food in different parts of the country. **For example,** in the Northwest there is a lot of fish.

Unit 6
Physical Exercise

Grammar
- Present Progressive: Statements
- Present Progressive: *Yes / No* Questions
- Present Progressive: Information Questions

Vocabulary

CD 1 TRACK 42 **Read and listen. Then circle the people who are exercising.**

1. take a shower
2. swim
3. run
4. go for a walk
5. sit
6. play tennis
7. practice tennis
8. play soccer
9. watch a soccer game
10. ride a bike
11. do exercises
12. go home

Listening

A  **43** Listen to Maria and Jenny's conversation. Look at the chart. Who is doing the activities? Check (✓) the correct answers.

	SWIMMING	RIDING A BIKE	RUNNING	PLAYING TENNIS
Mom is . . .	✓			
Dad is . . .				
Bob is . . .				

B **44** Read and listen again. Write the missing words. Use the words in the box.

| aren't watching | ~~doing~~ | he's running | is riding |

Maria: What's he _____*doing*_____?
1.

Jenny: He's out riding his bike.

Maria: What? Dad _____ a bike!
2.

Jenny: Yup.

Maria: Amazing. . .Well, is Bob at home?

Jenny: Nope.

Maria: Wait, let me think . . . _____.
3.

Jenny: No, he's playing tennis.

Maria: Bob? Playing tennis? Are you kidding? It's

Sunday afternoon, and he and Dad

_____ a soccer game on TV?
4.

Physical Exercise 65

Grammar to Communicate 1

PRESENT PROGRESSIVE: STATEMENTS

Subject	Be	Verb + –ing	Subject	Be	Not	Verb + –ing
I	am		I	am		
He She It	is	working.	He She It	is	not	working.
We You They	are		We You They	are		

Look

Use the present progressive to talk about things happening now.

We use contractions in conversation:
I'm working, he's working, we're working.

A Look at the pictures. What are the people wearing? Complete the sentences with the correct form of *wear*.

1. The man _____is wearing_____ white sneakers.

2. The women _____ tennis whites.

3. The man _____ a blue helmet.

4. The girls _____ black shorts.

5. The women _____ blue track suits.

Look

If a verb ends in –e, drop the –e and add –ing:
exercise   exercising

If a verb ends in 1 vowel + 1 consonant, double the consonant and add –ing:
run   running

B Write the –ing forms of the verbs. Follow the patterns of the verbs in each column.

go	_going_
eat	_eating_
play	_____
walk	_____

exercise	_exercising_
practice	_practicing_
ride	_____
take	_____

run	_running_
sit	_____
swim	_____

C Complete the sentences with the correct form of the verbs. Use contractions with pronouns.

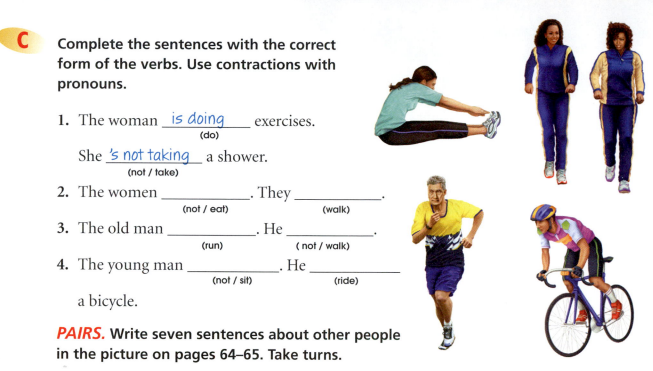

1. The woman <u>is doing</u> exercises.
   (do)

   She <u>'s not taking</u> a shower.
   (not / take)

2. The women _____. They _____.
   (not / eat)   (walk)

3. The old man _____. He _____.
   (run)   (not / walk)

4. The young man _____. He _____
   (not / sit)   (ride)

   a bicycle.

PAIRS. Write seven sentences about other people in the picture on pages 64–65. Take turns.

TIME to TALK

PAIRS. Look at the pictures. Talk about what the people are doing. What is wrong with the pictures? Make three affirmative and three negative sentences.

Example:
A: *The woman is running. She is not wearing sneakers.*

Grammar to Communicate 2

PRESENT PROGRESSIVE: YES / NO QUESTIONS AND SHORT ANSWERS

Be	Subject	Verb + –ing	Affirmative			Negative		
Am	I			I	**am.**		I	**am not.**
Is	he she it	**working?**	Yes,	he she it	**is.**	No,	he she it	**isn't.**
Are	we you they			we you they	**are.**		we you they	**aren't.**

 A   Answer the questions with true information. Write short answers.

1. Are you swimming right now?   ___No, I'm not.___

2. Is your teacher talking to your family?   ___No, she's not. OR No, he's not.___

3. Are you exercising right now?   _____

4. Are you learning English now?   _____

5. Are you and a friend talking right now? _____

6. Is a friend sitting near you?   _____

7. Are your classmates taking a shower?   _____

8. Is your best friend working today?   _____

B   Read the sentences. Write questions.

1. **A:** I'm not running.

   B: ___Are you walking?___
          (walk)

2. **A:** They're not playing tennis.

   B: _____
          (play soccer)

3. **A:** She's not eating ice cream.

   B: _____
          (eat cookies)

4. **A:** I'm not talking to my friend.

   B: _____
          (talk to your neighbor)

5. **A:** He's not practicing tennis.

   B: _____
          (practice baseball)

6. **A:** We're not exercising at home.

   B: _____
          (exercise in a park)

> ## Look
> The word order is different for statements and questions.
>
> They are running.   She is running.
>
> Are they running?   Is she running?

C   Look at the pictures. Write questions. Put the words in the correct order.

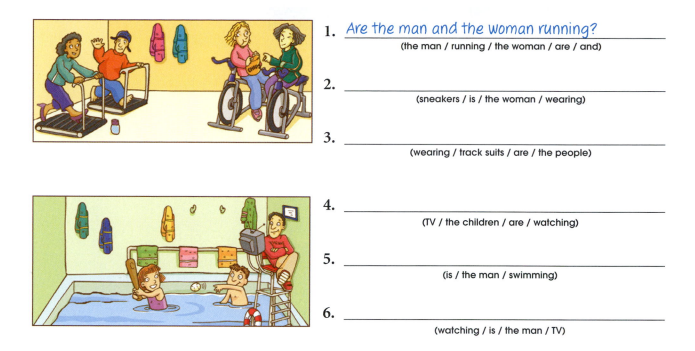

1. <u>Are the man and the woman running?</u>
   (the man / running / the woman / are / and)

2. _____
   (sneakers / is / the woman / wearing)

3. _____
   (wearing / track suits / are / the people)

4. _____
   (TV / the children / are / watching)

5. _____
   (is / the man / swimming)

6. _____
   (watching / is / the man / TV)

PAIRS. Ask and answer the questions above.

Example:

A: *Are the man and woman running?*
B: *Yes, they are.*

**TIME to TALK**

GROUPS. Student A: Choose a verb from page 64. Act it out for the other students. Can they guess the verb? Answer their questions with "Yes, I am" or "No, I'm not."
GROUP: Try to guess Student A's verb. Ask questions. Now another student acts out a verb. Continue until every student in the group has acted out two verbs.

Example:

Group: *Are you playing tennis?*
A: *No, I'm not.*
Group: *Are you swimming?*
A: *Yes, I am.*

Grammar to Communicate 3

PRESENT PROGRESSIVE: INFORMATION QUESTIONS				
Wh– word	**Be**	**Subject**	**Verb + –ing**	**Answers**
What	am	I	**eating?**	Cake.
Where	are	you we	**going?**	To his office.
Why	is	he she		Because it´s late.
Who	are	they	**calling?**	Their friends.

  A   Complete the questions. Use *is* or *are* and *you, he, she, we,* or *they*.

1. **A:** I'm reading.

   B: What <u>are you</u> reading?

2. **A:** Maria's playing tennis.

   B: Who _____ playing tennis with?

3. **A:** The students are talking to the teacher.

   B: Why _____ talking to the teacher?

4. **A:** Tom is swimming.

   B: Where _____ swimming?

5. **A:** I'm going home.

   B: Why _____ going home?

6. **A:** The children and I are eating.

   B: What _____ eating?

B   Write questions. Use the present progressive. Then answer the questions with the words in the box.

A track suit   Because she's late   I'm exercising   With some friends
At the health club   Dan   ~~Jeremy~~

1. <u>Who is Sylvia talking to?</u>   <u>Jeremy.</u>
   (who / Sylvia / talk to)

2. _____   _____
   (what / you / do)

3. _____   _____
   (where / you / exercise)

4. _____   _____
   (who / Paul and Jake / play soccer with)

5. _____   _____
   (why / your mother / run)

6. _____   _____
   (what / the boy / wear)

C **45** **Read Jean and Alice's conversation. Then write the missing questions. Use *What, Where, Who,* and *Why*. Listen and check your answers.**

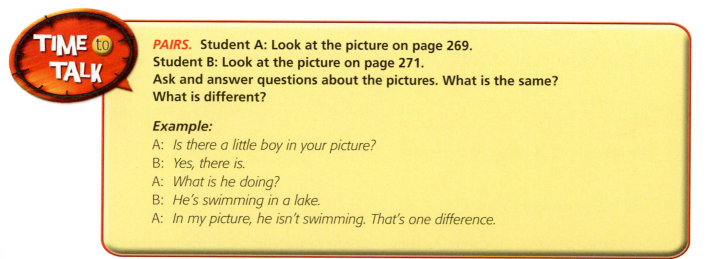

Alice: Hi? Jean? This is Alice. Is Rita there?

Jean: No, she's not.

Alice: ___What's she doing?___
       1. (do)

Jean: She's playing tennis with Sue.

Alice: How about Tom? Is he at home?

Jean: No, he's not.

Alice: _____
              2. (do)

Jean: He's playing soccer.

Alice: _____
             3. (play with)

Jean: With Phil and some other friends.

Alice: _____
                4. (play)

Jean: At Sandy Field.

Alice: Sandy Field? _____ at Sandy Field?
                        5. (play)

Jean: Because another team is playing at Bradley Field today.

Alice: _____
              6. (eat)

Jean: Me? I'm eating an apple . . . And why are you asking so many questions today?

TIME to TALK

PAIRS. **Student A: Look at the picture on page 269.**
Student B: Look at the picture on page 271.
Ask and answer questions about the pictures. What is the same?
What is different?

Example:
A: *Is there a little boy in your picture?*
B: *Yes, there is.*
A: *What is he doing?*
B: *He's swimming in a lake.*
A: *In my picture, he isn't swimming. That's one difference.*

Physical Exercise
71

Grammar

🔘 46 **Correct the conversation. There are seven mistakes. The first mistake is corrected for you. Then listen and check your answers.**

Mike: Hi, Tina. It's me, Mike. What ~~you are doing~~ *are you doing*?

Tina: I'm read a book.

Mike: Where are you?

Tina: At the health club.

Mike: Why you reading a book at the health club?

Tina: I'm sitting in the café. I'm waiting for Sara.

Mike: Are she exercising?

Tina: No, she not. She's taking a shower. Oh, she's coming now.

Sara: Hi, Tina! . . . Who is you talking to?

Tina: I talking to Mike.

Dictation

🔘 47 **Listen. You will hear five sentences. Write them on a piece of paper.**

Speaking

PAIRS. Read the sentences. Write a conversation for each sentence.

1. You're sitting in my seat.
2. Your dog is eating my flowers.
3. You're using my tennis ball.
4. Your daughter is swimming in the pool alone.
5. You're drinking my coffee.
6. Your telephone is ringing.

Example:
A: *Excuse me. You're sitting in my seat.*
B: *No, I'm not.*
A: *Yes, you are. Here's my ticket.*
B: *Oh, you're right. I'm sorry.*

WRAP-UP. Now perform one conversation for the class. Can they guess where you are?

Listening

A **48** **Listen. Reporters at the Summer Olympics are talking about three sports. Circle the pictures of the sports they talk about.**

Look

win = to be first in a game or race
athlete = a person who plays sports

tennis

marathon

volleyball

swimming

cycling

soccer

B **49** **Listen again. Match the countries of the athletes with the sports. Use one sport two times.**

_____ **1.** Kenya   **a.** tennis

_____ **2.** Canada   **b.** the marathon

_____ **3.** Japan   **c.** swimming

_____ **4.** Brazil

TIME to TALK

GROUPS. **Make a list of popular sports. If you don't know the name of a sport in English, ask your teacher or use a dictionary. Then answer the questions.**

1. Who are some famous athletes of the sports on your list? What countries are they from?

2. Is your country famous for any sport? Which sport(s)?

3. What are your favorite sports? Why?

Reading and Writing

Reading

A Read the reports from sports events. What are the sports? Write the sport above each paragraph.

PARAGRAPH 1 _____

Twenty-two girls are playing today. The players on our team are wearing black shorts and red T-shirts. The other players are wearing black shorts and blue T-shirts. Today's game is really interesting because there's an excellent player out there—Janet Abu. . . . And she's *kicking* the ball right now! The girls on our team are trying to get the ball. It's not easy for them!

PARAGRAPH 2 _____

There are many people here at the game today. Some people are standing. Some people are sitting. Some people are eating hot dogs. They are talking and laughing. It's very noisy. Dirk Bailey is standing and *holding* the ball. Most of his *teammates* are standing in the *field* behind him. Mickey Montoya from the other team is holding a bat. He's waiting for the ball. I am, too! It's so exciting!

B Read the sentences. Look at the italic words. Then find them in the paragraphs. Circle the letter of the sentence that has a similar meaning.

1. You are *kicking* a ball.
   a. You are using your hands.
   b. You are using your feet.

2. You are playing in a *field*.
   a. You are playing in a large outdoor area.
   b. You are playing in a large indoor room.

3. You are *holding* a ball.
   a. The ball is near your feet.
   b. The ball is in your hand.

4. Your *teammates* are standing in the field.
   a. They are watching your team.
   b. They are playing the game with you.

Prewriting

Watch or go to a sporting event or a place with a lot of activity (for example, a busy shopping mall). What is happening? Make a list of action verbs.

Writing

Write a report about what you saw. Use the reports on page 74 as a model. Do not write the place or the activity.

> ## Writing Tip
>
> Sometimes a person is doing two actions in one sentence.
>
> Write the word *and* between the *-ing* verbs. Do not repeat *are* or *is*.
>
> Example: Many people are sitting and watching.
>
> NOT Many people are sitting and ~~are~~ watching.

_____

_____

_____

_____

_____

_____

_____

_____

_____

_____

_____

_____

_____

_____

PAIRS. Show your report to your partner. Can he or she guess the activity?

Unit 7
Do's and Don'ts

Vocabulary

 **50** Read and listen.

1. finish dinner
2. start dinner
3. turn on
4. ask for something
5. take the food
6. touch
7. move a chair
8. put the food on the table
9. turn off
10. ask someone
11. wait for the bus

Listening

A CD 1 TRACK **51** **Listen. Why is Matthew's mother unhappy? Check (✓) all of the reasons.**

❏ 1. Matthew is listening to music.

☑ 2. Matthew is watching TV and doing homework.

❏ 3. Matthew is calling a friend.

❏ 4. Matthew's room is messy.

❏ 5. Matthew is eating in his bedroom.

B CD 1 TRACK **52** **Read and listen again. Write the missing words. Use the words in the box.**

don't	her	me	~~Turn~~

Mother: You aren't doing your homework. You're watching TV! _____Turn_____ it off right now!
$\qquad$ 1.

Matthew: But I am doing my homework . . .

Mother: So where is it?

Matthew: Here.

Mother: OK, now listen to _____. First,
$\qquad$ 2.
finish your homework. Do it right now, and _____ be careless. Then, clean
$\qquad$ 3.
your room. Make your bed and put your clothes in the closet. Don't put them under your bed, like last time.

Matthew: Yes, Mom.

Mother: Oh, and one more thing. Don't touch the telephone!

Matthew: But Sylvia is waiting for me to call!

Mother: Well, too bad. Call _____ tomorrow.
$\qquad$ 4.

Do's and Don'ts 77

Grammar to Communicate 1

IMPERATIVES				
Affirmative		**Negative**		
Verb		*Do + Not*	Verb	
Be	**quiet.**	**Don't**	**watch**	**TV.**
Sit	**down.**		**smoke.**	

Look

Say *please* to be polite.
Please be quiet.
Be quiet, please.

A Match the pictures with the sentences.

b 1. Be careful. The food is hot.

____ 2. Exercise every day.

____ 3. Close your mouth, please.

____ 4. Please open your books.

____ 5. Don't move your head.

____ 6. Don't turn on the water.

B Rewrite the sentences with *Don't*. Use the words in the box.

| close   run   stand   ~~talk~~ |

1. Be quiet.   Don't talk.
2. Sit down.   _____
3. Walk.   _____
4. Open the door.   _____

Make the sentences affirmative. Use the words in the box.

| Be careful   Be early   Be neat   ~~Turn off~~ |

5. Don't turn on the light.   Turn off the light.
6. Don't be late.   _____
7. Don't be careless.   _____
8. Don't be messy.   _____

78   Unit 7

C The people in the first sentence are doing something wrong. What do the people in the second sentence say? Use the words in the box.

be quiet	~~drink~~	eat	run	smoke	turn on

1. Andy is drinking soda.

   His dentist says, ___"Don't drink soda."___

2. The teenagers are waiting for their mother at her office. They are very noisy.

   The receptionist says, _____

3. The children are running in the hospital.

   The doctor says, _____

4. The little boy is eating in the store.

   The salesperson says, _____

5. Nancy is smoking in the restaurant.

   The waitress says, _____

6. The students are sitting in a room with no light.

   Their teacher says, _____

TIME to TALK

PAIRS. **What do the signs below mean? Where do you usually see each sign? Who are the signs for? Use the verbs in the box.**

eat	drink	smoke	use	~~wash~~	wear

Example:
A: *Sign 1 is in restaurant restrooms. It means "Wash your hands." It's for the cooks and waiters.*
B: *Sign 1 is also in hospitals. It's for the doctors and nurses.*

Now compare your answers with your classmates' answers.

Grammar to Communicate 2

PREPOSITIONS

Put the		Preposition	
	cat	**on**	the rug.
	shoes	**under**	the table.
	picture	**above**	
	chair	**behind**	
	rug	**in front of**	
	wastebasket	**near**	
	paper	**in**	the wastebasket.

A Look at the pictures. Frank's mother sees his room. What does she say? Complete the sentences with the words in the box.

BEFORE   AFTER

| books | chair | clothes | rug | telephone | wastebasket |

1. Put the _telephone_ on the desk.
2. Put the _____ under the bed.
3. Put the _____ on the shelf.
4. Put the _____ behind the door.
5. Put the _____ in front of the desk.
6. Put the _____ in the closet.

B Where do people usually put these things? Circle the correct preposition.

1. Put the wastebasket **behind** / **on** the door.
2. Put your clothes **in** / **in front of** your room.
3. Put the picture **above** / **under** the bed.
4. Put your shoes **in** / **under** the closet.
5. Put the chair **above** / **in front** of the window.
6. Put the food **on** / **behind** the table.

Complete the sentences. Use the prepositions *at, for,* and *to.*

1. Molly, be nice __to__ your sister.
2. Molly, wait _____ your brother.
3. Molly, listen _____ your teacher.
4. Molly, look _____ the cute boy.
5. Molly, write _____ your grandmother.
6. Molly, ask _____ some money.
7. Molly, talk _____ your father.

Look

Some verbs need prepositions after them.
Listen to him.
Write to me.
Talk to us.
Ask for it.
Wait for them.
Look at the board.

PAIRS. Molly is sixteen. Which sentences do you think Molly's mother says? Which sentences do you think Molly's friend says?

TIME to TALK

ON YOUR OWN. Where are the things below in your room at home? Draw them on page 270. Do not show your drawing to your partner.
Student A: Now tell Student B where to draw the things in your room.
Student B: Listen and draw things in your classmate's room on page 272.
Student A: Check Student B's picture. Is it correct? Then change roles.

Example:
A: *Put the sofa in front of the windows.*

Grammar to Communicate 3

OBJECT PRONOUNS		
	Noun	
Take	John.	
	Debra.	
	the bus.	
	John and me.	
	Debra and John.	

	Object Pronoun
Take	**him.**
	her.
	it.
	us.
	them.

Look

Pronouns

Subject	Object
I	me
you	you
he	him
she	her
it	it
we	us
they	them

 A   Rewrite the sentences. Replace the underlined words with words from the box.

Anna   David   ~~the answers~~   the conversation   your classmates

1. Read <u>them</u>.   Read the answers.
2. Listen to <u>it</u>.   _____
3. Wait for <u>her</u>.   _____
4. Don't ask <u>him</u>.   _____
5. Don't talk to <u>them</u>.   _____

Now replace the underlined words with an object pronoun.

6. Help <u>Mrs. Wu</u>.   Help her.
7. Play <u>the music</u>.   _____
8. Watch <u>the children</u>.   _____
9. Don't touch <u>the plates</u>.   _____
10. Go with <u>Mr. Montero</u>.   _____

B   Complete the sentences. Use an object pronoun.

1. Gabriel and I are going to a café. Come with ___us.___
2. I'm talking. Listen to _____.
3. Here are the answers. Read _____.
4. Don't do the homework now. Do _____ at home.
5. You're sitting next to Julia. Work with _____.
6. Your classmates are doing the same exercise. Ask _____ for the answers.
7. Tony isn't at work today. Call _____ at home.

C 🔘 **53** **Complete the conversation.**
Then listen and check your answers.

Ana: What exercises are you doing?

Tomás: B and C.

Ana: Are _____ difficult?
                  1. (they / them)

Tomás: _____'m not sure.
                  2. (I / Me)

           _____'m starting _____ now. Sit down and help _____.
           3. (I / Me)   4. (they / them)   5. (I / me)

Ana: Okay. Hmm. _____ are difficult.
                          6. (They / Them)

Tomás: David's a good student. Ask _____ for help.
                                           7. (he / him)

Ana: _____'s not in class today.
           8. (He / Him)

Tomás: Then ask _____.
                      9. (she / her)

Ana: Who?

Tomás: Safira. _____'s your friend, right?
                    10. (She / Her)

Ana: Yes, she is. Hey, Safira! Help _____ with Exercises B and C.
                                             11. (we / us)

Safira: _____'m busy.
           12. (I / Me)

GROUPS. Talk about Do's and Don'ts for the classroom. For each rule, write one sentence with a noun. Write the sentence again with a pronoun. Make a list.

Example:
A: *Here's a Do rule. Listen to the teacher.*
B: *Yes. Listen to **her.***
C: *Here's a Don't rule. Don't write in the book.*
A: *Yes. Don't write in **it.***

Now compare your lists to the other groups' lists. Which group has the most sentences?

Do's	Don'ts
Listen to the teacher.	Don't talk in class.

Grammar

Find the mistake in each sentence. Circle the letter and correct the mistake.

1. Put the chair next to she.
   A   B   C

   Correct: _*Put the chair next to her.*_

2. Children, stand in front your desks.
            A   B   C

   Correct: _____

3. No listen to him.
   A   B   C

   Correct: _____

4. Please wait to me.
   A   B   C

   Correct: _____

5. Don't talk to we.
   A   B   C

   Correct: _____

6. Turning off the TV, please.
   A   B   C

   Correct: _____

Dictation

 54 Listen. You will hear five sentences. Write them on a piece of paper.

Speaking

PAIRS. **Choose one situation and write a conversation. Then perform your conversation for the class.**

Situation 1

Student A: You are a mother or father. Your son or daughter is listening to loud music and playing computer games. He or she isn't doing homework.

Student B: You are the son or daughter.

Situation 2

Student A: You are a teacher. You are teaching an English class. One student is not listening to you. He is listening to music and drawing pictures in a notebook. His English book is not open. The student's feet are on the desk in front of him or her.

Student B: You are the student.

Example:
A: *Listen to me! Turn off that music!*
B: *But Mom! I'm busy! . . .*

Listening

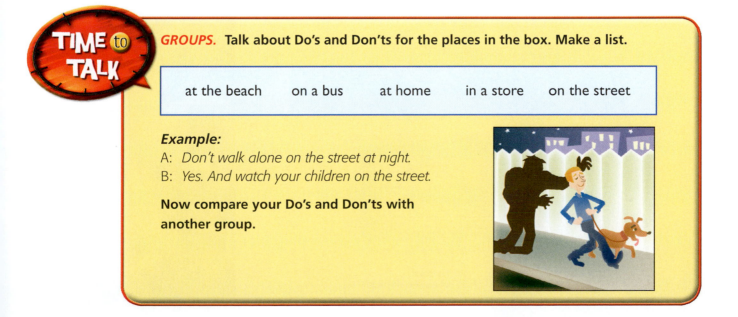

A CD 1 TRACK **55** Listen. You will hear six conversations. Check (✓) the correct answers. (Be careful! There are two extra answers.)

WHO IS SPEAKING?	A DENTIST	A DOCTOR	A POLICE OFFICER	A CAB DRIVER
conversation 1				
conversation 2				
conversation 3				

WHERE ARE THE PEOPLE?	AT THE AIRPORT	IN A CAR	ON AN AIRPLANE	ON THE STREET
conversation 4				
conversation 5				
conversation 6				

B CD 1 TRACK **56** Listen again to the conversations. For each sentence, write *T* (true), or *F* (false).

_____ **1.** The man is friendly. (Conversation 1)

_____ **2.** The man is not listening to the woman. (Conversation 2)

_____ **3.** The man is working. (Conversation 3)

_____ **4.** The people are standing on the street. (Conversation 4)

_____ **5.** The woman is a waitress. (Conversation 5)

_____ **6.** The woman is going. The man is staying. (Conversation 6)

TIME to TALK

GROUPS. Talk about Do's and Don'ts for the places in the box. Make a list.

| at the beach | on a bus | at home | in a store | on the street |

Example:
A: *Don't walk alone on the street at night.*
B: *Yes. And watch your children on the street.*

Now compare your Do's and Don'ts with another group.

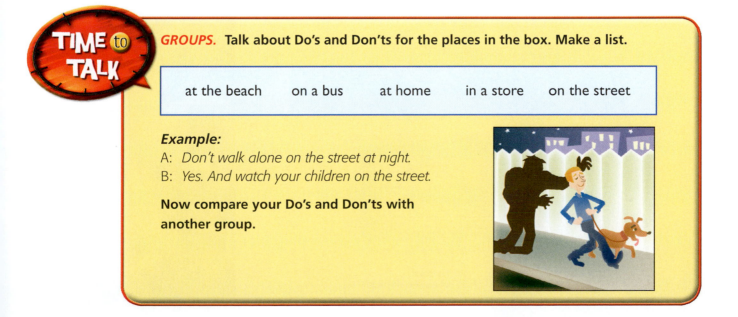

Reading and Writing

Reading

Read the instructions. Who are they for? Match the pictures with the instructions. Write the correct letters.

1. _____

(H) INSTRUCTIONS

- Put on a hospital gown.
- Make a list of questions to ask the doctor.
- Keep your insurance card with you.
- Do not keep money in your room.
- Be ready to take more medical exams.

a. science laboratory

2. _____

- Wear safety glasses at all times.
- Wear a lab coat over your clothes.
- Do not wear open-toed shoes.
- Do not wear shorts.

b. patient in hospital

3. _____

May 13, 2006

- Do not take a shower or go swimming for three days.
- Do not lift anything heavy.
- Call the nursing staff at 111-222-6777 with any questions.
- Come to the hospital immediately if get a fever.

Dr. _____

c. fire

4. _____

- Walk to the nearest exit.
- Do not run.
- Use the stairs.
- Do not use the elevator.

d. patient leaving hospital

Prewriting

Read the paragraph about Albania.

Here is some advice for your trip to Albania. First, go to Tirana. It's a nice city. There are many restaurants and cafés, and Albanian food is very good. Shish kebab and meatballs are two popular dishes. Try them! Then go to an outdoor café and have coffee. Second, visit Kruja. It is a beautiful old town in the mountains. But don't drive there. The mountain roads are sometimes dangerous. Take the bus. Next, visit Saranda. It is a small city near Corfu, Greece. There are beautiful beaches, and the sea is deep, clean, and blue. Finally, learn some words in Albanian. The Albanian people are kind and friendly, but many of them do not speak English.

Writing

Write a paragraph for a travel guide to your country. Write about the Do's and Don'ts. Use the paragraph above as a model.

Writing Tip

If two adjectives describe one noun, write the word *and* between the adjectives. Do not use any commas (,).

Example: The Albanian people are kind and friendly.
NOT The Albanian people are kind✗and friendly.

Unit 8
Possessions

Vocabulary

CD 2 TRACK 2 **Read and listen. Then circle the things you see that are in your room.**

1. painting
2. calendar
3. radio
4. alarm clock
5. keys
6. glasses
7. record player
8. speakers
9. camera
10. records
11. CD player
12. CDs
13. cell phone
14. wallet
15. contact lenses
16. computer
17. credit card
18. digital camera
19. DVD player
20. DVDs

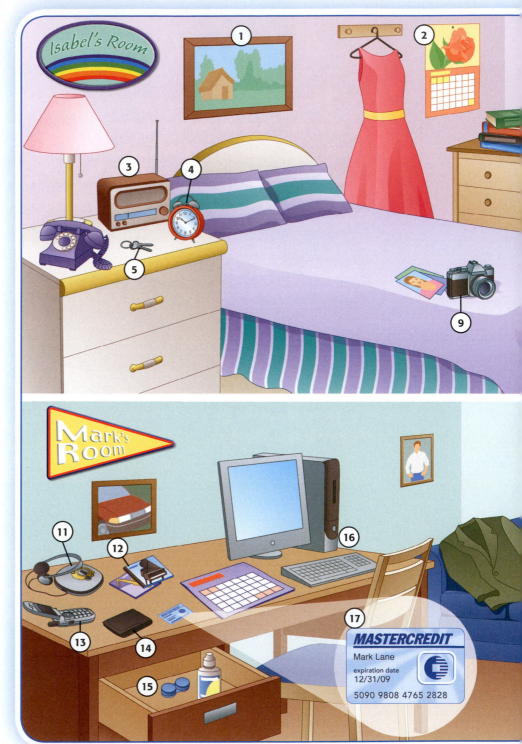

Listening

A  **3** **Listen. Two friends are in a store. Check (✓) the things that they see.**

- ✓ a camera
- ❏ a stereo
- ❏ speakers
- ❏ an alarm clock

- ❏ a credit card
- ❏ a radio
- ❏ a cell phone
- ❏ a DVD player

B CD 2 TRACK **4** **Read and listen again. Write the missing words. Use the words in the box.**

mine	These	this	those	~~yours~~

Saleswoman: That's mine. It's not for sale.

Bob: But what is it?

Saleswoman: It's a radio. We have other radios over there.

Sammi: Amazing . . . it's so thin—like a piece of paper! Is this ___yours___ too?
1.

Saleswoman: No, it isn't. Phil, is _____ cell phone yours?
2.

Phil: No, it's not _____.
3.

Bob: Hey, that cell phone is mine. And _____ keys are mine too.
4.

Sammi: _____? Here you are. And are these your sunglasses?
5.

Possessions **89**

Grammar to Communicate 1

THIS / THAT

Adjective	Noun			Pronoun	
This	flower	is white.	→	**This**	is white.
That	flower	is red.	→	**That**	is red.

THESE / THOSE

Adjective	Noun			Pronoun	
These	flowers	are pink.	→	**These**	are pink.
Those	flowers	are purple.	→	**Those**	are purple.

A Look at the pictures. Complete the sentences. Use the adjectives *This* or *That*.

1. ___This___ cell phone is modern.

2. _____ necklace is cheap.

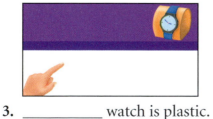

3. _____ watch is plastic.

4. _____ phone is old.

5. _____ necklace is expensive.

6. _____ watch is gold.

B Rewrite the sentences from Exercise A. Use the pronouns *This* or *That*.

1. _This is modern._

2. _____

3. _____

4. _____

5. _____

6. _____

C **5** Complete the questions. Use *this*, *that*, *these*, or *those* and *is* or *are*. Then listen and check your answers.

> **Look**
>
> Use *it* to answer questions with *this* or *that*.
>   A: What's **this**?   B: **It's** a book.
>
> Use *they* to answer questions with *these* or *those*.
>   A: What are **those**?   B: **They're** books.

A: What's _this?_

B: It's a wallet.

A: What are _____?

B: They're rings.

A: What's _____?

B: It's a backpack.

A: What are _____?

B: They're sunglasses.

A: What are _____?

B: They're earrings.

A: What's _____?

B: It's a radio.

D **6** Complete the compliments. Use *That* or *Those,* and *is* or *are.* Use *a* if necessary. Then listen and check your answers.

1. _____That is a_____ nice ring.

2. _____ beautiful earrings.

3. _____ nice watch.

4. _____ beautiful sunglasses.

Now talk to other students. Make compliments about their possessions.

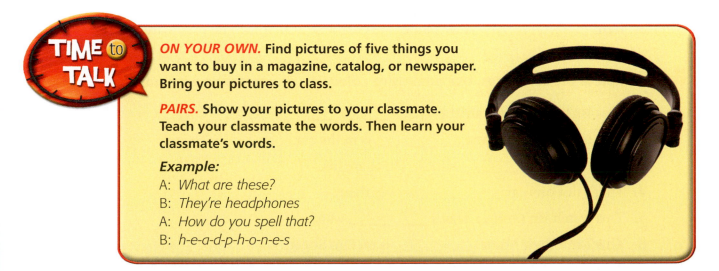

TIME to TALK

ON YOUR OWN. **Find pictures of five things you want to buy in a magazine, catalog, or newspaper. Bring your pictures to class.**

PAIRS. **Show your pictures to your classmate. Teach your classmate the words. Then learn your classmate's words.**

Example:
A: *What are these?*
B: *They're headphones*
A: *How do you spell that?*
B: *h-e-a-d-p-h-o-n-e-s*

Grammar to Communicate 2

POSSESSIVE ADJECTIVES AND POSSESSIVE PRONOUNS

		Possessive Adjective	Noun				Possessive Pronoun
That	is	**my**	book.	→	That	is	**mine.**
		your					**yours.**
		his					**his.**
Those	are	**her**	books.	→	Those	are	**hers.**
		our					**ours.**
		their					**theirs.**

Look

Possessive pronouns can replace singular or plural nouns.
This is his book. **Mine is** over there.
Those are my books. **Yours are** over there.

 A Look at the pictures. Complete the sentences. Use *mine, yours, his, hers, ours,* or *theirs.*

1. **Makiko:** John, is that camera __yours__?
2. **John:** Yes, the camera is _____.
3. **Greta:** Daddy, is the little dog _____?
4. **Charlene and Tom:** This car is _____.
5. **Ben:** Their names are Charlene and Tom. The prizes are _____.

B Complete the sentences. Use possessive adjectives or possessive pronouns.

1. This isn't my digital camera. That's __mine__.
2. This isn't her cell phone. _____ is in the car.
3. Those aren't _____ shoes. These are his.
4. That's not our car. _____ is over there.
5. This watch isn't mine. That's _____ watch.
6. That's not their home. _____ is on Elm Street.

Complete the conversations. Use possessive adjectives or possessive pronouns. Then listen and check your answers.

1. **A:** Are these glasses ____yours?____

   B: Yes, they are.

2. **A:** Are these Nicole's glasses?

   B: No. _____ are different.

3. **A:** Hello. I'm Ming Lee and this is

   _____ wife, Chiao-lun.

   B: It's nice to meet you.

4. **A:** _____ name is Ed.

   What's _____?

   B: Hi, Ed. I'm Stella.

5. **A:** Is that the children's dog?

   B: No. _____ is black.

6. **A:** Is that a picture of you and Chris?

   B: Yes. And that's _____ home.

7. **A:** Who's the woman with Ari?

   B: That's _____ wife.

8. **A:** Is Ari's home in Boston?

   B: No. _____ is in Cambridge.

   His brother's is in Boston.

Rewrite Speaker B's answers. Replace the underlined words with possessive pronouns. Then listen and check your answers.

1. **A:** Here's your book.

   B: That's not <u>my book</u>.

   ____That's not mine.____

2. **A:** Bill and Sue, your dogs are nice.

   B: Those dogs aren't <u>our dogs</u>.

   _____

3. **A:** Are those our records?

   B: No, these are <u>your records</u>.

   _____

4. **A:** Is Anna's cell phone black?

   B: No, <u>her cell phone</u> is blue.

   _____

5. **A:** They can't find their keys.

   B: Are those keys on the table <u>their keys</u>?

   _____

6. **A:** Is that his car in front of the house?

   B: No, <u>his car</u> is at home.

   _____

TIME to TALK

GROUPS. Look at the possessions of the people in your group and make five sentences. Use the words in the box and your own ideas.

big	heavy	cheap	gold	old	plastic
small	light	expensive	silver	new	leather

Example:

A: *Alex's wallet is leather. Mine is plastic.*

B: *Yes, and his wallet is old. Yours is new.*

Grammar to Communicate 3

SIMPLE PRESENT: *HAVE*					
Subject	*Have*		Subject	*Have*	
I We You They	**have**	a radio.	He She It	**has**	a radio.

Look
I **don't have** a radio.
She **doesn't have** a radio.

A Which things in the picture do you have or not have? Write sentences.

1. I don't have a DVD player.   4. _____

2. _____   5. _____

3. _____   6. _____

PAIRS. Tell your partner the things that you have.

B Look at the pictures on pages 88–89. What things do Mark and Isabel have? Complete the sentences. Use the correct names and *has* or *have*.

1. Mark and Isabel have paintings.   5. _____ DVDs.

2. Isabel has a CD player.   6. _____ calendars.

3. _____ cameras.   7. _____ a radio.

4. _____ a cell phone.   8. _____ glasses.

C Write sentences about your classmates. Use the words in the boxes.

One student	has	a book	an eraser	a pen	a CD player
Some students	have	books	erasers	pens	CD players
A lot of students		a dictionary	a notebook	a pencil	an earring
All the students		dictionaries	notebooks	pencils	earrings

1. <u>A lot of students have notebooks.</u>

2. _____

3. _____

4. _____

5. _____

6. _____

PAIRS. Compare sentences with a classmate.

TIME to TALK

GROUPS. What possessions do you have? Find out if people in your group have the same things. Talk about the things in the box and your own ideas.

apartment	cat	house	old car	a lot of books
bike	dog	motorcycle	piano	a lot of clothes
bird	guitar	new car	truck	a lot of shoes

Example:
A: *I have a cat. Her name is Chili.*
B: *I have a cat, too.*
C: *Me, too!*
D: *I have a dog. His name is Max.*

Now tell the class about your group.

Example:
E: *Angelo, Rami, and Nellie have cats. Sal has a dog.*

Review and Challenge

Grammar

CD 2 TRACK 9 Complete the conversation. Use the words in the box. Then listen and check your answers. (Be careful! There are three extra words.)

has	have	her	hers	mine	my	that	th~~e~~se	they	this

Carrie: Are ___these___ your earrings?
1.

Nadia: Yes, _____ are. And these are _____ rings.
2.   3.

Carrie: They're nice. And is _____ your cell phone over there on the table?
4.

Nadia: No, _____ is my cell phone.
5.

Carrie: Maybe it's Ann's phone. She _____ a red phone.
6.

Nadia: No, it's not _____. Her phone is in her bag.
7.

Dictation

CD 2 TRACK 10 Listen. You will hear five sentences. Write them on a piece of paper.

Speaking

GROUPS. Learn a few words in a new language from your classmates. Student A: point to things in the room. The group asks and answers questions about the words in other languages. Use *this*, *that*, *these*, and *those*.

Example:
A: *What are these?*
B: *In English, these are called keys.*
   In French, they're <u>clefs</u>.
C: *And in Spanish, they are* <u>llaves</u>.
   What is that?
D: *In English, that's called an earring.*
   In Russian, it's sergá.

earring

Listening

CD 2 TRACK

A 11 **Listen. Where are the people? Match the conversations with the places in the pictures.**

_____ **1.** Conversation 1

_____ **2.** Conversation 2

_____ **3.** Conversation 3

_____ **4.** Conversation 4

CD 2 TRACK

B 12 **Listen again. Complete the sentences. Circle the correct answers.**

Conversation 1

The woman is eating   **a.** with a male friend.   **b.** with a female friend.

Conversation 2

The briefcase is the   **a.** woman's briefcase.   **b.** man's briefcase.

Conversation 3

There are some sneakers in   **a.** Jamie's room.   **b.** the living room.

Conversation 4

The man's car is   **a.** on the left side of the street.   **b.** on the right side of the street.

Write five of your favorite possessions on a piece of paper, and give the paper to your teacher. Do not write your name on the paper.

GROUPS. **Your teacher will give your group some papers. Match each paper to a student in another group. Explain your answers.**

Example:

A: _We think this is Ahmed's paper._
Teacher: _Why?_
B: _Well, he has a new car and he likes computers a lot._
Ahmed: _You're wrong. That's not mine._

MY FAVORITE POSSESSIONS

my record player
my computer
my computer games
my digital camera
my soccer ball

Reading and Writing

Reading

A   Read the paragraph. Then complete the insurance form.

My wife and I have two cameras and a CD player. My camera is a Makki 510. Hers is a Shannon 600. I have the serial number of mine, but not hers. The serial number of my camera is 888576213. My camera is digital, and it is worth about $700. Hers is not digital. It is worth about $200. Our CD player is a Rory E50. It is worth about $500. The serial number is 765890133.

STANDARD HOME INSURANCE APPLICATION FORM

Property Description

Please include the serial number and value. If you are not sure, write ?.

Quality	Description	Make	Model	Serial number	Value
1	digital camera		510		
1	camera-not digital			?	
1	CD player	Rory	E50		$500

B   Label the drawing. Write *make, model, serial number,* and *value.*

1. _____

$30.00

Makki 510

2. _____

3. _____

4. _____

Prewriting

Complete the insurance form. Write about your family's most important possessions.

STANDARD HOME INSURANCE APPLICATION FORM

Property Description

Please include the serial number and value. If you are not sure, write ?.

Quality	Description	Make	Model	Serial number	Value

Writing

Now write a paragraph. Describe your property for your insurance company. Use the paragraph on page 98 as a model.

> ## Writing Tip
>
> After we use a noun one time, we often use a pronoun the second time.
>
> Example: Our CD player is a Rory E50.
>
> **It** is worth $200.
>
> (It = Our CD player)

Game 2
Units 5–8

PLAYERS | 2 pairs of students

MATERIALS | 1 book
1 coin
2 markers (1 marker for each pair of students)

INSTRUCTIONS
▶ Put your markers on the START box. Pair 1 goes first.
▶ EACH PAIR: Toss the coin. Heads = Move 1 box. Tails = Move 2 boxes. Read the words in the box and look at the pictures. Complete the conversations.
Example: PICTURE 1
  1. Student A: How much is a package of cookies?
      Student B: It's two dollars.
▶ Make sure the other pair's conversation is correct.
▶ If your conversation is *not* correct, put your marker on the box from your last turn. If you land on the box that has the other pair's marker, move to the next box.
▶ Continue taking turns. The first pair to get to the FINISH box wins.

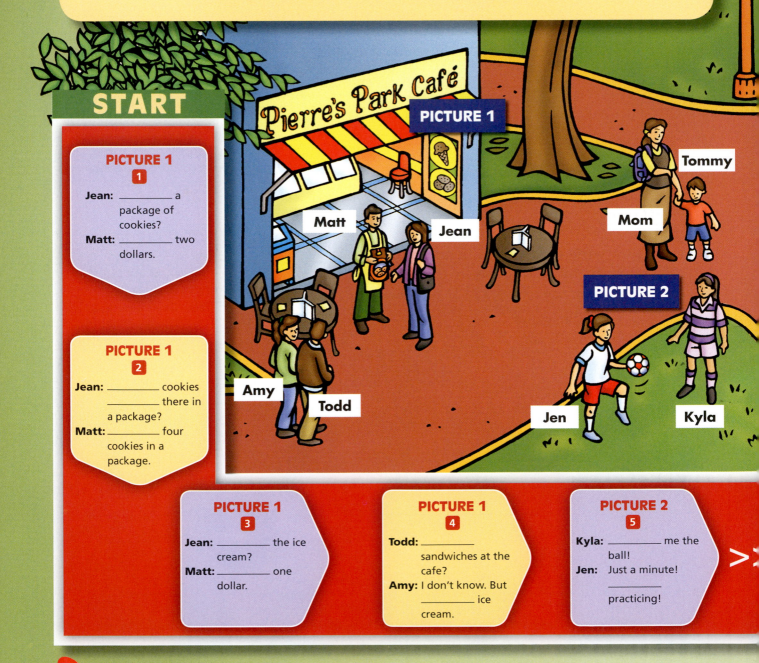

START

PICTURE 1
1
Jean: _____ a package of cookies?
Matt: _____ two dollars.

PICTURE 1
2
Jean: _____ cookies _____ there in a package?
Matt: _____ four cookies in a package.

PICTURE 1
3
Jean: _____ the ice cream?
Matt: _____ one dollar.

PICTURE 1
4
Todd: _____ sandwiches at the cafe?
Amy: I don't know. But _____ ice cream.

PICTURE 2
5
Kyla: _____ me the ball!
Jen: Just a minute! _____ practicing!

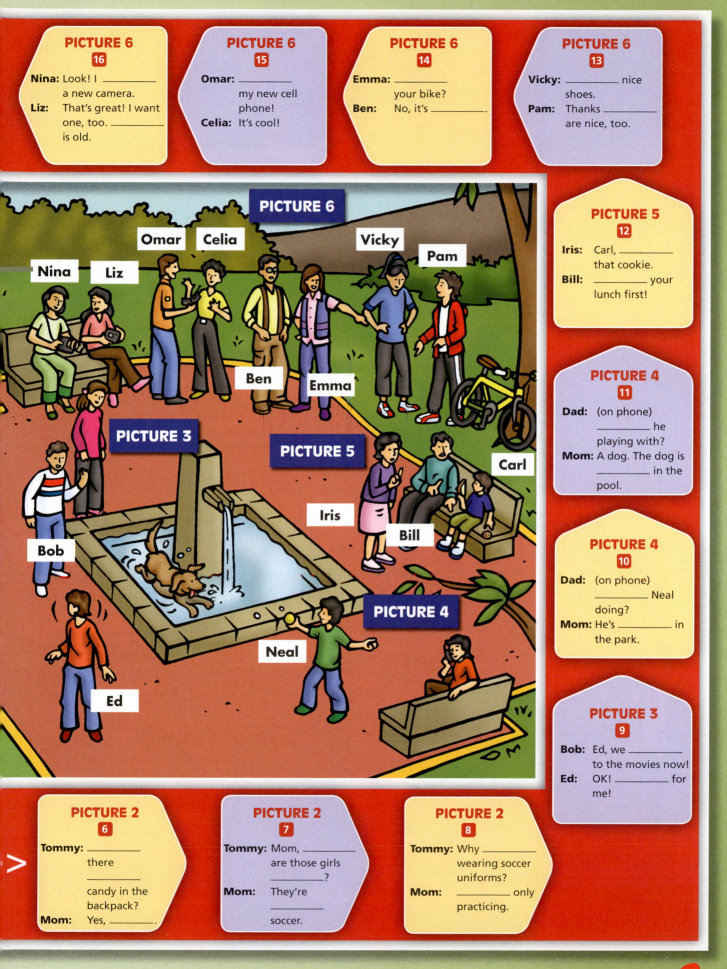

PICTURE 6
16
Nina: Look! I _____ a new camera.
Liz: That's great! I want one, too. _____ is old.

PICTURE 6
15
Omar: _____ my new cell phone!
Celia: It's cool!

PICTURE 6
14
Emma: _____ your bike?
Ben: No, it's _____.

PICTURE 6
13
Vicky: _____ nice shoes.
Pam: Thanks _____ are nice, too.

PICTURE 5
12
Iris: Carl, _____ that cookie.
Bill: _____ your lunch first!

PICTURE 4
11
Dad: (on phone) _____ he playing with?
Mom: A dog. The dog is _____ in the pool.

PICTURE 4
10
Dad: (on phone) _____ Neal doing?
Mom: He's _____ in the park.

PICTURE 3
9
Bob: Ed, we _____ to the movies now!
Ed: OK! _____ for me!

PICTURE 2
6
Tommy: _____ there _____ candy in the backpack?
Mom: Yes, _____.

PICTURE 2
7
Tommy: Mom, _____ are those girls _____?
Mom: They're _____ soccer.

PICTURE 2
8
Tommy: Why _____ wearing soccer uniforms?
Mom: _____ only practicing.

Game 2: Units 5-8

101

Unit 9
Routines

Grammar
- Simple Present: Affirmative Statements
- Simple Present: Spelling Rules
- Simple Present: Negative Statements

Vocabulary

CD 2 TRACK **13** Read and listen. Then circle the things you do every day.

1. stay up late

2. brush your teeth

3. sleep

5. have lunch

6. wash the dishes

7. take the bus

9. drink coffee

10. read a magazine

11. do the laundry

Listening

A 🔘 14 **Listen. Two people talk about work schedules in their countries. Which country is each sentence about? Write *F* (France), *J* (Japan) or *F, J* (both).**

_____ 1. Many people have long lunch breaks.

_____ 2. Many people eat lunch at home.

_____ 3. Most people start work at 8:00 or 8:30.

_____ 4. Most people have an hour for lunch.

_____ 5. Banks and shops aren't open on Mondays.

B 🔘 15 **Read and listen again. Write the missing words. Use the words in the box.**

doesn't	don't	~~have~~	works

Taka: Hey, Monique, you come from France, right?

Monique: Yes, why?

Taka: It says here that in France, most workers

_____*have*_____ a two-hour break for lunch. Is
1.

that true?

Monique: Well, it depends on the job, but in general, it's

true. Many people in France have lunch at

home. My mother, my sister, and I eat lunch

together every day. But my father _____
2.

in another city, so he _____ eat with us.
3.

Taka: Really? That's interesting. In Japan, we only

have an hour for lunch, so we _____ have
4.

time to go home. I think I like the French

way!

4. get up early

8. work

12. eat out

Grammar to Communicate ❶

SIMPLE PRESENT: AFFIRMATIVE STATEMENTS

Subject	Verb		Subject	Verb	
I			He She	**cooks**	a lot.
We You They	**cook**	a lot.	It	**works**	well.

A Make sentences about the people you know. Use the words in the box.

best friends	family and I	friends and I	mother
boyfriend	father	girlfriend	parents
children	friends	husband	wife

1. My _____ get up early.
2. My _____ stays up late.
3. My _____ eats out a lot.
4. My _____ sleeps late a lot.

5. My _____ works five days a week.
6. My _____ wash the dishes at night.
7. My _____ cooks in the evening.
8. My _____ go for a walk every day.

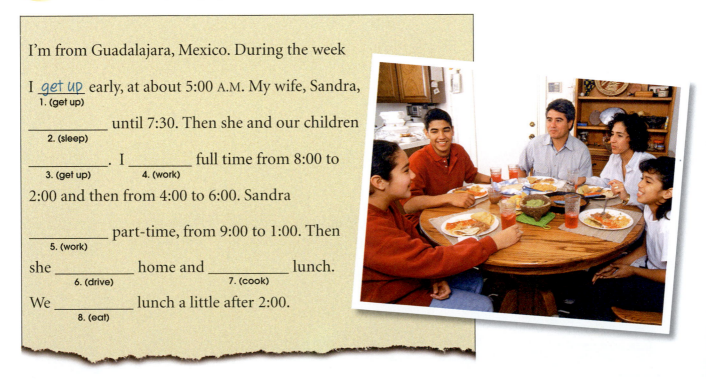

B Complete the paragraph.

I'm from Guadalajara, Mexico. During the week

I _get up_ early, at about 5:00 A.M. My wife, Sandra,
  1. (get up)

_____ until 7:30. Then she and our children
  2. (sleep)

_____. I _____ full time from 8:00 to
  3. (get up)   4. (work)

2:00 and then from 4:00 to 6:00. Sandra

_____ part-time, from 9:00 to 1:00. Then
  5. (work)

she _____ home and _____ lunch.
     6. (drive)   7. (cook)

We _____ lunch a little after 2:00.
    8. (eat)

C What do you think these people probably do? Write sentences. Use the verbs in the box and *a lot*.

| cook | eat out | play | sleep | ~~talk on the phone~~ | work |

1. Teresa and Angela are 16 years old.
   <u>They probably talk on the phone a lot.</u>

2. Billy is a three-month-old baby.
   _____

3. Melanie is a mother of six children.
   _____

4. Annie is five years old.
   _____

5. Sylvia and David Lin like good food.
   _____

6. Mark is a doctor.
   _____

PAIRS. Compare your answers. Do you agree? Then talk about the activities. Which activities do you do a lot?

Look

Time expressions

at night
every day
in the afternoon
in the morning
in the evening
on weekends

PAIRS. Tell your partner about the routines of five people you know. Use time expressions and the words in the boxes or your own ideas.

best friend	drink coffee
brother or sister	eat out a lot
children	get up late
English teacher	go for a walk
father	have lunch at home
grandparents	play computer games
mother	read magazines
neighbor	talk on the phone a lot
roommate	work full time

play computer games

Example:
A: *My best friend plays computer games every day.*

Grammar to Communicate 2

SIMPLE PRESENT THIRD PERSON SINGULAR: SPELLING RULES	
Example	**Spelling Rule**
study → studies He studies every day.	End of verb: consonant + –y Spelling: change y to i, add –es

Example	**Spelling Rule**
finish → finishes watch → watches miss → misses fix → fixes He misses his family.	End of verb: sh, ch, ss, x Spelling: Add –es

Look

We **go** to the movies a lot.
He **goes** to the movies a lot.

A Complete the sentences.

① ② ③ ④ ⑤

1. Ming _____ with her husband at night.
   (relax)

2. Ann _____ at sad movies.
   (cry)

3. Tina _____ lunch at 2:00 P.M.
   (finish)

4. Al _____ cars with Sal every day.
   (fix)

5. Lynn _____ her hair in the morning.
   (wash)

Look

Pronunciation of final -s
walks   /s/
comes   /z/
watches   /ɪz/

B

 CD 2 TRACK **16** Circle the verbs in the sentences. Then listen. What are the sounds of the verb endings? Check (✓) the correct column.

	/s/	/z/	/ɪz/
1. My daughter brushes her hair all the time.	❏	❏	❏
2. My mother reads the newspaper.	❏	❏	❏
3. My friend Sam drinks coffee.	❏	❏	❏
4. My sister takes the bus to work.	❏	❏	❏
5. My uncle washes his car once a week.	❏	❏	❏

C **PAIRS.** Change the underlined words in Exercise B to people you know. Read your sentences to your partner.

Example:
A: *My best friend brushes her hair all the time.*

D Look at the chart. It shows schedules in different countries. Complete the sentences with the correct words.

	COLOMBIA	SOUTH KOREA	IRAN	TAIWAN
start work	8:00 A.M.	9:00 A.M.	8:00 A.M.	9:00 A.M.
finish work	6:00 P.M.	6:00 P.M.	4:00 P.M.	5:00 P.M.
have lunch	12:00 – 2:00 P.M.	12:00 – 1:00 P.M.	12:00 – 1:00 P.M.	12:00 – 1:00 P.M.
go to school	7:00 A.M. – 3:00 P.M.	7:45 A.M. – 5:00 P.M.	8:00 A.M. – 3:30 P.M.	8:00 A.M. – 5:00 P.M.

1. Most students in South Korea _____*go to school*_____ for almost nine hours.

2. Most people in Taiwan _____ at 5:00 P.M.

3. Most people in Iran _____ at 8:00 A.M.

4. Rosa lives in Colombia. She _____ from 12:00 to 2:00 P.M.

5. Jae lives in South Korea. He _____ from 7:45 to 5:00 P.M.

6. Chia-Pei lives in Taiwan. She _____ at 9:00 A.M.

PAIRS. Talk about the schedules of people in your country.

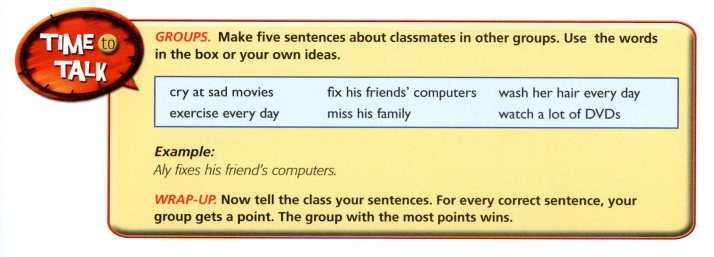

TIME to TALK

GROUPS. Make five sentences about classmates in other groups. Use the words in the box or your own ideas.

cry at sad movies	fix his friends' computers	wash her hair every day
exercise every day	miss his family	watch a lot of DVDs

Example:
Aly fixes his friend's computers.

WRAP-UP. Now tell the class your sentences. For every correct sentence, your group gets a point. The group with the most points wins.

Grammar to Communicate 3

SIMPLE PRESENT: NEGATIVE STATEMENTS

Subject	Don't	Verb		Subject	Doesn't	Verb	
I You We They	**don't**	**work**	every day.	He She It	**doesn't**	**work**	every day.

A Read the sentences. Write the correct names on the desks in the picture.

1. Ali sits behind Maria. He doesn't sit near a window or door.
2. Jin and Ozan sit next to Maria. They don't sit next to Ali.
3. Lin sits near the door. She doesn't sit in front of Jin.
4. Pedro and Ozan sit near the window. They don't sit next to Lin.

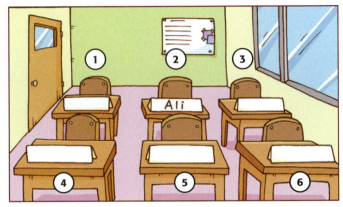

PAIRS. Look at the pictures on page 102–103. Write sentences about the things you do and don't do every day.

Example:
I cook every day. OR *I don't cook every day.*

B Complete the sentences. Use the negative form of the verb.

1. David goes out on Saturday night, but he ____doesn't go____ out on Sunday night.
2. Mr. and Mrs. Kim drink coffee, but they _____ tea.
3. I do the dishes every day, but I _____ the laundry every day.
4. The children have dinner at home, but they _____ lunch at home.
5. My friends and I play tennis, but we _____ soccer.
6. Ms. Li works on Mondays, but she _____ on Tuesdays.
7. I get up late on weekends, but I _____ late during the week.
8. Amy watches TV in the morning, but she _____ TV in the evening.

C Look at the chart. Make sentences about the people.

WEEKEND ACTIVITIES	CARLOS	ALICIA	PAUL	OLIVA
eat out	no	yes	yes	no
go to the movies	no	yes	yes	yes
play computer games	yes	no	no	yes
watch sports on TV	yes	no	yes	no

1. <u>Alicia and Oliva don't watch sports on TV.</u>
   (TV / Alicia and Oliva)

2. _____
   (eat out / Alicia and Paul)

3. _____
   (movies / Carlos)

4. _____
   (computer games / Alicia and Paul)

5. _____
   (sport on TV / Alicia)

6. _____
   (eat out / Carlos and Oliva)

PAIRS. Talk about your friends' activities on the weekend. Say what they do and don't do.

Look

too = also in affirmative responses
> A: Maria likes movies.
> B: John does, **too**.

either = also in negative responses
> A: Maria doesn't exercise
> B: I don't **either**.

PAIRS. Look at the pictures on pages 102–103. Make a story. What are the people's names? What do they do every day? What don't they do every day?

Example:
A: *Susie Li is a student. She stays up late every night.*
B: *She doesn't sleep much.*

Review and Challenge

Grammar

17 Correct the paragraph. There are seven mistakes. The first mistake is corrected for you. Then listen and check your answers.

        don't have

    My roommates and I ~~not have~~ the same routines. Julia get up late, at around 10:00 A.M. Katie and I get up early. Katie have class at 8:00 A.M., and I start work at 9:00 A.M. Julia don't work. She just takes two classes in the afternoon. She's lucky because she finishs early. Then she goes out with friends. She doesn't studies very much, and she doesn't cook. Katie and I study and goes to work every day. Julia's life is pretty good!

Dictation

18 Listen. You will hear five sentences. Write them on a piece of paper.

Speaking

GROUPS. Talk about the sentences below. For each sentence, write *T* (true), *F* (false), or *?* (not sure). If the sentence is false, change it to make it true.

                         don't speak

_F_ **1.** Most people in the U.S. ~~speak~~ two languages.

____ **2.** Most people in the U.S. watch soccer on TV.

____ **3.** Most people in the U.S. have two hours for lunch.

____ **4.** Most people in the U.S. ride a bike to work.

____ **5.** Most women in the U.S. don't work outside the home.

____ **6.** Most men in the U.S. don't do housework.

____ **7.** Most children in the U.S. don't wear uniforms to school.

____ **8.** Most teenagers in the U.S. have a part-time job.

housework

 110   **Unit 9**

Listening

A CD 2 TRACK **19** Listen. A radio reporter talks about how people around the world spend their time. Match the activities with the worldwide averages.

Look

► John works 40 hours a week. Paul works 50 hours a week. Sarah works 60 hours a week. On **average**, they work 50 hours a week.
$(40 + 50 + 60 = 150 \div 3 = 50)$
► % = **percent**.
► 2.5 = two **point** five

Activities

_e_ 1. hours of sleep a night

____ 2. hours of work a day

____ 3. percent of men who do housework

____ 4. percent of people who eat at home every day

____ 5. percent of men who cook

Worldwide Averages

a. 21%

b. 79%

c. 15%

d. 9.6

e. 7.4

B CD 2 TRACK **20** Listen again. Complete the sentences. Circle the correct verb.

1. People in Japan **sleep** / **don't sleep** a lot.

2. People in South Africa **work** / **sleep** 7.9 hours a day.

3. People in Argentina and Turkey **cook** / **work** a lot.

4. Men in Turkey and Egypt **do** /**don't do** a lot of housework.

5. Most women in Egypt **cook** / **work**.

TIME to TALK

Complete the sentences about your country.

1. On average, I think people in my country get _____ hours of sleep a night.

2. On average, I think people in my country work _____ hours a day.

3. I think _____% of people in my country eat at home every day.

4. I think _____% of men in my country do housework every day.

5. I think _____% of men in my country cook every day.

GROUPS. Compare your answers. Discuss any differences. Then tell the class about your countries.

Reading and Writing

Reading

A   Linda writes about her day for a study on how people spend their time. Read about her typical day. How are you and Linda different? Write two differences.

1. _____   2. _____

> **Describe how you spend your time on an average day.**
>
> I work in a hospital. My hours are from 11:00 P.M. to 7:00 A.M. Monday to Friday. I get home at 7:30 A.M. and drive my children to school. Then I go home and go to bed. I sleep only about 5 hours a day, from 9:00 A.M. to 2:00 P.M. My children get home from school at 3:00 I help them with their homework. Then we eat dinner together between 5:00 and 6:00. After dinner, we watch TV. They go to bed at 7:30 P.M. Then I read a magazine or talk to my friends on the phone. At about 9:00 P.M., I get ready for work. At 9:30 my husband comes home and we talk about our day for an hour. At 10:30 I leave for work.

B   Complete Linda's diary for the study. Use information from the paragraph in Exercise A.

> **Write your activities. Include the start and end times for each activity.**

Morning	Afternoon	Evening	Night
7:30	12:00 – 2:00	5:00 – 6:00	9:00 – 10:00
8:00 – 9:00 drive kids to school	3:00 – 5:00 help kids with their homework	6:00 – 6:30	9:30 – 10:30
9:00 – 12:00		7:30	10:30
		8:00 – 9:00	
			11:00 – 7:00 A.M.

Prewriting

Complete the diary with your daily activities.

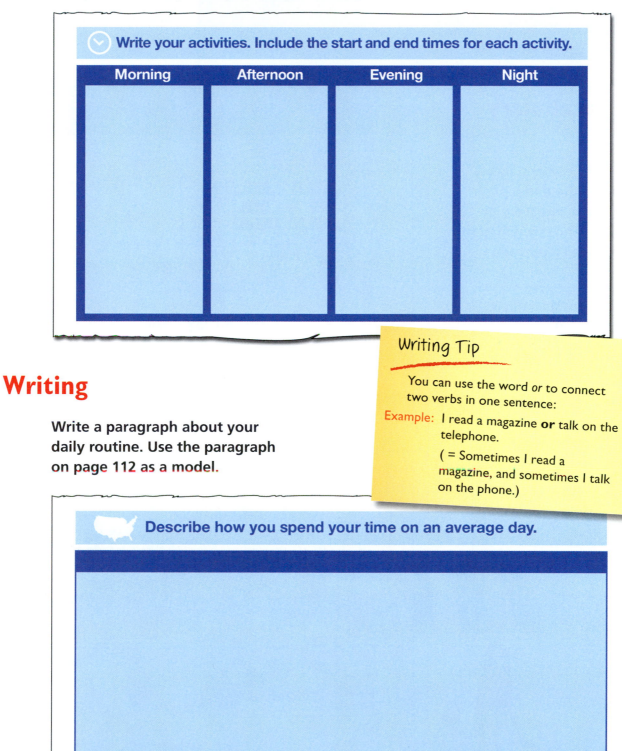

Write your activities. Include the start and end times for each activity.

Morning	Afternoon	Evening	Night

Writing

Write a paragraph about your daily routine. Use the paragraph on page 112 as a model.

Writing Tip

You can use the word *or* to connect two verbs in one sentence:

Example: I read a magazine **or** talk on the telephone.

(= Sometimes I read a magazine, and sometimes I talk on the phone.)

Describe how you spend your time on an average day.

Unit 10
Shopping

Vocabulary

CD 2 TRACK **21** Read and listen. What is the name of a department store or convenience store in your town? Tell a partner.

1. department store
2. on sale
3. spend money on
4. 25% off
5. sell
6. pay for
7. receipt
8. convenience store
9. open
10. close
11. cash

B. Altman's DEPARTMENT STORE

WOMEN'S

DRESSING ROOMS

ON SALE

TOYS

"ALL TOYS 25% OFF"

DOLLS $18
NOW $13.50

TRUCKS $20.⁰⁰
Now $15.⁰⁰

How will you pay for this?

Listening

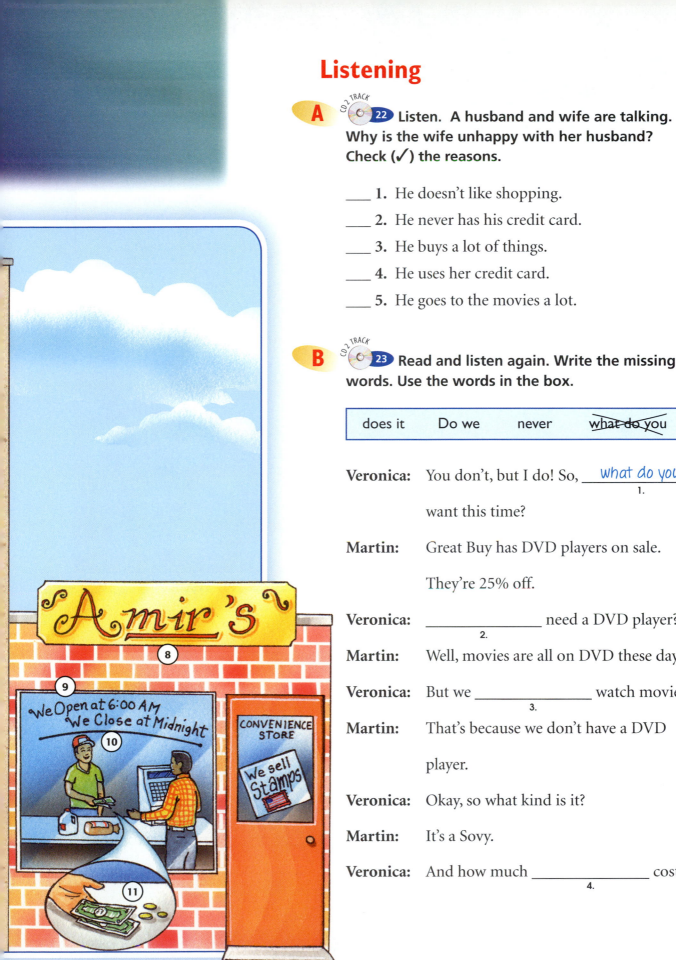

A 🔘 CD 2 TRACK **22** **Listen. A husband and wife are talking. Why is the wife unhappy with her husband? Check (✓) the reasons.**

___ 1. He doesn't like shopping.

___ 2. He never has his credit card.

___ 3. He buys a lot of things.

___ 4. He uses her credit card.

___ 5. He goes to the movies a lot.

B 🔘 CD 2 TRACK **23** **Read and listen again. Write the missing words. Use the words in the box.**

does it	Do we	never	~~what do you~~

Veronica: You don't, but I do! So, __what do you__
$\underset{1.}{}$
want this time?

Martin: Great Buy has DVD players on sale.

They're 25% off.

Veronica: _____ need a DVD player?
$\underset{2.}{}$

Martin: Well, movies are all on DVD these days.

Veronica: But we _____ watch movies.
$\underset{3.}{}$

Martin: That's because we don't have a DVD

player.

Veronica: Okay, so what kind is it?

Martin: It's a Sovy.

Veronica: And how much _____ cost?
$\underset{4.}{}$

Grammar to Communicate 1

FREQUENCY ADVERBS WITH THE SIMPLE PRESENT

Subject	Adverb	Verb			Subject	*Be*	Adverb	
I We You They	**always**	use	cash.		I	am		
					We You They	are	**always**	at the mall.
He She	**often**	uses	cash.		He She	is		
It	**never**	costs	a lot.					

Look

100%	always
90%	usually
70%	often
50%	sometimes
10%	hardly ever
0%	never

A Complete the sentences about shopping in your country. Use *always, usually, often, sometimes, hardly ever,* or *never.*

1. People _____ buy things from a catalog.
2. People _____ buy fruit at outdoor markets.
3. People _____ go shopping at malls.
4. People _____ buy bread at a supermarket.
5. People _____ go shopping on Sundays.
6. Stores _____ have sales.
7. Stores _____ close in the afternoon.
8. Stores _____ close for two weeks in the summer.

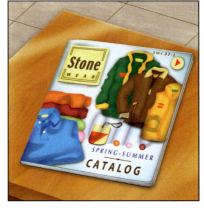

catalog

GROUPS. Compare your answers with students from other countries.

B Make sentences. Put the words in the correct order. Then check (✓) the sentences that are true about you.

❑ 1. ___I never buy food at a convenience store.___

(I / at a convenience store / buy / never / food)

❑ 2. _____

(buy / from a catalog / clothes / I / hardly ever)

❑ 3. _____

(at department stores / shop / my family and I / often)

❑ 4. _____

(on sale / I / things / usually / buy)

❑ 5. _____

(sometimes / pays for / my classmate / my lunch)

❑ 6. _____

(ask for / a / I / always / receipt)

C  CD 2 TRACK **24** **Linda Kelly talks about her job in a department store. Listen and complete the sentences. Use the adverbs from the box. Then listen again and check your answers. Some words may be used two times.**

Look
Frequency adverbs come after the verb *be*.
   Chin **is often** at the mall.
Frequency adverbs come before all other verbs.
   Chin **often goes** to the mall.

always	often	never	sometimes	usually

1. I _____ *am always* _____ friendly.
   (am)
2. The store _____ sales.
   (has)
3. I _____ late for work.
   (am)
4. The store _____ at 9:00.
   (opens)
5. The customers _____ nice.
   (are)
6. I love my job. It _____ boring.
   (is)
7. The customers _____ me questions.
   (ask)

TIME to TALK

ON YOUR OWN. Where do you buy the things in the chart? Write the names of the stores.

CLOTHES	SHOES	ELECTRONICS	FRUIT AND VEGETABLES	MEAT	TOILETRIES
	Pay Little				

GROUPS. Tell your classmates about where you shop, and talk about how often you shop at the places in your classmates' charts. Use frequency adverbs.

Example:
A: *I usually buy shoes at Pay Little.*
B: *Really? I hardly ever shop at Pay Little.*

Grammar to Communicate 2

SIMPLE PRESENT: YES / NO QUESTIONS AND SHORT ANSWERS

Do/Does	Subject	Verb			Affirmative				Negative		
Do	I we you they	**have**	food?	**Yes,**	I we you they	**do.**	**No,**	I we you they	**don't.**		
Does	he she it				he she it	**does.**		he she it	**doesn't.**		

A Read the chart. Complete the questions with *do* or *does*. Then answer the questions.

> **Look**
>
> Statements: Questions:
> They **need** a car. → **Do** they **need** a car?
> He **needs** a car. → **Does** he **need** a car?

	has:	needs:	wants:
ERIC	cell phone computer camera	new TV sunglasses new sneakers	new watch bike new computer games
SUSANNA	has: new car CD player computer	needs: cell phone new shoes alarm clock	wants: DVD player camera new CDs
SHEILA AND TONY	have: stereo TV old car	need: computer radio new phone	want: new car DVD player DVDs

1. ____Does____ Eric have a cell phone?   Yes, he does.
2. Eric, ____do____ you need a new camera?   No, I don't.
3. _____ Sheila and Tony want a TV?   _____
4. _____ Susana need a cell phone?   _____
5. Susana, _____ you have a new car?   _____
6. Tony, _____ you and Sheila have a stereo?   _____
7. _____ Eric want a computer?   _____
8. _____ Sheila and Tony want a DVD player?   _____
9. _____ Susana have a CD player?   _____
10. _____ Eric need a camera?   _____

B Complete the questions about the pictures. Then answer the questions.

1. <u>Does Trudy need</u> a new coat?   <u>Yes, she does.</u>
    (Trudy / need)
2. _____ the same clothes?   _____
    (the sisters / have on)
3. _____ a lot of ties?   _____
    (Jeff / have)
4. _____ the jackets?   _____
    (the children / want)
5. _____ a lot?   _____
    (the bathing suit / cost)
6. _____ her husband's new suit?   _____
    (the woman / like)

C Write a new question about each picture in Exercise B. Use the words in the box. Write your questions on a piece of paper.

have the same hairstyle	need new jackets	spend a lot on clothes
like cheap clothes	need a new tie	want a new bathing suit

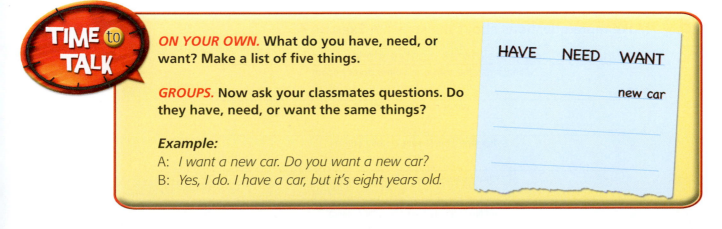

TIME to TALK

ON YOUR OWN. What do you have, need, or want? Make a list of five things.

GROUPS. Now ask your classmates questions. Do they have, need, or want the same things?

Example:
A: *I want a new car. Do you want a new car?*
B: *Yes, I do. I have a car, but it's eight years old.*

HAVE	NEED	WANT
		new car

Grammar to Communicate 3

SIMPLE PRESENT: INFORMATION QUESTIONS					
Wh– word	Do / Does	Subject	Verb	Answers	
What	**do**	I you we they	**need?**	A cell phone.	
How often	**does**	he	**go?**	Every day.	
What time		it	**start?**	8:00 P.M.	

Look

We also use *What kind of* + noun
What kind of car do you want?

A Read the mall directory. Match the questions with the answers.

Directory

Books
1. Read Away
   8:30-8:00
2. Story Time
   9:00-8:00

Cameras
1. Mikko's
   9:00-9:00
2. Andover Pictures
   11:00-7:00

Electronics
1. Costwise
   11:00-10:00
2. Stereo Plus
   10:00-9:00

Children's Clothes
1. Little Angel
   10:00-7:30
2. Happy Time
   10:00-6:00

Shoes
1. Pretty Feet
   10:00-8:00
2. Easy Fit
   11:00-9:00

Jewerly
1. Mia Gold
   9:00-7:00
2. Silver Lining
   9:00-8:00

_f_ **1.** What does Little Angel sell?   **a.** 8:00.

____ **2.** What do people buy at Andover Pictures?   **b.** 8:30.

____ **3.** What time does Read Away open?   **c.** jewelry.

____ **4.** What time do the bookstores close?   **d.** electronics.

____ **5.** What do Stereo Plus and Costwise sell?   **e.** cameras.

____ **6.** What does Silver Lining sell?   **f.** children's clothes.

B Make more questions about the stores in Exercise A.

1. _What time do the children's clothes stores open?_
   (What time / the children's clothes stores / open)

2. _____
   (What / Mikko's / sell)

3. _____
   (What time / the jewelry stores / open)

4. _____
   (What / people / buy / at Story Time)

5. _____
   (What time / Pretty Feet / Easy Fit / close)

C CD 2 TRACK 25 **Read the conversations. Write questions. Use *What*, *What kind*, *How much*, and *How often* and the verbs in the box. Then listen and check your answers.**

~~cost~~	go	have	like	sell

1. **A:** I like the T-shirt in the catalog.

   B: _How much does it cost?_

   A: It's $15.66 including tax.

2. **A:** You have a big car, right?

   B: No, I don't.

   A: _____

   B: I have a very small car.

3. **A:** Julie doesn't like gold earrings.

   B: _____

   A: Silver.

4. **A:** Makis and Lit Brothers are good stores.

   B: _____

   A: Clothes, jewelry, umbrellas, handbags—a lot of different things.

5. **A:** My daughter goes to the mall a lot.

   B: _____

   A: Every weekend.

Pia's	
1 T-shirt	$15.00
sales tax	.66
	$15.66

TIME to TALK

GROUPS. One student says what he or she wants or needs. The other students ask as many questions as possible. Continue until everyone asks and answers questions.

Example:
A: *I need a new TV.*
B: *What kind of TV do you want?*
A: *I want a 30-inch flat-screen.*
C: *How much do they cost?*
A: *They're on sale for $399 at Great Buy.*

Review and Challenge

Grammar

Find the mistake in each sentence. Circle the letter and correct the mistake.

1. Those stores usually are busy.
   A   (B)   B

   Correct: *Those stores are usually busy.*

2. You like these black shoes?
   A   B   C

   Correct: _____

3. How much does the big TV costs?
   A   B   C

   Correct: _____

4. What kind of cell phone John want?
   A   B   C

   Correct: _____

5. Do you have always a lot of money?
   A   B   C

   Correct: _____

Dictation

CD 2 TRACK 26 **Listen. You will hear five sentences. Write them on a piece of paper.**

Speaking

PAIRS. **Choose one of the situations and write a conversation.**

> **Situation 1**
> *Customer:* It's your friend's birthday. You want to buy your friend a gift. Ask questions about things in a store.
> *Salesman:* You want to help the customer. Answer questions about things in the store. Ask the customer questions about what his or her friend wants and needs.

> **Situation 2**
> *Parent:* Your son needs a computer for school. You don't know anything about computers.
> *Friend:* You know a lot about computers. Help your friend.

Example: *(Situation 1)*
A: *How much is that jacket?*
B: *It's $32.40 with tax. What color does your friend like? Does he like green?*

Now perform the conversation for the class.

Listening

A  **Listen. Where are the people? Match the conversations with the places.**

_____ Conversation 1

_____ Conversation 2

_____ Conversation 3

_____ Conversation 4

B  **Listen again. Write the questions you hear in each conversation.**

Conversation 1: How much _does the flat screen TV cost?_

Conversation 2: What _____ ?

Conversation 3: What kind _____ ?

Conversation 4: Where _____ ?

TIME to TALK

GROUPS. Where do you shop? How often do you shop? What do you buy? How much do things cost? Ask and answer questions. Use the places in the box.

buy things from a home shopping network	shop at a convenience store
go to the mall	shop at an outdoor market
order things from a catalog	shop online

Example:

A: _How often do you go to the mall?_

B: _I usually go to the mall every Saturday._

A: _What do you buy there?_

B: _Sometimes I buy clothes or CDs. I often look and don't buy anything. How about you? Do you go to the mall a lot?_

Reading and Writing

Reading

A   Read the newsletter. Where are yard sales? Check (✓) the correct answer.

❑   in shopping malls   ❑   in front of people's houses   ❑   in stores

New to the U.S.
A NEWSLETTER FOR NEWCOMERS

Do you have anything in your home that you don't need or want? For example, do you have an old television, or clothes that you don't wear anymore? Do you want some extra money? Have a yard sale!

What is a yard sale? At these sales, people sell their old things. On warm weekend mornings, the sellers put the things for sale on tables in front of their house or apartment. Then they wait for their customers. Where do the customers come from? On weekends, people often drive around and look for yard sales. Yard sales usually start at 8:00 or 9:00 A.M.

What kinds of things do people sell at yard sales? They sell everything! They sell furniture,

electronics, clothes, children's toys, CDs, and jewelry. People like yard sales because the prices are usually great–and there's no sales tax! Buyers and sellers talk about the price. If the buyer likes the price, he usually pays the seller in cash. Sellers sometimes take a check, but they never take a credit card.

B   Read the newsletter again. Answer the questions. Write complete sentences.

1. What kinds of things do people buy at yard sales?

   They buy electronics, clothes, furniture, children's toys, CDs, and jewelry.

2. Do things at yard sales usually cost a lot of money?

   _____

3. When do people usually have yard sales?

   _____

4. What time do yard sales usually start?

   _____

5. How do buyers pay for the things they want?

   _____

Prewriting

Read the paragraph about outdoor markets.

> In my country, outdoor markets are a popular way of shopping. The market near my home is open every Thursday from 7:00 in the morning until noon. I buy a lot of fruit and vegetables there, but people also buy clothes, shoes, CDs, and many other things there. I like outdoor markets because they always have fresh fruit and vegetables.

Writing

Write a paragraph about shopping in your country. Use the paragraph above as a model.

Writing Tip

Use *because* to give a reason for something. *Because* connects the fact and the reason in one sentence.

Example: (fact) Outdoor markets are popular **because** they always have fresh fruit and vegetables. (reason)

New to _____

A NEWSLETTER FOR NEWCOMERS

Unit 11
Holidays and Special Occasions

Grammar
- Direct and Indirect Objects
- Simple present: Information Questions
- *Who* as Subject and Object

Vocabulary

🎵 CD 2 TRACK **29** Read and listen. Then circle the things that people do on special occasions.

1. birthday
2. have a party
3. make a cake
4. thank someone
5. invite someone to a party
6. get flowers
7. visit
8. give a gift
9. groom
10. bride
11. relatives
12. wedding
13. dance
14. host
15. guest
16. hostess
17. celebrate
18. invitation

Listening

A 🔊 **30** **Listen. Petra is talking about her birthday. Circle the things that Petra tells Julie.**

1. (She misses her family.)
2. She usually has a small party.
3. The party is at her house.
4. Her friends send cards.
5. She gets some gifts.

B 🔊 **31** **Read and listen again. Write the missing words. Use the words in the box.**

do you	~~How do you~~	makes	me cards

Petra: Oh, this weekend is my first birthday alone—my family and friends aren't here. I really miss them.

Julie: Oh, that's hard. So . . . _How do you_
1.
usually celebrate your birthday?

Petra: Well, my friends send _____, and
2.
all of my relatives call me.

Julie: Do you have party?

Petra: Oh, yes. We always have a big party.

Julie: Who _____ invite?
3.

Petra: My friends, my parents' friends, my sisters' friends, and my relatives.

Julie: Wow. You need a big place for a party like that. Where do you usually have it?

Petra: Oh, we have a big house.

Julie: And who _____ the food for all
4.
those people?

Hi, grandma!

7

13

14

Thank you for playing at the wedding.

You are cordially invited to celebrate the wedding of Miss Jane Miller and Mr. John Torres

17

18

Holidays and Special Occasions

Grammar to Communicate 1

DIRECT AND INDIRECT OBJECTS WITH PREPOSITIONS

Subject	Verb	Direct Object	Preposition	Indirect Object
I	send	**a gift** **it**	to	**my friend.** **her.**

DIRECT AND INDIRECT OBJECTS WITHOUT PREPOSITIONS

Subject	Verb	Indirect Object	Direct Object
I	send	**my friend** **her**	**a gift.**

A   **Underline the direct object. Circle the indirect object.**

1. Do you give a <u>birthday present</u> to (your father)?
2. Do you send birthday cards to your friends?
3. Do you give money to your parents?
4. Do you make birthday cakes for your friends?
5. Do you get gifts for your teachers?
6. Do you buy flowers for your mother?

B   **Rewrite the questions from Exercise A. Write the indirect objects.**

1. Do you give ___your father___ a birthday present?
2. Do you send _____ birthday cards?
3. Do you give _____ money?
4. Do you make _____ birthday cakes?
5. Do you get _____ gifts?
6. Do you buy _____ flowers?

PAIRS.   **Ask and answer the questions above.**

C   **Complete the sentences. Use *to* or *for*.**

Look

I **send** a gift **to** her.
I **give** a gift **to** her.
I **buy** a gift **for** her.
I **get** a gift **for** her.

1. I send cards __to__ 100 people.
2. I buy presents _____ my husband.
3. I make a special dinner _____ my wife.

4. I get a present _____ my mother.
5. I give money _____ my nieces and nephews.

   128   Unit 11

D **Read the first sentence. Complete the second sentence. Put the words in the correct order.**

1. Parents give their children birthday presents.

   Children often <u>give birthday presents to their parents.</u>
   (their parents / birthday presents / give / to)

2. Men often send women flowers.

   Women don't usually _____
   (send / to / them / men)

3. Children hardly ever give money to their parents.

   Parents often _____
   (give / to / their children / money)

4. Children often make cards for their parents.

   Parents don't usually _____
   (them / their / make / for / children)

5. Mothers often make birthday cakes for their children.

   Children don't usually _____
   (birthday cakes / make / for / their mothers)

6. Parents often have birthday parties for their children.

   Children don't usually _____
   (their parents / have/ for / parties)

PAIRS. **Which sentences above are true about your country? Talk with a partner.**

PAIRS. **Ask and answer five questions about gifts. Use the words in the box and your own ideas.**

boyfriend / girlfriend	father / mother	candy	computer games
brother / sister	friends	CDs	flowers
children / daughter / son	husband /wife	clothes	toys

Example:
A: *Do you give your mother a gift on her birthday?*
B: *Yes, I do.*
A: *What do you give her?*
B: *I usually give her flowers.*

Grammar to Communicate 2

SIMPLE PRESENT: INFORMATION QUESTIONS

Wh- word	Do / Does	Subject	Verb		Answers
How	**do**	you	**celebrate**	Thanksgiving?	We visit our relatives, and we eat special food.
		we			
When		they			On November 23rd.
Where	**does**	he			At his grandparents' home.
Why		she			She likes to see her family.

A Complete the questions. Use *do* or *does*.

1. When _____do_____ Americans celebrate Thanksgiving?

2. How _____ Americans celebrate Thanksgiving?

3. Where _____ Gina celebrate Thanksgiving?

4. Why _____ Gina celebrate Thanksgiving in Seattle?

Read the answers. Write matching questions from above.

1. When do Americans celebrate Thanksgiving?   On the fourth Thursday in November.

2. _____   Families have a special dinner.

3. _____   With her parents in Seattle.

4. _____   Her parents live there.

B CD 2 TRACK 32 Read the conversations. Complete the questions about Father's Day. Then listen and check your answers.

1. **Ted:** We celebrate Mother's Day to show that we love our mothers.

   Lia: Why _do you celebrate Father's Day?_

   Ted: To show that we love our fathers, of course!

2. **Ted:** We celebrate Mother's Day on the second Sunday in May.

   Lia: When _____?

   Ted: On the third Sunday in June.

3. **Ted:** We celebrate Mother's Day in different ways. Most people send cards.

   Lia: How _____?

   Ted: We send cards on Father's Day, too.

4. **Ted:** Mothers often get flowers.

   Lia: What _____?

   Ted: Fathers often get ties.

C Write questions about Chinese New Year. Use *when, where, how,* and *why.* Use *why* two times.

Chinese New Year   envelopes

1. <u>When does the celebration begin?</u>   It begins on New Year's Eve.
   (the celebration / begin)

2. _____   They have a special dinner.
   (families / celebrate New Year's Eve)

3. _____   They don't. They stay up all night.
   (people / go to bed)

4. _____   Because they get gifts of money.
   (children / like the New Year)

5. _____   They put it in little red envelopes.
   (adults / put the money)

6. _____   Because red is a lucky color in China.
   (adults / use red envelopes)

TIME to TALK

GROUPS. Talk about how you usually celebrate the New Year in your country. Ask and answer five questions. Use the words in the box and your own ideas.

New Year's resolutions = a promise to yourself to do something next year

| dance | eat special food | make New Year's resolutions | stay up late |

Example:
A: *How do you celebrate the New Year holiday in your country?*
B: *We have a big party, and we go to our relatives' homes.*

Grammar to Communicate 3

WHO AS SUBJECT

Subject	Verb	Object	Answers
Who	invites	the guests?	The hostess does.
Who	gives	gifts?	The guests do.

WHO AS OBJECT

Object	Do / Does	Subject	Verb	Answers
Who	does	the hostess	invite?	The guests.
	do	the guests	give gifts to?	To the bride.

A **Underline the subjects. Then write questions with *Who*.**

1. <u>Children</u> visit their neighbors.

    <u>Who visits their neighbors?</u>

2. The neighbors buy candy.

    _____

3. The children wear costumes.

    _____

4. The children say "Trick or Treat!"

    _____

5. The neighbors give candy.

    _____

> ### Look
> When *who* is the subject of a question, always use a singular verb.
> Who visit<u>s</u> their neighbors?
> The children.

B **Complete the questions with the words in the box and *do* or *does*.**

give	go	have	make	~~visit~~

1. Who __do__ the children __visit__ ?
2. Who _____ your brother always _____ to Halloween parties with?
3. Who _____ the neighbors _____ candy to?
4. Who _____ his mother _____ costumes for?
5. Who _____ schools sometimes _____ parties for?

Halloween costume

C **Read the answers and write the questions. Put the words in the correct order.**

1. _____ *Who usually pays for the wedding?* _____   The bride's parents do.
    (for the wedding / usually pays / Who)

2. _____   Relatives and friends.
    (Who / they / invite / do / to the wedding)

3. _____   The bride's family and
    (sees / the bride / before the wedding / Who)   girlfriends do.

4. _____   The bride does.
    (white clothes / Who / at the wedding / wears)

5. _____   With their parents.
    (do / the bride and groom / Who / sit with)

PAIRS. Ask the questions above. Answer with information about weddings in your country.

Example:
A: *Who pays for the wedding?*
B: *The bride's parents usually pay.*

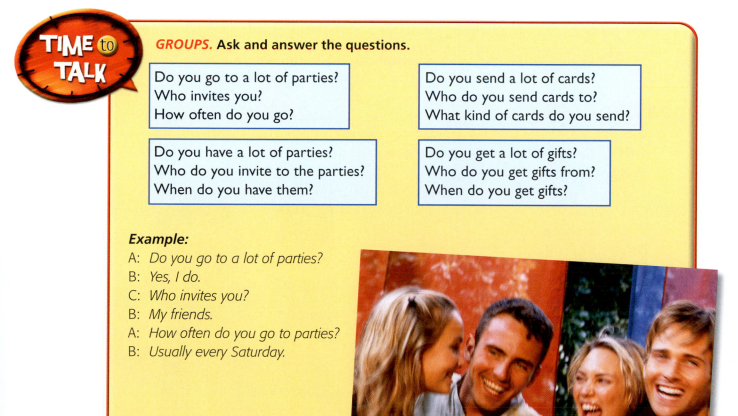

TIME to TALK

GROUPS. Ask and answer the questions.

Do you go to a lot of parties?
Who invites you?
How often do you go?

Do you send a lot of cards?
Who do you send cards to?
What kind of cards do you send?

Do you have a lot of parties?
Who do you invite to the parties?
When do you have them?

Do you get a lot of gifts?
Who do you get gifts from?
When do you get gifts?

Example:
A: *Do you go to a lot of parties?*
B: *Yes, I do.*
C: *Who invites you?*
B: *My friends.*
A: *How often do you go to parties?*
B: *Usually every Saturday.*

Review and Challenge

Grammar

Find the mistake in each sentence. Write the letter in the blank and correct the mistake.

__B__ 1. How <u>you do</u> <u>celebrate</u> the holiday?   Correct: _How do you celebrate the holiday?_
       A   B   C

_____ 2. When <u>do you</u> give <u>to your wife flowers</u>?   Correct: _____
         A   B   C

_____ 3. <u>Who</u> <u>does buy</u> candy <u>for her</u>?   Correct: _____
         A   B   C

_____ 4. Who <u>do</u> she <u>send</u> cards <u>to</u>?   Correct: _____
             A   B   C

_____ 5. <u>Why</u> <u>does</u> she <u>likes</u> the holiday?   Correct: _____
         A   B   C

_____ 6. <u>I</u> give <u>to</u> <u>her</u> a lot of gifts.   Correct: _____
         A   B   C

Dictation

 33 **Listen. You will hear five sentences. Write them on a piece of paper.**

Speaking

GROUPS. **How do people in your country celebrate the occasions in the box? Ask and answer questions.**

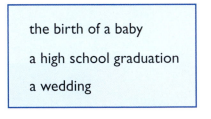
the birth of a baby

a high school graduation

a wedding

Example:
A: *How do you celebrate a wedding in India?*
B: *Well, the day before the wedding, the groom's mother and sisters go to the bride's house. They bring the bride gifts like jewelry and fruit . . .*

134   Unit 11

Listening

wrap a gift

receive a gift

A **34** **Listen. A reporter talks about gift giving in different parts of the world. Check (✓) the places she talks about.**

    ❑ Asia   ✓ China   ❑ Europe   ❑ Mexico   ❑ North America

    ❑ Brazil   ❑ Egypt   ❑ Japan   ❑ The Middle East   ❑ South America

B **35** **Read the sentences. Listen again to the report. Write the correct places from Exercise A. Then listen again and check your answers.**

1. People give gifts with two hands.   _China and Japan_

2. People give gifts with their right hand.   _____

3. People don't wrap gifts in white paper.   _____

4. People don't wrap gifts in purple paper.   _____

5. People don't give knives as gifts.   _____

TIME to TALK

GROUPS. **Ask and answer the questions about gift giving in your country.**

1. When do people in your country give gifts?
2. Who do they give gifts to?
3. What kinds of gifts do people give or never give?
4. What color paper do people in your country wrap gifts in?

Example:
A: *When do people in your country give gifts?*
B: *They give gifts on birthdays and at Christmas.*

Tell the class about gift giving in your group.

Reading and Writing

Reading

A Read the information about Valentine's Day. Do you have a similar holiday in your country? Write the name of the holiday. _____

New to the U.S.
A NEWSLETTER FOR NEWCOMERS

Volume XXXIII

Valentine's Day

In the United States, Valentine's Day is a popular holiday. Valentine's Day is always on February 14. On Valentine's Day people celebrate love and friendship. Husbands and boyfriends often give gifts to their wives or girlfriends. Sometimes women buy presents for men. People usually buy chocolate candy and flowers. Red roses are for true love. Pink roses are for new love. Yellow roses are for friendship. Many people give cards. Small children often buy or make them. Then they take them to school. They give them to their friends.

B Read the answers to questions about the reading. Then write the questions.

> **Look**
>
> When *who* is the object of a question, the preposition comes at the end.
> **Who** do you buy cards **for?**
> **Who** does she go to parties **with?**

1. *What do Americans celebrate on Valentine's Day?*
    They celebrate love and friendship.

2. _____
    Americans celebrate Valentine's Day on February 14.

3. _____
    Women sometimes buy presents for men.

4. _____
    Yellow roses are for friendship.

5. _____
    They make cards for their friends.

Prewriting

Think of your favorite holiday in your country. Write answers to these questions about the holiday. Write on a piece of paper.

- When is the holiday?
- How do people celebrate the holiday?
- Who do you celebrate the holiday with?
- Why is this your favorite holiday?

Writing

Write a paragraph about a holiday in your country. Use the paragraph on page 136 as a model.

New to _____

A NEWSLETTER FOR NEWCOMERS

Volume XXXIII

Writing Tip

The adverbs *sometimes*, *often*, and *usually* can go in the middle or at the beginning of a sentence. When the adverb comes at the beginning of the sentence, a comma (,) follows it.

Example: **Sometimes,** women buy presents for men.

Women **sometimes** buy presents for men.

At Work

Grammar
- Simple Present and Present Progressive
- Stative Verbs
- *Like / Need / Want* + Infinitive

Vocabulary

CD 2 TRACK **36** Read and listen. Then circle the people, places, and activities that you often see.

1. be off
2. manager
3. have experience
4. interview
5. day-care center
6. day-care worker
7. take care of children
8. make an appointment
9. co-worker
10. real estate agent
11. make money
12. paycheck

Listening

37 **Listen. Check (✓) the true statements.**

❏ **1.** Doris is talking to her friend.

❏ **2.** Liz usually works on Mondays.

❏ **3.** Doris works on Tuesdays.

❏ **4.** Doris works on Saturdays.

B **38** **Read and listen again. Write the missing words. Use the words in the box.**

| doing | ~~don't~~ | has | I'm working | to work | works |

Mr. Yu: Yes, Doris? Please, come in. So, what are you doing here today? You ___don't___ usually work on Mondays, do you?
1.

Doris: No, _____ for Liz today. She's visiting her mom in the hospital.
2.

Mr. Yu: Oh, that's right. How is her mother _____?
3.

Doris: She's doing very well.

Mr. Yu: Oh, that's good. So, what's up?

Doris: Well, my husband _____ a new job, and he _____ on Tuesdays now, too. And we don't have day care on Tuesdays.
4.
5.

Mr. Yu: So are you asking me for Tuesdays off?

Doris: Oh no, I need _____ 40 hours a week. We need the money . . .
6.

Grammar to Communicate 1

SIMPLE PRESENT

Subject	Verb		Do / Does	Subject	Verb	
I You We They	work	every day.	Do	you I we they	work	every day?
He She It	works		Does	he she it		

PRESENT PROGRESSIVE

Subject	Be	Verb + -ing		Be	Subject	Verb + -ing	
I	am			Are	you		
You We They	are	working	now.	Am	I	working	now?
				Are	we they		
He She It	is			Is	he she it		

A Complete the sentences. Use the correct form of the verbs.

1. The boy _____is getting_____ a haircut.
                (get)

2. The barber _____ the boy's hair.
                (cut)

3. The barber _____.
                (work)

4. The boy _____ in a chair.
                (sit)

5. The boy _____ a blue smock.
                (wear)

Look

Contractions:
I **don't work** every day.
He **doesn't work** every day.
I**'m not working** today.
She**'s not working** today.
We**'re not working** today.

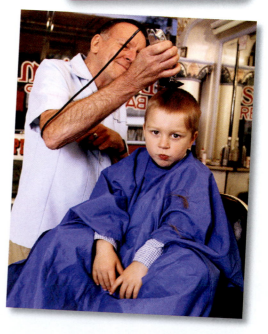

PAIRS. Look at the picture on pages 138-139. Talk about Jack and Teresa. What do they do every day? Where are they right now? What are they doing?

B Look at the pictures on pages 138-139. Answer the questions. Use the simple present or the present progressive.

Look at the pictures on pages 138-139.

1. What does Jack do?   _He's a real estate agent._

2. What does Jack do every day?   _____

3. What is Jack doing right now?   _____

4. Where does Teresa work?   _____

5. What is Teresa doing right now? _____

6. What is Kim doing?   _____

> **Look**
>
> Use the simple present for routines.
>
> Use the present progressive for actions happening now.
>
> **I work** at a bank three time a week.
>
> **I'm working** right now.

C CD 2 TRACK 39 Complete the sentences. Use the simple present or the present progressive. Use contractions where possible. Then listen and check your answers.

Tim: Hi, Dana. This is Tim. What's up? What _____are you doing?_____
                                                    1. (you /do)

Dana: I _'m eating_____ lunch.
              2. (eat)

Tim: Really? But it's only 11:00. _____ lunch this early every day?
                                          3. (you/ have)

Dana: Yeah, usually. I _____ work early, at 7:00, so I'm always hungry
                            4. (start)

at this time. And my boss _____ out around 11:00, so it's
                            5. (go)

always quiet. What _____ right now?
                      6. (you/do)

Tim: I _____. I _____ to a movie.
            7. (drive)   8. (go)

Dana: A movie? But it's Monday! Why aren't you at work?

Tim: I _____ the first Monday of every month off.
            9. (have)

TIME to TALK

PAIRS. Talk about four people you know. What do they do? Where do they live? What are they probably doing right now?

> What do they do? = What is their job?

Example:

A: *My father lives in California. He's a real estate agent. He sells houses, but he's not selling houses now. This week he's on vacation. He's probably at the beach.*

Grammar to Communicate 2

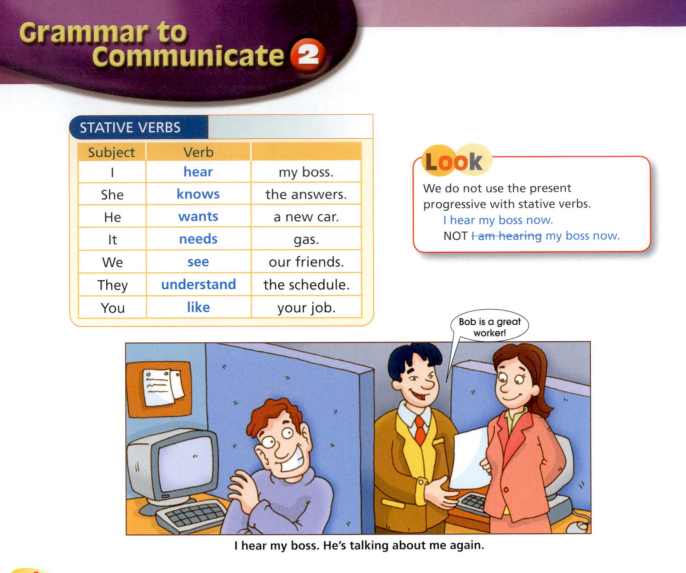

STATIVE VERBS		
Subject	**Verb**	
I	**hear**	my boss.
She	**knows**	the answers.
He	**wants**	a new car.
It	**needs**	gas.
We	**see**	our friends.
They	**understand**	the schedule.
You	**like**	your job.

Look

We do not use the present progressive with stative verbs.
I hear my boss now.
NOT ~~I am hearing~~ my boss now.

> Bob is a great worker!

I hear my boss. He's talking about me again.

A Circle the stative verb in each sentence.

1. I (hear) the manager. She's talking to my co-workers. She talks to them every Friday.

2. I see the mechanic. He's fixing my car. He fixes cars every day.

3. Mia's eating with a co-worker now. They often eat together. Mia likes her co-worker.

4. Jackie wants lunch. Her secretary is buying it for her. She often buys Jackie's lunch.

5. Jim is working today. He works seven days a week. He needs a day off.

6. They know their boss's wife. They are talking to her right now. They talk to her a lot.

B Circle the correct form of the verb for each sentence.

1. Take my car. **I'm not needing /**(**I don't need**)it right now.

2. Don't get me a sandwich. **I'm having / I have** a sandwich in my bag.

3. Please help me. **I don't understand / I'm not understanding** this.

4. Who are those people? **Do you know / Are you knowing** them?

5. Listen. **Do you hear / Are you hearing** that?

6. Don't buy any coffee for Emily. **She's not liking / She doesn't like** coffee.

C Write sentences about yourself. Write negative statements where necessary.

1. ___I have a good job.___ OR ___I don't have a good job.___
   (I / have / a good job)

2. _____
   (My teacher / know / my family)

3. _____
   (My friend / have / a nice office)

4. _____
   (My family and I / need / a vacation)

5. _____
   (I / need / a cup of coffee / right now)

D Look at the picture. Then write sentences. Use the simple present or the present progressive.

1. ___Ahmed drives a cab 8 hours every day.___
   (Ahmed / drive a cab / 8 hours every day)

2. _____
   (Ahmed / drive / now / not)

3. _____
   (He / not / at night / drive)

4. _____
   (He and his family / eat dinner)

5. _____
   (He / have / two sons)

6. _____
   (Ahmed / like / his job)

TIME to TALK

PAIRS. Read the questions. Match the questions with the people in the box. Then ask and answer the questions. Then talk about other things that people ask or say.

1. Do you want paper or plastic?
2. What do you want on your sandwich?
3. Where are you going?
4. Who knows the answer to number 3?
5. Who's calling, please?
6. How often do you brush your teeth?

| cab driver | cashier | dentist | receptionist | teacher | waiter |

Example:
A: *"Do you want paper or plastic?" I think a cashier asks that.*
B: *Yes, in a supermarket. She also says, "Do you have a store card?"*

Grammar to Communicate 3

LIKE / NEED / WANT + INFINITIVE

Subject	Verb	Infinitive	
I	like	to work	hard.
You We They	need want	to get	a job.
She	likes	to work	hard.
He	wants	to get	a good job.
It	needs	to be	

Look

We can use an infinitive or a noun after the verbs *like*, *need*, and *want*.

I want <u>to make</u> a lot of money.
infinitive

I want a <u>vacation</u>.
noun

A Check (✓) the sentences that have infinitives. Then underline the infinitives.

☑ 1. Do you want <u>to get</u> a new job?

❏ 2. Do you want a new job?

❏ 3. The manager wants to meet you.

❏ 4. You need to call in the morning.

❏ 5. Do I need to ask questions?

❏ 6. You need an appointment.

❏ 7. They want people with experience.

❏ 8. Does the manager want to see me?

❏ 9. He likes his boss.

❏ 10. Does he like to interview people?

B Leo has a job interview tomorrow morning. What does he need to do? Make sentences with the words in the box. Write the sentences in the correct columns.

ask questions about the job	find information about the job	go to bed early
be on time	get a haircut	talk about his experience
eat a good breakfast	get up early	wear nice clothes

THE DAY BEFORE THE INTERVIEW	THE MORNING OF THE INTERVIEW	AT THE INTERVIEW
		He needs to ask questions about the job.

PAIRS. Compare sentences. Are your sentences in the same columns?

C Write sentences about yourself and people you know. Use the words in the box with the correct form of *want* or *need*.

I	doesn't need	to buy a house
My co-worker	doesn't want	to change jobs
My co-workers	don't need	to get a college degree
My family	don't want	to get married
My friend	need	to move to a different city
My friends	needs	to speak excellent English
	want	to take a vacation
	wants	

1. _A friend of mine wants to change jobs._

2. _____

3. _____

4. _____

5. _____

6. _____

TIME to TALK

GROUPS. Talk about three future goals. What do you want to do? What do you need to do?

Example:
A: *I like to fix things. I want to be plumber, but first I need to finish high school.*
B: *I like cars. I need a car for my job. I want to buy a used car. First I need to save $1,000.*

WRAP-UP. Now tell the class about the people in your group.

Example:
C: *Nikos likes to fix things. He wants to be plumber. First he needs to finish high school. And Alex likes cars. He needs a car for his job.*

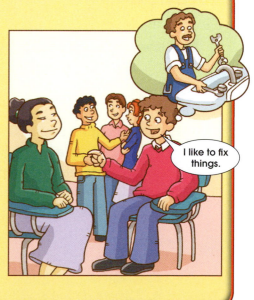

I like to fix things.

Review and Challenge

Grammar

CD 2 TRACK 40 Find and correct seven mistakes. The first mistake is corrected for you. Then listen and check your answers.

Caroline: ~~Do you wait~~ *Are you waiting* for me?

Bill: Yes, I am. I need talk to you.

Caroline: Why you need to talk to me?

Bill: It's about Jake. Is he here today?

Caroline: Yes. He cleans up right now. Why?

Bill: He is wanting more hours, but we aren't needing extra workers right now.

Caroline: So tell him.

Bill: But he has a new baby. He is needing the money now.

Caroline: Mason doesn't want to work on Saturdays. Maybe Jake wants to work then.

Bill: That's a good idea.

Dictation

CD 2 TRACK 41 Listen. You will hear five sentences. Write them on a piece of paper.

Speaking

PAIRS. Imagine that you are looking for a new job. Follow these steps:
1. Make a list of five questions a job interviewer might ask. Use the simple present or the present progressive.
2. Ask and answer the questions.
3. Change roles.

Example:
A: *Do you have a job now?*
B: *Yes, I do.*
A: *Where do you work?*
B: *I work at a shoe store.*
A: *Why are you looking for a new job? . . .*

Listening

A 42 **Listen. Mrs. Pineiro is looking for a job. Who is she talking to? Check (✓) the correct answer.**

❏ A job interviewer

❏ The manager at Little Friends

❏ A woman who helps people find jobs

❏ Mrs. Anderson

B CD 2 TRACK 43 **Read the statements about Mrs. Pineiro. Write *T* (true) or *F* (false) for each statement. Listen again and check your answers.**

___F___ **1.** Her children do not go to school.

_____ **2.** She wants to work two hours a week.

_____ **3.** She wants to work in the afternoon.

_____ **4.** She has a high school diploma.

_____ **5.** She doesn't drive.

_____ **6.** She lives near Little Friends.

_____ **7.** She comes from a small family.

_____ **8.** She wants to work at Little Friends.

TIME to TALK

GROUPS. **Discuss the questions about your country.**

1. Do a lot of women have jobs outside the home?
2. What kinds of jobs do women usually have?
3. What kinds of jobs do women almost never have?
4. Do you think some jobs are good only for women or for men? Which jobs? Why?

Now tell the class the interesting things that you learned from your discussion.

Example:

A: *In Chen's country, a lot of women have jobs outside the home. They work on farms and in factories . . .*

Reading and Writing

Reading

A   Imelda Aquino has an appointment with a career counselor. Read the paragraphs and answer the questions.

1. How is Imelda like you? _____

2. How is she different from you? _____

> My name is Imelda Aquino. I live in Jersey City. I come from the Philippines. My first language is Tagalog, but I also speak Spanish. I am learning English now.
>
> In the Philippines I was an elementary school teacher at Baluarte Elementary School in Iloilo City for five years. I have a bachelor's degree in education from the University of the Philippines. Right now I am working part-time as a cashier at Lucky's Supermarket.
>
> I am looking for a job as a teacher's aide. I like children and I like to teach. In the future, I want to teach in an elementary school.

B   Complete the form with information about Imelda.

COUNSELING & CAREER SERVICES

Today's Date: __3/19/06__   Name: __Imelda Aquino__

List any foreign languages that you speak: _____

COUNSELING & CAREER SERVICES

Educational Background

Check (✓) all that apply. Write the institution's name and location, as well as your major field of study.

	Name and location of institution	Major
☑ Graduated from high school	Pasay City High School, Pasay City	–
❑ Associate's Degree	–	–
☑ Bachelor's Degree	University of Philippines, Manila	education
❑ Master's Degree (or higher)	–	–
❑ Other? Please explain.	–	–

Work Experience

Employer	Job title or position	Years employed

Future Plans

What are your educational and career goals?

_____

Prewriting

Fill in the form with information about yourself.

COUNSELING & CAREER SERVICES

Today's Date: _____   Name: _____

List any foreign languages that you speak: _____

Educational Background

Check (✓) all that apply. Write the institution's name and location, as well as your major field of study.

	Name and location of institution	Major
❏ Graduated from high school	_____	_____
❏ Associate's Degree	_____	_____
❏ Bachelor's Degree	_____	_____
❏ Master's Degree (or higher)	_____	_____
❏ Other? Please explain.	_____	_____

Work Experience

Employer	Job title or position	Years employed
_____	_____	_____
_____	_____	_____
_____	_____	_____

Future Plans

What are your educational and career goals?

_____

_____

Writing

Write about your goals on a piece of paper. Use the paragraphs on page 148 as a model.

Use the paragraphs on page 148 as a model.

> ### Writing Tip
>
> A paragraph has one topic. If you start a new topic, start a new paragraph. Look at the reading on page 148. Each paragraph has a different topic:
>
> Paragraph 1 = personal information
> Paragraph 2 = education and work
> Paragraph 3 = future plans

Game 3
Units 9-12

PLAYERS | 4 students

MATERIALS | 1 book
1 coin
2 markers (1 marker for each pair of students)

INSTRUCTIONS
▶ Put your markers on the START box.
▶ Student A: Toss the coin. Heads = Move 1 box. Tails = Move 2 boxes.
▶ Make a statement or question about the picture in the box.
▶ Students B, C, D: Make sure Student's A statement or question is correct. Now make new statements or questions about Student A's picture.

> **POINTS FOR CORRECT ANSWERS**
> statement = 1 point   *yes / no* question = 2 points   information question = 3 points

Example: PICTURE 1

Student A: He plays computer games on weekends. (1 point)
Student B: Does he play computer games on weekends? (2 points)
Student C: What does he do on weekends? (3 points)

▶ Student B: Now take your turn. Students A, C, D: make questions and statements about Student B's picture.
▶ Students: If your answer is not correct, put your marker back on the box from your last turn. If you land on another student's box, move your marker to the next box.
▶ Continue taking turns until you get to the FINISH box. The student with the most points wins.

START

1
play computer games / on weekends

5
Lisa / get up early / in the morning

>>

2
not / cost / $100

3
guests / usually / gifts / bride and groom

4
Joe / get a haircut / right now

8 Alex / want / go on vacation

9 Margo / drink 10 cups of coffee / everyday

10 convenience store / never / close / 9 P.M.

7 Joe and Val / celebrate / Thanksgiving

FINISH

Is 12 o'clock good for you?

Dan

16 make an appointment / right now

Birthday Party!
Saturday October 12th, 4 p.m.

Luisa   Mark

11 invite / birthday party

6 Cory / brush his teeth / after breakfast

15 Louise / always / get flowers / on her birthday

Résumé EXPERIENCE

12 Sue / have / a lot of experience

14 boys / not / like / the ties

13 Pam / not / do housework / in the afternoon

Unit 13
Feelings and Opinions

Grammar

- Simple Past of *Be*: Statements
- Simple Past of *Be*: Yes / No Questions
- Simple Past of *Be*: Information Questions

Vocabulary

CD 2 TRACK 44 **Read and listen. Circle the positive words. Underline the negative words.**

1. angry
2. rude
3. in a bad mood
4. noisy
5. slow
6. dirty
7. terrible food
8. worried
9. crowded
10. wonderful food
11. good service
12. in a good mood
13. clean

The food is wonderful!

152 Unit 13

Listening

A 〔CD 2 TRACK 45〕 **Listen. Check (✓) the good things about Angel's vacation last week.**

- ❏ **1.** the location of his mother-in-law's house
- ❏ **2.** the people at the beach
- ❏ **3.** the price of the airline tickets
- ❏ **4.** the warm water
- ☑ **5.** the weather

B 〔CD 2 TRACK 46〕 **Read and listen again. Write the missing words. Use the words in the box.**

How much	~~How was~~	was	Were	weren't	Were they

David: I love Miami. <u>How was</u> the weather?
1.

Angel: It was wonderful. And my mother-in-law's

house is only about ten minutes from the

beach. We were there every day from 9:00 to

4:00. The water _____ really warm.
2.

David: Great . . . _____ were the airline
3.

tickets? _____ expensive?
4.

Angel: No, they _____ . They were only
5.

$159 from New York.

David: Wow, that's cheap _____ your kids
6.

with you?

Angel: Of course! It was spring vacation so they

were off all week.

Feelings and Opinions **153**

Grammar to Communicate 1

SIMPLE PAST OF *BE*: STATEMENTS

Subject	Be	
I He She It	**was**	at home.
You We They	**were**	

Subject	Be	Not	
I He She It	**was**	not	at work.
You We They	**were**		

Contractions

was + not → **wasn't**

were + not → **weren't**

There	Be		
There	**was**	a lot of	food.
	were	three	kids.

There	Be + Not		
There	**wasn't**	any	food.
	weren't		kids.

A Complete the sentences about yesterday at 1:00 P.M. Use *was* or *were*.

1. I ___was___ at work. My co-workers and I ___were___ busy.

2. My daughter and her friend _____ at home all day. They _____ bored.

3. My husband _____ at a restaurant with a co-worker. They _____ at lunch.

4. My neighbors _____ at home. They _____ sick.

5. My sister _____ late for lunch. My mother and father _____ worried.

B Look at the calendar. Match the dates on the left with the time expressions on the right.

___b___ 1. June 7   **a.** last month

_____ 2. June 7, 6 P.M. **b.** yesterday

_____ 3. June 6   **c.** yesterday morning

_____ 4. June 7, 8 A.M. **d.** yesterday afternoon

_____ 5. May 8   **e.** yesterday evening

_____ 6. June 7, 10 P.M. **f.** last night

_____ 7. June 1   **g.** last week

_____ 8. June 7, 1 P.M. **h.** the day before yesterday

today

C Write true sentences about yourself. Use time expressions from Exercise B.

1. I was bored ___last night___.
2. I was late _____.
3. I was sick _____.
4. The homework wasn't easy _____.
5. My lunch wasn't very good _____.

bored

Complete the sentences. Use *was, were, wasn't,* or *weren't.*

6. I _____ in a good mood yesterday evening.
7. The weather _____ wonderful yesterday.
8. My friends _____ scared last night.
9. The teacher _____ angry last week.
10. My neighbors _____ worried last month.

scared

D Complete the sentences. Circle the correct form of the verbs.

1. There **was** / **were** some dirty dishes in my bedroom. My mother was angry.
2. There **was** / **were** a fire in our building yesterday. We were scared.
3. There **was** / **were** two big tests last week. I was worried.
4. There **wasn't** / **weren't** any good movies on TV last night. I was bored.
5. There **wasn't** / **weren't** any homework last week. The students were in a good mood.
6. There **wasn't** / **weren't** any clean shirts in my father's closet. He was in a bad mood.

TIME to TALK

PAIRS. Tell your classmate about the last time you were at one of these events.

| children's birthday party | graduation | large party | wedding |

Example:
A: *I was at a children's birthday party last week. The party was for my son's best friend. There were about ten kids at the party. The weather wasn't great, so the party was inside. The children were in a good mood . . .*

Grammar to Communicate 2

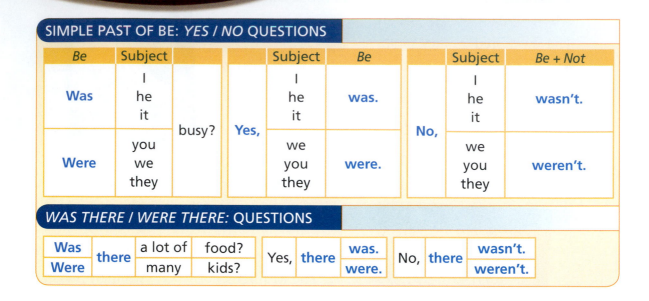

SIMPLE PAST OF BE: *YES / NO* QUESTIONS								
Be	*Subject*			*Subject*	*Be*		*Subject*	*Be + Not*
Was	I he it	busy?	**Yes,**	I he it	**was.**	**No,**	I he it	**wasn't.**
Were	you we they			we you they	**were.**		we you they	**weren't.**

WAS THERE / WERE THERE: QUESTIONS									
Was	**there**	a lot of	food?	**Yes,**	**there**	**was.**	**No,**	**there**	**wasn't.**
Were		many	kids?			**were.**			**weren't.**

A Look at the pictures on pages 152–153. Answer the questions about last night at Del Fino's and Vinnie's restaurants.

	DEL FINO'S	VINNIE'S
1. Was the food good?	No, it wasn't.	Yes, it was.
2. Were the waiters polite?		
3. Were the customers angry?		
4. Was the service fast?		
5. Were the plates clean?		
6. Was the restaurant noisy?		
7. Was the cook in a good mood?		

B Write questions. Put the words in the correct order.

1. _____Was the teacher nice?_____
   (the / Was / nice / teacher)

2. _____
   (Was / crowded / classroom / the)

3. _____
   (homework / Was / the / difficult)

4. _____
   (Were / long / classes / your)

5. _____
   (at night / classes / your / Were)

6. _____
   (tests / easy / Were / the)

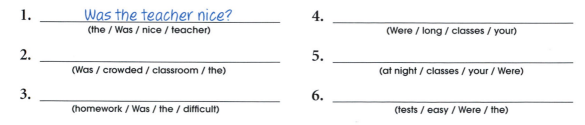

PAIRS. Think of a class you were in. Ask and answer the questions above.

C Complete the questions. Use *Was there* or *Were there*. Then complete the answers.

1. _____Were there_____ a lot of people?   Yes, _____there were._____

2. _____ good food?   Yes, _____

3. _____ a line?   No, _____

4. _____ a lot of different dishes on the menu?   Yes, _____

5. _____ a lot of salespeople?   No, _____

6. _____ a lot of cheap things?   Yes, _____

PAIRS. Which questions are about a restaurant? Which questions are about a store? Which questions are about both?

Example:

A: *I think number 1 is about a restaurant or a store.*

PAIRS. Look at the pictures. Imagine you were at these places last weekend. Ask and answer questions about your weekend.

Example:

A: *I was at Hector's Café last weekend.*

B: *How was it?*

A: *It was OK. The coffee was good and the weather was nice. But there were a lot of people! It was crowded.*

Grammar to Communicate 3

SIMPLE PAST OF *BE*: INFORMATION QUESTIONS

Wh- word	*Be*	Subject		Answers
When	was	the party?		On Saturday night.
Why		the party	on Saturday?	Saturday was my birthday.
Where	were	you	last night?	I was at the movies.
How		the children	yesterday?	They were very good.

A Write questions. Use *How* and the words in the box.

~~class~~   school   the party   work   your day

1. You weren't in class yesterday. You call a classmate and ask:

   A: _How was class?_____

2. It's 8:00 P.M. Your mother had a long day. You ask:

   A: _____

3. It's 4:00 P.M. Your son is home from school. You ask:

   A: _____

4. It's Sunday. Your friend was at a party last night. You ask:

   A: _____

5. It's 6:00 P.M. Your husband or wife is home from work. You ask:

   A: _____

PAIRS. Ask and answer the questions above. Use the expressions in the Look Box.

Example:
A: *How was class?*
B: *Pretty bad. The test was difficult.*

> **Look**
> really good = very good
> pretty good = good
> pretty bad = bad
> really bad = very bad

B **PAIRS.** Complete the questions with *was* or *were*. Then think about the last time you were in another city or country. Ask and answer the questions.

1. Where __were__ you?

2. When _____ you there?

3. Who _____ with you?

4. Why _____ you there?

5. How _____ it?

6. How long _____ you there?

C CD 2 TRACK **47** Complete the conversation. Use *Where*, *How*, *Who*, and *Why* and the correct form of *be*. Then listen and check your answers.

Matt: _____How was_____ your day yesterday?
1.

Bob: It was really good.

Matt: _____ you?
2.

Bob: I was at the beach.

Matt: But it was Thursday. _____
3.

you at the beach on Thursday?

Bob: Thursday's my day off.

Matt: _____ with you?
4.

Bob: My girlfriend and her mother.

Matt: Her mother? _____ her mother with you?
5.

Bob: Her mother likes the beach.

Matt: Oh . . . OK. _____ the beach?
6.

Bob: It was very nice. There weren't many people, and it was a beautiful day.

Matt: _____ the water?
7.

Bob: It was pretty cold. The water is always cold around here.

PAIRS. **Student A:** Look at the picture on page 270.
Student B: Look at the picture on page 272.
You were both on an airplane last weekend, but your experiences were very different. How were they different? Ask and answer questions.

Example:
A: *How was the weather on the day of your flight?*
B: *It was wonderful. It was a beautiful day. How was your weather?*
A: *It was terrible!*

Review and Challenge

Grammar

🔘 **48** **Complete the conversation. Use the words in the box. Then listen and check your answers. (Be careful! There is one extra answer.)**

| How | it | they | ~~was~~ | wasn't | were | weren't | what | Where |

Greg: I miss my old apartment. It ___was___ really nice.
1.

Pearl: _____ was it?
2.

Greg: On Cherry Street in Overbrook.

Pearl: Was _____ big?
3.

Greg: No, it _____. There _____ five
4.   5.

rooms, but _____ were small.
6.

Pearl: Were there a lot of stores in the neighborhood?

Greg: No, there _____. They were all far away.
7.

Pearl: So _____ was nice about the apartment?
8.

Dictation

🔘 **49** Listen. You will hear five sentences. Write them on a piece of paper.

Speaking

PAIRS. Write a short conversation for each question. Then perform one of your conversations for the class.

1. Why were you late this morning?
2. It's midnight. Where were you?
3. How was the movie?
4. Why weren't you in class yesterday?

Example:
A: *Why were you late this morning?*
B: *The traffic was terrible. . .*

 Unit 13

Listening

A CD 2 TRACK **50** Listen. What are the people talking about? Match the conversations with the topics. (Be careful! There are two extra topics.)

____ Conversation 1 **a.** a class

____ Conversation 2 **b.** a sports event

____ Conversation 3 **c.** a job interview

____ Conversation 4 **d.** a movie

                               e. a new DVD

                               f. a test

B CD 2 TRACK **51** Listen again. Complete the sentences about the conversations. Use the words in the box.

~~bad~~	difficult	great	sick
bored	easy	rude	worried

Conversation 1

1. The weather was ____*bad*____.

2. The questions were _____.

Conversation 2

3. She was _____.

4. The man behind her was _____.

Conversation 3

5. He was _____ at first.

6. The test was _____.

Conversation 4

7. The man wasn't there because he was _____.

8. The game was _____.

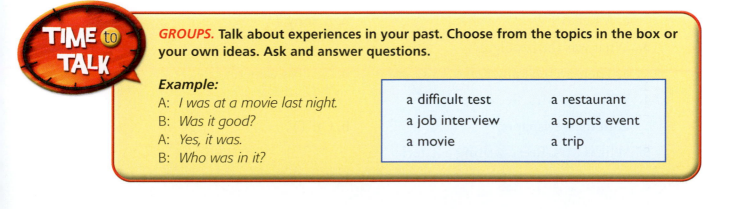

TIME to TALK

GROUPS. Talk about experiences in your past. Choose from the topics in the box or your own ideas. Ask and answer questions.

Example:
A: *I was at a movie last night.*
B: *Was it good?*
A: *Yes, it was.*
B: *Who was in it?*

a difficult test	a restaurant
a job interview	a sports event
a movie	a trip

Reading and Writing

Reading

A Read the letter. Check the word that describes Mrs. Reese's feelings.

❏ angry

❏ bored

❏ scared

❏ worried

George Harrison, Manager   1329 Market Street
Price Wise Electronics   Freemont, CA 94538
115 West Broadway
Freemont, CA 94538   June 28, 2006

  Dear Mr. Harrison:

In last week's newspaper, there was an ad for a sale on Saturday, June 26th, at your Freemont Store. The ad said Keiko TVs were $299.

I was at your store on Saturday morning. There were a lot of TVs, but there weren't any Keikos. Some TVs were on sale, but there weren't any for $299. The salesman said there was a mistake in the ad.

Was your ad wrong? Why weren't there any Keiko TVs for $299? I would like to buy a Keiko for the price in the ad. Please call me at (111) 917-2525. Thank you.

Sincerely,

Brenda Reese

Brenda Reese

B Circle the correct answers.

1. When was Mrs. Reese at Price Wise?

   a. On Friday morning.   **b.** On Saturday morning.

2. What did she want to buy?

   a. A Keiko TV.   **b.** A Sony TV.

3. What was the problem?

   a. There weren't any Keiko TVs.   **b.** No TVs were on sale.

4. Where did Mrs. Reese see the ad?

   a. In the newspaper.   **b.** On TV.

5. Why is Mrs. Reese writing a letter?

   a. She wants a TV for $299.   **b.** She doesn't want to pay for a TV.

Writing

Think about a time when you were unhappy with a business. Write a letter to the manager. Use the letter on page 162 as a model.

Writing Tip

Business letters look different from personal letters. Follow the instructions below.

Write your address here.

Write the recipient's name here.

Write the business address here.

Write today's date here.

_____

_____

_____

_____

_____

_____

_____

_____

Dear _____:

Write about these questions:
• Why are you unhappy?
• What happened?
• What do you want the recipient of this letter to do?

_____

_____

_____

_____

_____

_____

_____

Sincerely,

Sign your name here.

_____

_____

Print your name here.

Unit 14
Fact or Fiction?

Grammar
- Simple Past: Regular Verbs
- Simple Past: Irregular Verbs
- Simple Past: Negative Statements

Vocabulary

52 Read and listen. Circle the best newspaper headline for the story.

Gorilla on Canal Street

Police visit the city zoo

New job for zoo worker

1. forget the keys

2. leave the keys

3. get out

5. happen [*what happened?*]

6. lose his keys

8. catch

9. take back

Listening

A CD 2 TRACK 53 **Listen. Steve and Marie are talking about a story in yesterday's newspaper. Check (✓) the places Steve talks about.**

❑ a bus stop   ❑ a police station   ❑ a street

❑ a park   ❑ a small town   ❑ a zoo

B CD 2 TRACK 54 **Read and listen again. Write the missing words. Use the words in the box.**

didn't	~~ran~~	took	walked	watched

Marie: A gorilla?

Steve: Yeah, you heard me —a gorilla. First he

__ran__ into the park. Then he ran across
        1.

Canal Street. All the people in their cars

stopped and _____ him. Then he
                    2.

_____ to the bus stop, and stood next to
     3.

it. The people all screamed, but the gorilla

_____ move. He just stood there.
     4.

Marie: Oh, please!

Steve: Really! Look. It's in the paper. A policeman

took a picture of it.

Marie: Wow! That's really strange. Where

is he now? Is he back in the zoo?

Steve: Yes, the police caught him and _____
                                          5.

him back.

4. scream

7. chase

10. change jobs

Fact or Fiction? 165

Grammar to Communicate 1

Look

See page 262 for spelling rules with the Simple Past.

SIMPLE PAST: REGULAR VERBS			
Subject	**Verb + -ed**		**Time Expression**
I You He	work**ed**		last Saturday.
It	clos**ed**		last night.
We They	mov**ed**	to Miami	last year.

A Complete the sentences. Use the verbs in the box.

changed	~~lived~~	moved	started	worked

1. In 1995 I ___lived___ in **Los Angeles**.
2. In 1998 I _____ in **a restaurant**.
3. I _____ jobs **in 2003**.
4. I _____ to **Chicago in 2004**.
5. I _____ English class **in 2005**.

move

PAIRS. **Change the bold words in the sentences. Write true sentences about yourself on a piece of paper.**

Look

Pronunciation of final -ed
listen**ed**   /d/
cook**ed**   /t/
wait**ed**   /ɪd/

B **55** Circle the verb in each sentence. Then listen. What are the sounds of the verb endings? Check (✓) the correct column.

	/d/	/t/	/ɪd/
1. I (invited) friends home last month.	❏	❏	✔
2. I exercised the day before yesterday.	❏	❏	❏
3. I washed my hair last night.	❏	❏	❏
4. I started dinner at 6:00 last night.	❏	❏	❏
5. I cooked yesterday morning.	❏	❏	❏
6. I called my friend yesterday.	❏	❏	❏
7. I watched TV yesterday afternoon.	❏	❏	❏

C **PAIRS.** Change the time expressions in the sentences in Exercise B. Make the sentences true about yourself. Write them on a piece of paper. Read your sentences to your partner.

Example:

I invited friends home <s>last month</s>. *last Saturday*

D Read about Vincent's activities every day. Rewrite the sentences to talk about his day yesterday.

Every day	Yesterday
1. Vincent works every day.	1. <u>He worked yesterday.</u>
2. He fixes computers.	2. _____
3. He walks to the bus stop in the morning.	3. _____
4. He talks to his wife at lunchtime.	4. _____
5. He finishes work at 5:30.	5. _____
6. He plays with his baby son after dinner.	6. _____
7. He listens to the radio at night.	7. _____

PAIRS. Now circle the activities above that you did yesterday. Tell your partner.

Example:

A: *I worked yesterday. How about you?*
B: *I worked yesterday, too. I also listened to the radio.*

TIME to TALK

PAIRS. When did you last do the things in the box? Tell your partner. If you don't remember, say "I don't remember."

ask for directions	move
change jobs	play cards
clean your house	stay up late
cook	wash a car
invite someone to your house	watch a good movie
miss a bus	wait for a bus

miss the bus

Example:

A: *I waited for a bus yesterday. How about you?*
B: *Yesterday, I missed the bus, so I was late to school.*

Grammar to Communicate 2

SIMPLE PAST: IRREGULAR VERBS

Subject	Verb		Time Expression
I You He	**had**	dinner	last week.
It	**came**		last night.
We They	**did**	the dishes	yesterday.

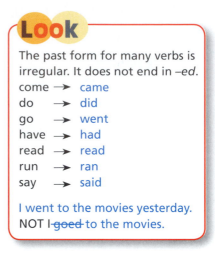

Look

The past form for many verbs is irregular. It does not end in *–ed*.
come → came
do → did
go → went
have → had
read → read
run → ran
say → said

I went to the movies yesterday.
NOT I ~~goed~~ to the movies.

A Match the simple present sentences with the simple past sentences.

_d_ 1. Sara's late for work.

____ 2. Sara's boyfriend is angry with her.

____ 3. Max is looking for a taxi.

____ 4. Max doesn't have his cell phone.

____ 5. Max's boss is talking to him.

____ 6. Sara doesn't have her bag.

____ 7. Sara doesn't know the person on the phone.

____ 8. Max didn't sleep much last night.

____ 9. Max wasn't at work yesterday.

a. She <u>called</u> the wrong phone number.

b. He <u>drank</u> two cups of coffee after dinner.

c. She <u>forgot</u> his birthday.

d. She <u>got up</u> late.

e. He <u>left</u> his cell phone at home.

f. He <u>made</u> a big mistake at work yesterday.

g. He <u>missed</u> the bus.

h. He <u>spent</u> the day with a friend.

i. She <u>took</u> the wrong bag.

B Write the simple past of the verbs. Look at the underlined verbs in Exercise A for help. Then check (✓) the correct column.

	SIMPLE PAST	REGULAR	IRREGULAR
call	called	✓	
drink	drank		✓
forget			
get up			
leave			
make			
miss			
spend			
take			

spend time with your family

C Write true sentences about yourself. Complete the sentences with time expressions.

1. I wrote a letter _____.
2. I heard a funny story _____.
3. I woke up early _____.
4. I lost something _____.

5. I knew the answers _____.
6. I went to the bank _____.
7. I saw a friend _____.
8. I ate out _____.

Write the simple past form of these verbs.

write __wrote__   wake _____   know _____   see _____

eat _____   hear _____   lose _____   go _____

D Some students did not do their homework. Below are the excuses or reasons they gave. Complete the sentences. Use the simple past form of the verbs.

1. The dog ___ate___ my homework.
       (eat)

2. I _____ my book.
   (lose)

3. I _____ the wrong page.
   (do)

4. I _____ the wrong book.
   (read)

5. I _____ my homework at home.
   (leave)

6. I _____ about it.
   (forget)

PAIRS. You are teachers. Which excuses do you believe?

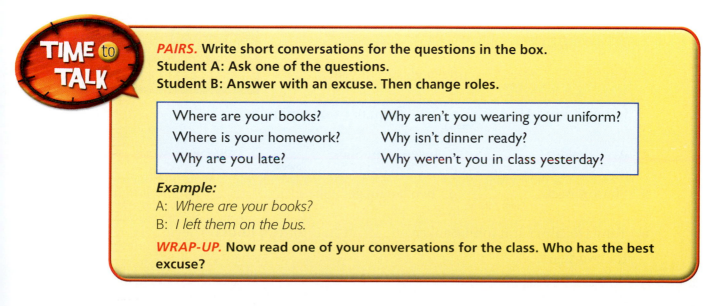

TIME to TALK

PAIRS. Write short conversations for the questions in the box.
Student A: Ask one of the questions.
Student B: Answer with an excuse. Then change roles.

Where are your books?	Why aren't you wearing your uniform?
Where is your homework?	Why isn't dinner ready?
Why are you late?	Why weren't you in class yesterday?

Example:
A: *Where are your books?*
B: *I left them on the bus.*

WRAP-UP. Now read one of your conversations for the class. Who has the best excuse?

Grammar to Communicate 3

SIMPLE PAST: NEGATIVE STATEMENTS			
Subject	*Did + Not*	Verb	
I You He It We They	**didn't**	**work**	last night.

Look

To make negative statements with the simple past, use *did* + *not* + verb.

He **didn't miss** the bus.
NOT He didn't ~~missed~~ the bus.

She **didn't lose** her keys.
NOT She didn't ~~lost~~ her keys.

A Make each sentence true about yourself. Circle the affirmative or negative form of the verb.

1. I **ate** / **didn't eat** breakfast at 3 A.M. yesterday.

2. I **stayed up** / **didn't stay up** all night last night.

3. I **got up** / **didn't get up** at 4:00 yesterday afternoon.

4. I **called** / **didn't call** ten people yesterday.

5. I **slept** / **didn't sleep** at work yesterday.

B Write a negative statement. Then write an affirmative statement.

1. Simon Ward ____didn't eat____ two hamburgers.
   (not / eat)

   He ____ate____ twenty hamburgers.
   (eat)

2. Sonya Keller _____ for twelve hours.
   (not / sleep)

   She _____ for two days.
   (sleep)

3. Bill Lau _____ fifteen glasses of water
   (not / drink)

   in two hours. He _____ them in twenty minutes.
   (drink)

4. Anna Valdez _____ seven sons. She _____ seventeen sons.
   (not / have) (have)

5. Sharon Beck _____ two languages. She _____ twenty languages.
   (not / study) (study)

6. Tony DePalma and John Banker _____ for two hours. They _____
   (not / walk) (walk)
   for two years.

C **Complete the story. Use the correct form of the verbs.**

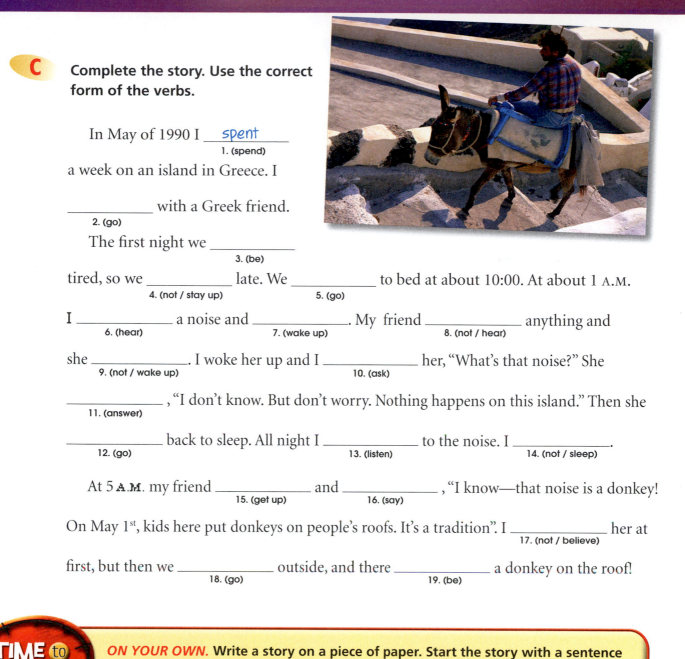

In May of 1990 I ___spent___
1. (spend)

a week on an island in Greece. I

_____ with a Greek friend.
2. (go)

The first night we _____
3. (be)

tired, so we _____ late. We _____ to bed at about 10:00. At about 1 A.M.
4. (not / stay up)   5. (go)

I _____ a noise and _____. My friend _____ anything and
6. (hear)   7. (wake up)   8. (not / hear)

she _____. I woke her up and I _____ her, "What's that noise?" She
9. (not / wake up)   10. (ask)

_____, "I don't know. But don't worry. Nothing happens on this island." Then she
11. (answer)

_____ back to sleep. All night I _____ to the noise. I _____.
12. (go)   13. (listen)   14. (not / sleep)

At 5 A.M. my friend _____ and _____, "I know—that noise is a donkey!
15. (get up)   16. (say)

On May 1st, kids here put donkeys on people's roofs. It's a tradition". I _____ her at
17. (not / believe)

first, but then we _____ outside, and there _____ a donkey on the roof!
18. (go)   19. (be)

TIME to TALK

ON YOUR OWN. Write a story on a piece of paper. Start the story with a sentence from the box. Talk about what happened next. Make as many negative statements as you can.

I drank two cups of coffee after dinner.	I lost my wallet.
I forgot my keys.	I made a mistake at work.
I forgot my wife's/husband's birthday.	I missed the bus.
I heard a strange noise.	My dog got out of the house and ran away.

PAIRS. Tell your story to your partner.

Example:

A: *I drank two cups of coffee after dinner, so I didn't sleep well. I didn't hear my alarm clock in the morning, so I didn't wake up on time. I was late, so I didn't . . .*

Review and Challenge

Grammar

Find the mistake in each sentence. Circle the letter. Then correct the mistake.

1. I change jobs last month.
   A B C

   Correct: _I changed jobs last month._

2. They goed to a restaurant and ate.
   A   B   C

   Correct: _____

3. We not see them last night.
   A   B   C

   Correct: _____

4. He didn't stayed here yesterday.
   A   B   C

   Correct: _____

5. You didn't did the dishes yesterday.
   A   B   C

   Correct: _____

6. She didn't works yesterday.
   A   B   C

   Correct: _____

Dictation

CD 2 TRACK **56** Listen. You will hear five sentences. Write them on a piece of paper.

Speaking

GROUPS. 1. **Look at pages 164–165. With a partner, practice telling the story.**
2. **Now choose an experience from the box. Tell your group a true story.**

a funny experience	a scary experience
a happy experience	a strange experience

Example:

A: *I had a funny experience two years ago. It was early in the morning. I got in my car to drive to work. I started the car, but then I heard a funny noise. I stopped the car. I looked in the engine. There was a cat in the engine!*

WRAP-UP. **Now choose the best story in the group and tell the class.**

Listening

A CD 2 TRACK **57** Listen to the radio report. Check (✓) the news you hear.

❏ international news   ❏ funny news   ❏ important news

B CD 2 TRACK **58** Listen again. Read the sentences. For each sentence, write *T* (true) or *F* (false).

Story 1

_____ **1.** A woman took a day off because she wanted to meet the U.S. president.

_____ **2.** Her boss wrote a note for her.

_____ **3.** The president signed her excuse note.

Story 2

_____ **1.** The little boy didn't want to go to school.

_____ **2.** The police officer was late for work.

_____ **3.** The driver of the car was seven years old.

TIME to TALK

PAIRS. Put the pictures in order. Write *1* for the first event that happened, *2* for the second event, and *3* for the last event. Then tell your partner the story.

GROUPS. Now tell your story to a group. Does everyone have the same story?

Fact or Fiction? 173

Reading and Writing

Reading

 A Read the police report in Exercise B. What happened? Circle the correct answer.

1. Somebody stole things from an office.

2. Somebody stole things from a person on the street.

3. Somebody stole things from an apartment.

steal / stole

B Read the report again. Then complete the missing information.

CITY OF CHANDLER POLICE

Stolen Property Report

Date of incident: _____

Witness's name(s): _____

Witness's address: 15 Linwood Ave., #4A, Chandler, TX

Witness's phone number: 111-987-5236

Description of suspect: Include hair color, eye color, race, weight, height, clothing, etc. _____

_____

_____

Description of incident:

On May 30, 2006, at 9:30 P.M my neighbors, Wendy and Harry Chen, heard a loud noise in my apartment. I was at work, so they called the police. Then they watched my apartment door. They saw a man at the door of my apartment. He was white and had black hair. He was about 6 feet tall. He had on jeans and an orange shirt. He ran away with my TV and a large bag. When I got home at 10:00 P.M., the Chens went with me into my apartment. The kitchen window was broken, and the apartment was a mess. The burglar took my Sovy 14 inch TV, $300 in cash, and two gold rings.

Stolen items: What did the suspect take? If you don't know, write "?"

Description	Make	Model	Serial #	Value
	Sovy		?	$200

Prewriting

GROUPS. **Talk about crimes. Ask and answer these questions with your group:**

• What crimes have happened to you or people you know?
• What other local crimes have you read or heard about?
• When and where did the crime happen?
• What exactly happened?

Take notes during your discussion. Write on a piece of paper.

Writing

Complete the police report. You can write about a true crime from your group discussion, or an imaginary one. Use the police report on page 174 as a model.

CITY OF CHANDLER POLICE

Stolen Property Report

Date of incident: _____

Witness's name(s): _____

Witness's address: _____

Witness's phone number: _____

Description of suspect: Include hair color, eye color, race, weight, height, clothing, etc. _____
_____
_____

Description of incident:
_____
_____
_____
_____
_____
_____
_____

Stolen items: What did the suspect take? If you don't know, write " *?* "

Description	Make	Model	Serial #	Value

Unit 15
Life Stages

Grammar
- Simple Past: *Yes / No* Questions
- Simple Past: Information Questions
- Information Questions with *Who* and *What* as Subject
- *How long ago / How long*

Vocabulary

CD 3 TRACK **2** Read and listen. Then circle the life stages that happen to most people in your country.

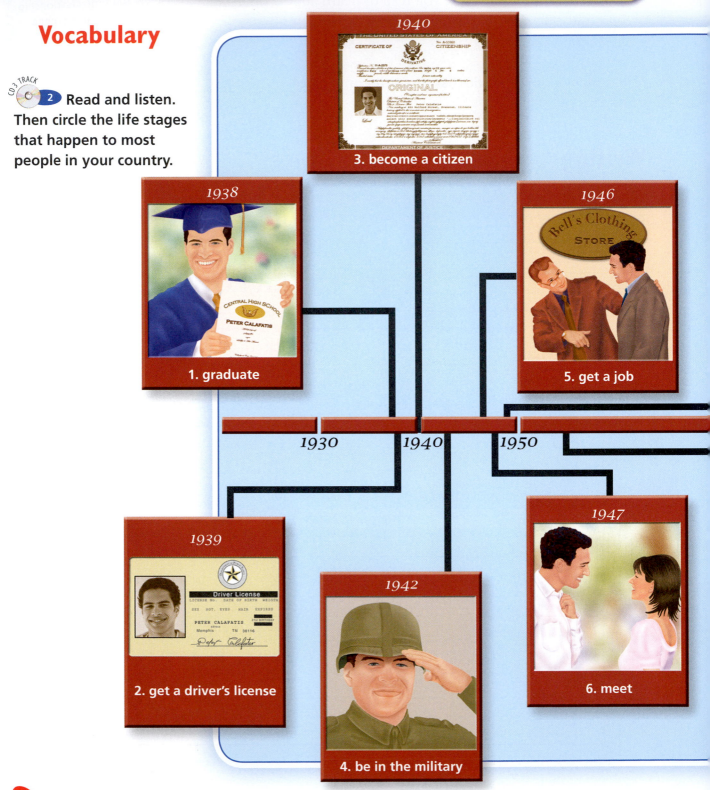

1940

3. become a citizen

1938

1. graduate

1946

5. get a job

1930   1940   1950

1939

2. get a driver's license

1942

4. be in the military

1947

6. meet

Listening

CD 3 TRACK **A** **3** **Listen. Paul and Jean talk about their lives. Match the information with the person. Write** *P* **(Paul) and** *J* **(Jean).**

_____ **1.** He became a citizen.   _____ **4.** His wife had a baby.

_____ **2.** He got a new job.   _____ **5.** He got married.

_____ **3.** He bought a house.   _____ **6.** He moved.

CD 3 TRACK **B** **4** **Read and listen again. Write the missing words. Use the words in the box.**

A year ago	~~ago~~	Did you keep	How long	What did

Jean: So, how long ____*ago*____ did you get
1.
married?

Paul: _____. We had a small
2.
wedding—just our relatives and a few
friends.

Jean: Well, congratulations!

Paul: Thanks, but that's not all. We had a baby
last month.

Jean: A baby? That was fast! _____ you
3.
have—a girl or a boy?

Paul: A boy—Jason.

Jean: Oh that's great! . . . Where are you living?
_____ your old apartment?
4.

Paul: No, we bought a house in Malden. It
needs work but it didn't cost a lot.

Jean: Wow, that's a big change. _____
5.
did you live in Boston?

1975

9. have an accident

1949

7. get married

1960   1970

1952

8. have a baby

1976

BELL'S CLOTHING
Store

30
years
of
service

10. retire

Life Stages **177**

SIMPLE PAST: *YES / NO* QUESTIONS

Did	Subject	Verb		Short Answers						
Did	I you he we they	**live**	there a long time?	**Yes,**	I you he we they	**did.**	**No,**	I you he we they	**didn't.**

A Answer the questions with true information. Use short answers.

> **Look**
>
> Did you **go fishing** a lot? See page 265 for a list of other expressions with *go* + verb + *-ing*

When you were a child . . .

1. . . . did you live in a big city?   <u>Yes, I did. OR No, I didn't.</u>

2. . . . did you walk to school? _____

3. . . . did you go swimming a lot? _____

4. . . . did your mother have a job? _____

5. . . . did your grandparents live with you? _____

6. . . . did you and your family go fishing? _____

PAIRS. Ask and answer the questions above.

B Complete the conversations. Use *did* or *didn't*.

1. **A:** <u>Did Lynn read a lot last summer?</u>

                       (Lynn / read / a lot last summer)

   B: <u>Yes, she did. She read Harry Potter books.</u>

                       (yes / she / read / Harry Potter books)

2. **A:** _____

                       (Robert / go fishing / with his father last year)

   B: _____

                       (no / he / go / with his uncle)

3. **A:** _____

                       (Karen / have / a full-time job last year)

   B: _____

                       (no / she / have / a part-time job)

4. **A:** _____

                       (Jason / go swimming / at the beach yesterday)

   B: _____

                       (no / he / visit / his grandparents)

C   Complete the questions. Use *was*, *were*, or *did*.

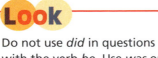

Look

Do not use *did* in questions with the verb *be*. Use *was* or *were*.

Were you a good student?
Yes, I **was**. / No, I **wasn't**.

Did you **like** school?
Yes, I **did** / No, I **didn't**.

1. ____*Were*____ you a happy child?

2. ____*Did*____ you spend a lot of time with your cousins?

3. _____ you tall for your age?

4. _____ you have a best friend?

5. _____ you friendly with your neighbors?

6. _____ you take care of a younger brother or sister?

7. _____ you do a lot of housework?

8. _____ you a serious child?

PAIRS. **Ask and answer the questions above.**

TIME to **TALK**

GROUPS. Ask and answer five questions about your childhood. Use the words in the boxes or your own ideas.

When you were a child, did you . . . ?

get up early every day	have lunch at home
go bowling	live on a farm
have a pet	spend a lot of time with relatives

Were you . . . ?

curious	friendly	lonely	noisy
cute	funny	neat	shy

WRAP-UP. Now tell the class about your partner.

Example:
A: *When he was a child, Manuel lived on a farm. He got up early every day.*
   He was a friendly boy . . .

Grammar to Communicate 2

SIMPLE PAST: INFORMATION QUESTIONS

Wh- Word	Did	Subject	Verb		Answers
What		I	**buy?**		A car.
Where	**did**	you			At Jake's Cars.
When		they	**get**	the car?	In October.
Why		she			For work.

INFORMATION QUESTIONS WITH *WHAT* AND *WHO* AS SUBJECT

Wh- Word	Verb		Answers
What	**happened?**		We had an accident.
Who	**called**	the police?	My friend did.

A Complete the questions. Use *Where, When, Who, How,* or *How old.*

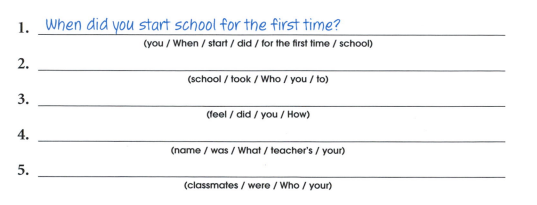

1. _____Where_____ did you drive the first time? (In Atlanta.)

2. _____ taught you to drive? (My father.)

3. _____ did you feel? (I was scared.)

4. _____ were you? (I was 18.)

5. _____ did you get your license? (In 1999.)

PAIRS. Talk to someone who has a driver's license. Ask the questions above.

B Write questions about your first day at school. Put the words in the correct order.

1. __When did you start school for the first time?__
   (you / When / start / did / for the first time / school)

2. _____
   (school / took / Who / you / to)

3. _____
   (feel / did / you / How)

4. _____
   (name / was / What / teacher's / your)

5. _____
   (classmates / were / Who / your)

C

Read the answers. Then write questions about the underlined words. Use *What, Where, When, Who, Why, How much,* or *How old.*

1. <u>Where did Loretta get her first job?</u>

   Loretta got a job <u>in a café</u>. Her sister worked there, too.

2. _____

   Loretta got the job <u>in 1992</u>.

3. _____

   <u>She made coffee and sandwiches</u> at the café.

4. _____

   She was <u>16</u>.

5. _____

   She got a job <u>because she needed the extra money</u>.

6. _____

   The café was <u>near her home</u>.

7. _____

   She met her <u>boyfriend</u> at the café.

8. _____

   She left the café <u>in 1995</u>.

PAIRS. Talk about the first time you did something. Ask and answer questions. Use the ideas in the box or your own ideas.

bought your first car	got your first job	moved away from home
flew on an airplane	met your husband/wife	spoke English for the first time

Example:
A: *I got my first job in a restaurant when I was 15.*
B: *What did you do there?*

Grammar to Communicate 3

HOW LONG AGO / HOW LONG: INFORMATION QUESTIONS

How Long Ago	Did				Time Expression	Ago
How long ago	did	you meet?		We met	ten years five days two minutes	**ago.**

How Long	Did				For	Time Expression
How long	did	they stay?		They stayed	**for**	ten years. five days. two minutes.

A Complete the sentences with *for* or *ago*.

1. Linda was a high school student twenty years __ago__.

2. She was married fifteen years _____.

3. Linda studied at a university _____ four years.

Look

Two days ago   For two days   Now

Sunday   Monday   Tuesday

becoming a citizen

4. Linda took English classes in her country _____ a year.

5. Linda became a citizen a year _____.

6. Linda didn't have a car a few years _____.

7. Linda didn't stay at her first job _____ a long time.

B Change the underlined words in the sentences. Use *for* or *ago*.

1. Tran was born <u>in 1970</u>.   _Tran was born (X) years ago._

2. He lived in Vietnam <u>from 1970 to 1985</u>.   _He lived in Vietnam for fifteen years._

3. He graduated from college <u>in 1995</u>.   _____

4. He worked in an office <u>from 1997 to 1998</u>.   _____

5. He got married <u>in 1999</u>.   _____

6. He became a father <u>in 2001</u>.   _____

PAIRS. Now talk about three important events in your life. Use *for* or *ago*.

Example:

A: *I lived in Cuba for ten years.*

C Read about Arnold Schwarzenegger's life. Write questions. Then answer the questions.

Timeline:
- 1947 — was born in Austria
- 1963 — started his bodybuilding career
- 1965 — went into the army
- 1966 — left the army
- 1968 — moved to the U.S.
- 1970 — made his first movie
- 1975 — retired from bodybuilding
- 1979 — graduated from the University of Wisconsin
- 1983 — became a U.S. citizen
- 1986 — married Maria Shriver
- 2003 — became governor of California

1. How long did Arnold Schwarzenegger live in Austria?   For twenty-one years.
   (How long / Arnold Schwarzenegger / live / in Austria)

2. How long ago did he move to the United States?   _____
   (How long ago / he / move / to the United States)

3. _____   _____
   (How long ago / he / graduate from college)

4. _____   _____
   (How long / was / he / in the army in Austria)

5. _____   _____
   (How long ago / he / get married)

6. _____   _____
   (How long / he / work / as a bodybuilder)

7. _____   _____
   (How long ago / he / become / governor of California)

TIME to TALK

ON YOUR OWN. Draw a timeline for your life. Use the timeline in Exercise C as a model. Use the ideas in the box or your own ideas.

became a U.S. citizen	got a green card	moved to a new place
bought a car	got a job	started English classes
bought a house	got married	was in the military
came to the United States	had a child	went to school

PAIRS. Now exchange timelines with your partner. Ask and answer questions with *How long* and *How long ago*.

Review and Challenge

Grammar

A 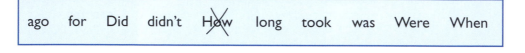 **5** Complete the conversation. Use the words in the box. Then listen and check your answers. (Be careful! There are two extra words.)

ago	for	Did	didn't	H~~ow~~	long	took	was	Were	When

Meg: ___How___ long ago did you come to the United States?
1.

Aida: I came here 15 years ago. My first home

_____ in Los Angeles.
2.

Meg: How _____ did you live there?
3.

Aida: I was there _____ two years.
4.

Meg: _____ you work there?
5.

Aida: No, I didn't. I _____ classes.
6.

Meg: _____ did you move here?
7.

Aida: Three years _____.
8.

Los Angeles

Dictation

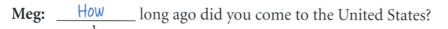 **6** Listen. You will hear five sentences. Write them on a piece of paper.

Speaking

PAIRS. Student A: Look at the timeline about Bruce Lee's life on page 271.
Student B: Look at the timeline on page 273. Ask and answer questions to complete the timeline. Use *where, when, who, what,* and *how long ago*.

Example:
A: *Where was Bruce Lee born?*
B: *He was born in San Francisco. When was he born?*

Kung Fu master Bruce Lee in
***Enter the Dragon,* 1973**

Listening

 A **7** **Listen. A reporter is interviewing Mariela Lopez. What did Ms. Lopez do? Check the correct answer.**

❏ She painted.

❏ She wrote a book.

❏ She got married two times.

Frida and Diego Rivera, 1931, one of Frida Kahlo's paintings

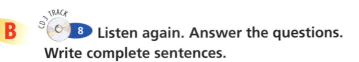 **B** **8** **Listen again. Answer the questions. Write complete sentences.**

1. Who was Frida Kahlo?

   She was an artist.

2. Where was she from?

   _____

3. What happened to her when she was 18?

   _____

4. Who did she get married to?

   _____

5. How long were they married?

   _____

6. When did she die?

   _____

GROUPS. Talk about the past of someone famous in your country or someone important in your life. Ask and answer questions.

Example:
A: *George Washington was the first president of the United States.*
B: *When did he become president?*
A: *I'm not sure about the date, but it was over 200 years ago.*

Reading and Writing

Reading

A A student interviewed her grandmother and wrote about her. Read the story. Check (✓) the best title for the story.

❏ A Love Story   ❏ A Handsome Man   ❏ Many Children

My grandmother was born on January 17, 1909, in New York City. She had three brothers. She was the only girl in her family. She was tall and pretty, and she liked to dance. She was a very good dancer.

In the summer of 1929, she went on a vacation with some friends. They stayed at a big hotel. At a dance at the hotel, she met a tall, handsome man. He asked her to dance, and seven days later, they got married. It was the beginning of a very long love story.

In 1987, after 58 years of marriage, three sons, and six grandchildren, my grandfather died. He was 82 years old. Today, my grandmother still likes to dance, but she misses her favorite dance partner.

B Match the topic with the paragraph.

_____ 1. Paragraph 1   **a.** after her grandfather's death

_____ 2. Paragraph 2   **b.** before her grandmother's marriage

_____ 3. Paragraph 3   **c.** her grandmother and grandfather's first meeting

Prewriting

Think of a person who is 60 years old or older. Write ten questions to ask about his or her past. Then interview the person. Write the answers.

1. <u>Where were you born?</u>
   <u>László was born in Budapest, Hungary, in 1940.</u>

2. _____
   _____

3. _____
   _____

4. _____
   _____

5. _____
   _____

Writing

Write about the life of the person you interviewed. Write one paragraph for each important part of the person's life. Use the story on page 186 as a model.

Writing Tip

We often start a sentence with a time expression. Put a comma (,) between the time expression and the subject.

Example:

<u>In the summer of 1929</u>, she went to the mountains with some friends.

Grammar

- *Be going to*: Statements
- *Be going to*: Yes / No Questions
- *Be going to*: Information Questions

Vocabulary

CD 3 TRACK 9 Read and listen. Then circle the things that you are going to do tomorrow.

1. leave the house
2. stay at home
3. buy groceries
4. pick up someone
5. take someone somewhere
6. go on a picnic
7. tonight
8. have people over
9. play cards

RON

Listening

A CD 3 TRACK **10** **Listen. What does Amir want to do? Check (✓) the correct answer.**

❏ 1. He wants to use his mother's car.

❏ 2. He wants to go to a soccer game.

❏ 3. He wants to pick up his uncle.

❏ 4. He wants to go to a birthday party.

B CD 3 TRACK **11** **Read and listen again. Write the missing words. Use the words in the box.**

| going to | to do | We're not | ~~When are you~~ |

Mom: Are you going to stay the whole weekend?

_____When are you_____ going to leave?
　　　　　　1.

Amir: Sunil's _____ pick me up after
　　　　　　　　　　2.

school on Friday.

Mom: On Friday? When are you going _____
　　　　　　　　　　　　　　　　　　　　　3.

your homework?

Amir: On Sunday night.

Mom: What time are you going to be home on

Sunday?

Amir: Don't worry. _____ going to be late.
　　　　　　　　　　　　4.

We're going to leave San Jose in the morning.

Mom: And where are you going to stay?

Amir: With Sunil's uncle. He lives there.

Mom: What's his name? Do I know him?

Amir: Yes, Mom, you met him at Sunil's birthday

party.

Looking Ahead 189

Grammar to Communicate 1

FUTURE WITH *BE GOING TO*: STATEMENTS

Subject	Be	Going to	Verb	Subject	Be + Not	Going to	Verb
I	am			I	am not		
He It	is	going to	stop.	He It	is not	going to	stop.
We You They	are			We You They	are not		

Look

Contractions:
I **'m not** going to go.
He **isn't** going to go.
We **'re** going to go.
We **aren't** going to go.

A Look at the weather chart for different cities. Write sentences about the weather tomorrow.

City	Today	F/C	Tomorrow	F/C
Beijing	cloudy	61/16°	windy sunny	62/17°
Mexico City	sunny	81/27°	sunny	81/27°
Moscow	snow windy	32/0°	snow	38/3°
São Paulo	humid	90/32°	cloudy	88/31°
Toronto	rain	46/8°	rain	51/10°
Weather Chart Key				
windy =	cloudy =		sunny =	
humid =	snow =		rain =	

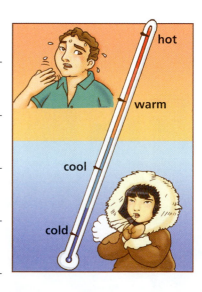

1. Xihua lives in Beijing. It's cloudy and cool today.
   <u>It's going to be sunny and windy tomorrow.</u>

2. Flor lives in Mexico City. It's sunny today. It's warm.
   _____

3. Mariya lives in Moscow. It's windy today. It's snowing.
   _____

4. Jarbas lives in São Paulo. It's humid today. It's hot.
   _____

5. Paulette lives in Toronto. It's raining today. It's cool.
   _____

hot

warm

cool

cold

B Look at Exercise A. What are the people going to do tomorrow? Complete the sentences. Use *be going to*.

1. Mariya ___is going to take___ her children to school.
   (take)

2. Mariya's children ___are not going to ride___ their bikes to school.
   (not / ride)

3. Paulette says, "I _____ tennis."
   (not / play)

4. Paulette says, "My children _____ their umbrellas."
   (take)

5. Flor and her husband _____ to the park.
   (go)

C Write sentences with *be going to*. Use the words in the box or your own ideas.

be late	go outside	play soccer	wear sunglasses
drive to work	go to the laundromat	watch a movie at home	wear a T-shirt

1. It's going to be cloudy and cool tomorrow.

   People ___aren't going to wear sunglasses.___

   I ___'m going to wear a jacket.___

2. It's going to be sunny and hot tomorrow.

   My family and I _____

   My friend _____

3. It's going to snow tomorrow.

   Children _____

   I _____

4. It's going to rain tomorrow.

   I _____

   The bus _____

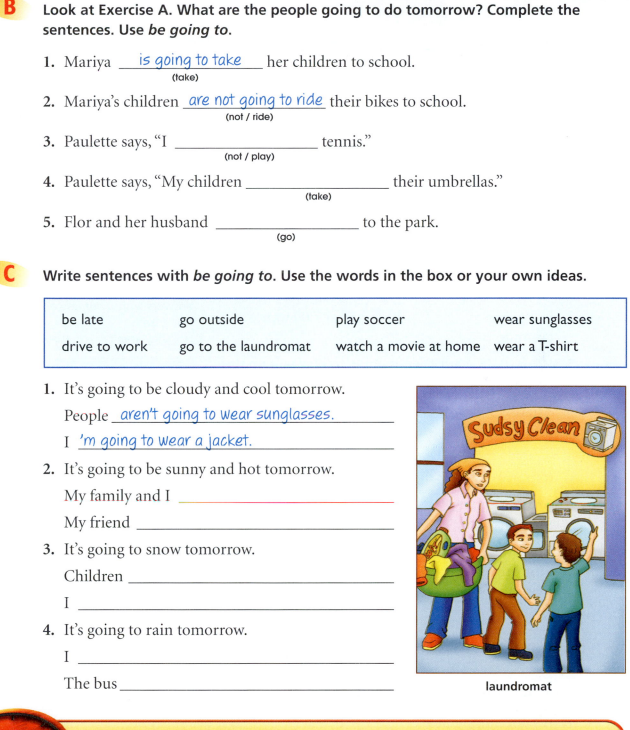

laundromat

PAIRS. Look at the weather report in your local newspaper. What is the weather going to be like for the next few days? What are you going to do? What are you not going to do? Tell your partner.

Example:

A: *It's going to be hot and humid tomorrow. Are you going to go to the beach?*

B: *No, I'm not. I'm going to class.*

Grammar to Communicate ❷

FUTURE WITH *BE GOING TO*: YES / NO QUESTIONS

Be	Subject	*Going to*	Verb	Short Answers					
Am	I			Yes,	you	**are.**	No,	you	**aren't.**
Is	she it	**going to**	**stop?**		she it	**is.**		she it	**isn't.**
Are	you we they				I	**am.**		I'm	**not.**
					we they	**are.**		we they	**aren't.**

 A **Complete the questions with the missing words.**

1. _____Are_____ you going to go on a picnic next week?

2. Is it going _____ be sunny at 7:00 tomorrow evening?

3. _____ your friends going to pick you up this evening?

4. Are you _____ to go to the laundromat tomorrow?

5. _____ your school going to be open tomorrow?

6. Are you going _____ play cards tonight?

7. Is the weather _____ to be good tomorrow?

8. _____ you going to have people over this weekend?

Look

There are two negative short answers with *is not* and *are not*.

No, it **isn't**.   No, it**'s not**.
No, they **aren't**.   No, they**'re not**.

PAIRS. **Ask and answer the questions above.**

B **Look at the sentences. Write questions.**

1. It's not raining now.   _____Is it going to rain_____ soon?

2. The children aren't studying now.   _____ later?

3. I'm not doing the dishes now.   _____ later?

4. John isn't using the phone now.   _____ soon?

5. We aren't going to the movies now.   _____ later?

6. The bus isn't leaving now.   _____ soon?

192 Unit 16

C Write future time expressions. Use *this, tomorrow,* and *next* with the words in the box.

morning	afternoon	evening	night	week	year	month

(morning is crossed out)

this	***tomorrow***	***next***
this morning	tomorrow morning	next week
_____	_____	_____
_____	_____	_____
_____	_____	
_____		

D Write questions. Use the correct form of *be going to*. Then answer the questions with true information.

1. _Are you going to eat out tomorrow night?_   _Yes, I am._ OR _No, I'm not._
   (you / eat out / tomorrow night)

2. _____   _____
   (you / take an English class / next year)

3. _____   _____
   (it / be / hot / this month)

4. _____   _____
   (you / go to the laundromat / tonight)

5. _____   _____
   (you / be / busy / next week)

6. _____   _____
   (your teacher / work / next month)

7. _____   _____
   (a new shopping mall / open / here / this year)

TIME to TALK

ON YOUR OWN. Think of three plans. How are you going to prepare for them? Make a list of sentences.

PAIRS. Read your sentences to your partner. Can your partner guess what you are going to do? Then changes roles.

Example:
A: *Next month, I'm going to order a cake.*
B: *Hmm—I need more information.*
A: *OK. I'm going to buy a white dress.*
B: *Oh! Are you going to get married?*
A: *Yes, I am. I'm going to get married in April.*

Grammar to Communicate 3

BE GOING TO: INFORMATION QUESTIONS					
Wh- word	Be	Subject	Going to	Verb	Answers
Where	**are**	we	**going to**	**sleep?**	At my house.
What		you		**do?**	I'm going to buy food.
When	**is**	he		**go?**	In two hours.
How long		it		**work?**	For a week.
How much				**cost?**	$25.00.

WHAT / WHO AS SUBJECT				
What / Who	Be	Going to	Verb	Answers
What	**is**	**going to**	**happen?**	He's going to drive us.
Who			**drive?**	Paul is going to drive.

A Complete the questions. Use *How much, When,* or *Who.*

1. _____Who_____ is going to get married?   Martha and Ed.

2. _____ are they going to get married?   Next August.

3. _____ is the wedding going to cost?   A lot of money.

4. _____ is going to pay?   Martha's parents.

5. _____ are they going to have a baby?   In one year.

PAIRS. Which questions are not polite to ask in American culture? In your culture?

B Read and circle the correct answers.

1. **Lucy:** Your daughter is 20, right? When is she going to graduate from college?

   Fran: In twenty years./ In two years.

2. **Lucy:** So your wife is pregnant! When is she going to have the baby?

   Brad: In one month. / In one year.

3. **Lucy:** Your husband is 65 now, right? When is he going to retire?

   Rita: In three minutes. / In three years.

4. **Lucy:** When is your son going to get married?

   Tony: In six months. / In sixty years.

> **Look**
>
> Use *in* with a period of time.
> **I'm going to get a haircut in three days.**

pregnant

C Answer the questions with true information. Use *in* and time expressions.

1. When are you going to have a day off?   <u>In a month.</u>

2. When are you going to retire?   _____

3. When are you going to celebrate your birthday?   _____

4. When are you going to get a haircut?   _____

5. When are you going to go to the dentist?   _____

D Write questions. Use the correct form of *be going to*.

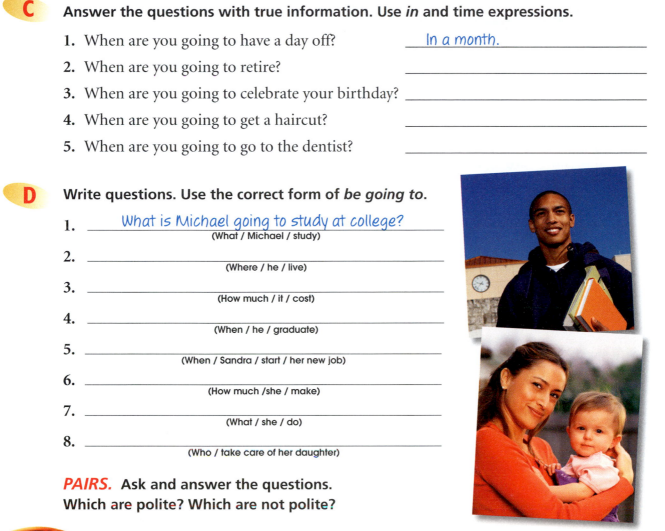

1. <u>What is Michael going to study at college?</u>
    (What / Michael / study)

2. _____
    (Where / he / live)

3. _____
    (How much / it / cost)

4. _____
    (When / he / graduate)

5. _____
    (When / Sandra / start / her new job)

6. _____
    (How much /she / make)

7. _____
    (What / she / do)

8. _____
    (Who / take care of her daughter)

PAIRS. Ask and answer the questions.
Which are polite? Which are not polite?

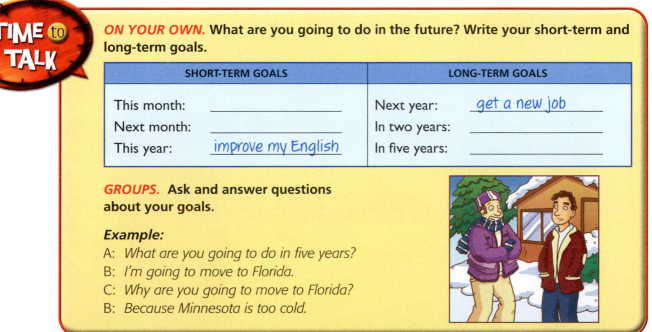

TIME to TALK

ON YOUR OWN. What are you going to do in the future? Write your short-term and long-term goals.

SHORT-TERM GOALS		LONG-TERM GOALS	
This month:	_____	Next year:	<u>get a new job</u>
Next month:	_____	In two years:	_____
This year:	<u>improve my English</u>	In five years:	_____

GROUPS. Ask and answer questions about your goals.

Example:
A: *What are you going to do in five years?*
B: *I'm going to move to Florida.*
C: *Why are you going to move to Florida?*
B: *Because Minnesota is too cold.*

Review and Challenge

Grammar

Complete the conversation. Use the words in the box. Then listen and check your answers. (Be careful! There are four extra words.)

| am | are | be | ~~go~~ | going | He | He's | is | start | to | We | We're |

Steve: Are you going to ____go____ out tonight?
1.

Ted: No, I'm going _____ stay at home. My brother _____ going to come
                           2.   3.
  over. _____ going to play cards. Do you want to come?
                4.

Steve: No. I don't like cards.

Ted: Are you sure? Jan and Kate _____ going to come over, too.
                                       5.

Steve: Do you mean Jan Richards? Is she going to _____ at your place tonight?
                                                  6.
  Um . . . What time is the game going to _____?
                                  7.

Ted: Why? Are you _____ to come? But you don't like cards!
                     8.

Dictation

Listen. You will hear five sentences. Write them on a piece of paper.

Speaking

GROUPS. **Imagine you have one year to travel around the world. Where are you going to go? Ask and answer questions. Use the words in the box and your own ideas.**

| Where . . . (go) | Who . . . (go with) | How long . . . (stay) |
| When . . . (go) | What . . . (do) | What . . . (see) |

Example:
A: *Where are you going to go?*
B: *First, I'm going to go to Egypt.*

Sphinx and pyramid in Egypt

Listening

A  **14 Listen to the weather report. What day is it? Check (✓) the correct answer.**

❏ Wednesday
❏ Thursday
❏ Friday
❏ Saturday
❏ Sunday

B **15 Listen again. What is the weather going to be like? Complete the chart.**

	WEDNESDAY	THURSDAY	FRIDAY	SATURDAY	SUNDAY
sunny	✓				
cloudy					
windy					
rainy					
cold					
cool					
warm	✓				
hot					
humid					

TIME to TALK

ON YOUR OWN. Think of a city you know well or that you have information about. Imagine you are going to visit the city.

GROUPS. Talk to your group about your trip. What does the city look like? What are you going to do there? What are you going to wear? How are you going to travel there? Can your group guess the city?

Example:

A: *It's a beautiful warm city with beaches.*
B: *Are you going to go to Miami?*
A: *No, I'm not.*
C: *How are you going to get there? Are you going to drive?*
A: *No, I'm going to fly.*
C: *Are your go to travel to San Juan?. . .*

Reading and Writing

Reading

A   Read the weekend calendar. Check (✓) the things that are going to happen on Saturday.

    ❏ an art exhibit   ❏ a dance   ❏ a movie   ❏ a picnic

COMMUNITY CALENDAR: FRIDAY, MAY 6–SUNDAY, MAY 8

Friday, May 6	Saturday, May 7		Sunday, May 8
Art exhibit Picasso's Life and Work 5–9 P.M., City Museum $5	NYC Firefighters Annual Picnic 12–2 P.M. Prospect Park Free—bring a dish to share	Cinco de Mayo Celebrate this Mexican holiday 9 P.M., Flushing Meadows Park, Free Music	Special event for Mother's Day Read to your mom! 3–5 P.M., Public Library— Children's Room Free
Outdoor movie *Beauty and the Beast* 7 P.M., Central Park Free		NYC Police Department Ball Dinner and Dance 8 P.M.–midnight Sheraton Ballroom	

B   Read about the people. Then look at the calendar and answer the questions.

1. Seth is 6 years old. He loves to read. What is he going to do on Mother's Day?
   He is probably going to go to the library with his mother.

2. Mrs. Fremont is married to a NYC firefighter. Where is she going to have lunch on Saturday?
   _____

3. Mr. and Mrs. Sangha are going to go to the art exhibit. How much are they going to pay?
   _____

4. Ms. Chen is a police officer. Where are she and her boyfriend going to be on Saturday night?
   _____

5. Lisa Gutierrez is from Mexico. She loves music. What is she going to do on Saturday?
   _____

6. Mr. Amadou works on Saturday and Sunday, but he has Friday night off. Where is he going to take his 5-year-old son on Friday evening?
   _____

Prewriting

Read the note. Then find a calendar of events from your local newspaper. Read about the events, and plan a nice weekend.

Puerto Rican Day Parade

Hi Barbara,
How are you doing? Do you have any plans for the weekend? Are you and Hank going to go to the Puerto Rican Day Parade? There's going to be a band with live music in the city on Saturday. Dan's going to be in the parade, so I'm going to take the kids. My mother's going to come over and take care of the baby. The weather report says it's going to be beautiful. Call me and we can make plans.

Liz

Writing

Write a note to a friend. Write what you are going to do this weekend. Use the note above as a model.

Writing Tip

We often use contractions in informal writing such as letters, notes, or e-mails to friends or relatives.

Example: Dan's going to be in the parade.

Game 4
Units 13-16

PLAYERS | 2 students

MATERIALS | 1 book
1 coin
2 markers

INSTRUCTIONS
▶ Put your markers on the START box.
▶ Student A: Toss the coin. Heads = Move 1 box. Tails = Move 2 boxes.
▶ Look at the picture in the box. Answer the question.
▶ Student B: Make sure Student A's statement is correct. Then make another statement about Student A's picture. Each student gets one point for a correct answer.
Example: PICTURE 1
   Student A: There were a lot of cars.
   Student B: It was hot.
▶ Student B: Now take your turn. Toss the coin and move to a new box.
▶ Students: If your answer is not correct, put your marker on the box from your last turn.
▶ If you land on the other student's box, move your marker to the next box.
▶ Continue taking turns until you get to the FINISH box. The student with the most points wins.

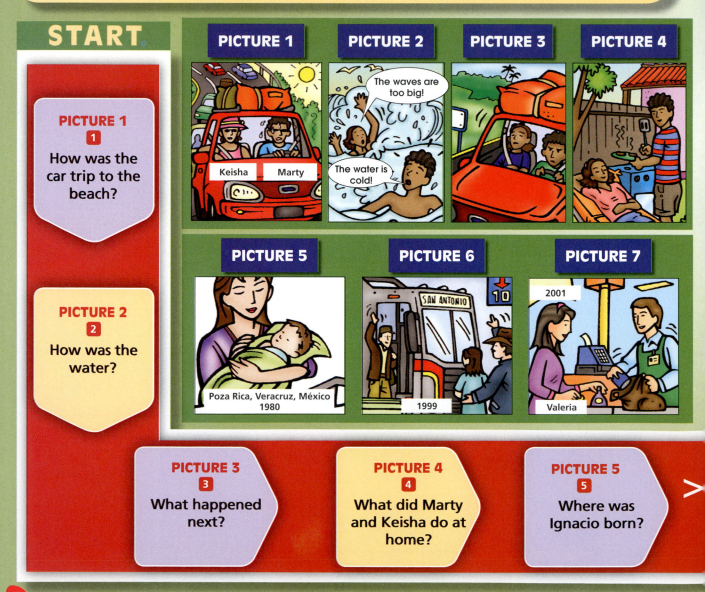

START

PICTURE 1
1
How was the car trip to the beach?

PICTURE 2
2
How was the water?

PICTURE 3
3
What happened next?

PICTURE 4
4
What did Marty and Keisha do at home?

PICTURE 5
5
Where was Ignacio born?

PICTURE 1
Keisha   Marty

PICTURE 2
The waves are too big!
The water is cold!

PICTURE 3

PICTURE 4

PICTURE 5
Poza Rica, Veracruz, México 1980

PICTURE 6
SAN ANTONIO
10
1999

PICTURE 7
2001
Valeria

Unit 17
Health

Grammar
- *Should*: Affirmative and Negative Statements
- *Should*: Yes / No Questions
- *Should*: Information Questions

Vocabulary

CD 3 TRACK

16 **Read and listen. Then circle the health problems you have today.**

1. prescription
2. get a prescription
3. see a doctor
4. take someone's temperature
5. pharmacist
6. have the flu
7. hurt
8. have a pain
9. sneeze
10. have allergies
11. put on a Band-Aid
12. have a cut
13. have a cough

Listening

A 🔘 **17** Listen. Abby is talking to her mother-in-law, Glenda. Check (✓) the statements that are true.

❏ 1. Abby had a baby a month ago.
❏ 2. Abby's baby is sick.
❏ 3. It is cold outside.
❏ 4. Glenda likes Dr. Mendez a lot.
❏ 5. Glenda is worried about her grandson.
❏ 6. Abby wants to go out to lunch.

B 🔘 **18** Read and listen again. Write the missing words. Use the words in the box.

| should | ~~should we~~ | shouldn't | shouldn't be |

Abby: So, where ___should we___ go for lunch?
1.

Glenda: Go? Oh, I don't think we _____
2.
go out for lunch.

Abby: Why not?

Glenda: Well, the baby _____ around a
3.
lot of people. What if someone has a cold
and coughs on him?

Abby: But that's crazy!

Glenda: Really? I don't agree. Should we call the
doctor and ask?

Abby: No, we _____! He told me it
4.
was OK.

Glenda: Who told you? Dr. Mendez? Why should we
believe him? He's just a kid!

Grammar to Communicate ①

SHOULD: AFFIRMATIVE AND NEGATIVE STATEMENTS

Subject	Should	Verb	Subject	Should + Not	Verb
I You She We They	should	go out.	I You She We They	shouldn't	go out.

A Write a sentence from the box under each picture. If you need more room, write on a piece of paper. There can be more than one correct answer.

> He shouldn't go out in the hot sun.   He should put ice on his back.
>
> She should take some aspirin.   She shouldn't go to work.
>
> He should take some medicine.   She shouldn't eat anything.
>
> She should see a doctor.   He should take some aspirin.

1. Rose has a headache.

She should take some

aspirin.

2. Luz is nauseous.

_____

_____

3. Amit has a fever.

_____

_____

4. Arthur has heartburn.

_____

_____

5. Ramon has a backache.

_____

_____

6. Cecile has a stomachache.

_____

_____

B   Complete the sentences with *should* or *shouldn't*.

1. Alicia took her son's temperature. It is 102°F (38.8°C).

   a. _She should take her son to the doctor._
   (take her son to the doctor)

   b. _____
   (go to school)

2. Mike's son had a bike accident. His arm hurts a lot.

   a. _____
   (call the pharmacist)

   b. _____
   (go to the hospital)

3. Betty's daughter has a small cut on her finger.

   a. _____
   (put a Band-Aid on it)

   b. _____
   (call the doctor)

C   *PAIRS.* Give advice. Write sentences with *should* or *shouldn't*.

1. I have a backache.   _You should do exercises._
2. I have an earache.   _____
3. I have the flu.   _____
4. I'm tired all the time.   _____
5. My feet hurt.   _____
6. I have heartburn.   _____

TIME to TALK

GROUPS. Find out the meanings of the words in the chart. Then talk about what you should and shouldn't do for each problem and complete the chart.

IF YOU HAVE . . .	YOU SHOULD . . .	YOU SHOULDN'T . . .
a sore throat	gargle	_____
bad breath	_____	_____
insomnia	_____	_____
a sunburn	_____	_____

gargle

Grammar to Communicate ❷

SHOULD: YES / NO QUESTIONS										
Should	**Subject**	**Verb**			**Short Answers**					
Should	I you she we they	**call**	the doctor?	Yes,	I you she we they	**should.**	No,	I you she we they	**shouldn't.**

A **Answer the questions. Write short answers.**

1. Should people smoke?   <u>No, they shouldn't.</u>

2. Should people drink water every day?   _____

3. Should people eat a lot of red meat?   _____

4. Should people eat a lot of fruit and vegetables? _____

5. Should people drink a lot of alcohol?   _____

PAIRS. Compare your answers.

B **Read the sentences. Write questions. Use *should*.**

1. Mr. Smith has the flu.

   <u>Should he go to work?</u>
   (he / go / to work)

2. Mrs. Jones is 80 years old and healthy.

   _____
   (she / exercise)

3. Tran is 20 and healthy.

   _____
   (he / see / a doctor every month)

4. Ana is a 6-week-old baby.

   _____
   (her parents / take her / to the beach)

5. Mona and Jason just ate a big lunch.

   _____
   (they / go swimming)

6. Marcus is six. His temperature is 99° (37.2°C).

   _____
   (he / go / to school today)

> It's just a cold, right, Doc?

PAIRS. Ask and answer the questions above. Use short answers. Do you and your partner agree?

C   **Complete the questions. Use *should* and the verbs in the box.**

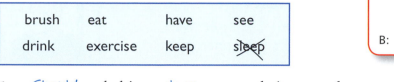

brush	eat	have	see
drink	exercise	keep	~~sleep~~

1. ___Should___ babies ___sleep___ on their stomachs or on their backs?
2. _____ you _____ once a week for two hours or every day for 30 minutes?
3. _____ children _____ a lot of milk or a lot of fruit juice?
4. _____ children _____ a lot of French fries or a lot of salad?
5. _____ you _____ a large meal for lunch or for dinner?
6. _____ you _____ a doctor or a dentist for a toothache?
7. _____ people with allergies _____ cats at home?
8. _____ you _____ your teeth before you eat or after you eat?

PAIRS. Ask and answer the questions above. Do you agree?

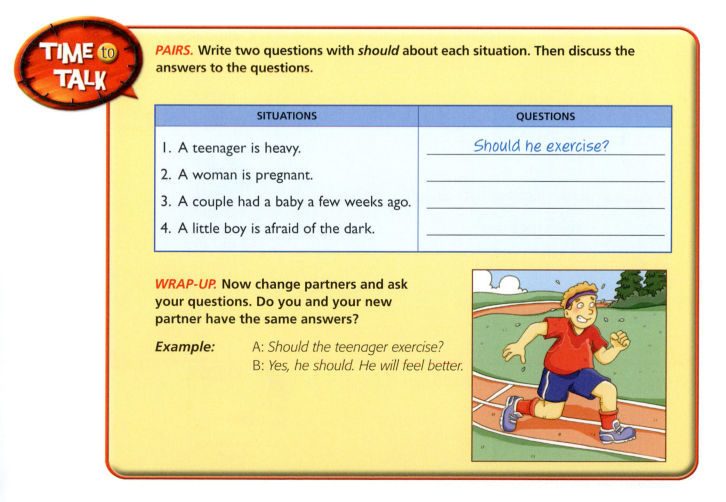

PAIRS. Write two questions with *should* about each situation. Then discuss the answers to the questions.

SITUATIONS	QUESTIONS
1. A teenager is heavy.	___Should he exercise?___
2. A woman is pregnant.	_____
3. A couple had a baby a few weeks ago.	_____
4. A little boy is afraid of the dark.	_____

WRAP-UP. Now change partners and ask your questions. Do you and your new partner have the same answers?

Example: A: *Should the teenager exercise?*
                B: *Yes, he should. He will feel better.*

Look

Use *or* in questions with two possible answers.
A: I need a prescription. Should I see the doctor **or** the nurse?
B: You should see the doctor.

Grammar to Communicate 3

Which medicine should I buy?

SHOULD: INFORMATION QUESTIONS

Wh- word		Should	Subject	Verb	Answers
Who			he	**ask?**	The pharmacist.
What		**should**	we	**do?**	Take some medicine.
Which	doctor		they	**see?**	Dr. Norion.

How long / How often	Should	Subject	Verb		Answers
How long	**should**	I	**take**	it?	For a week.
How often		you			Two times a day.

 A Complete the questions with *should* and *take*. Then match the questions with the answers.

<u> b </u> **1.** Mr. Lang has a cough.

Which medicine <u>should he take?</u>

a. Adnol Aspirin

_____ **2.** Lynn and Robert have heartburn.

Which medicine _____?

b. Bronchusin Cough Syrup

_____ **3.** Ruth and Steve have allergies.

Which medicine _____?

c. Bell's Children's Cough Syrup

_____ **4.** Alison's eight-year-old son has a cough.

Which medicine _____?

d. Tumex Antacid for Heartburn Relief

_____ **5.** Ms. Bryant has a headache.

Which medicine _____ ?

e. Viva Allergy Relief

B Complete the questions. Use *How often, Where, What, Who,* and *Should.*

1. _____How often should_____ people take aspirin?   Every four to six hours.

2. _____ a patient ask for   A doctor.
   medical advice?

3. _____ parents put medicine?   In a safe place, away from children.

4. A baby has a cold. _____ his   Baby cough syrup.
   mother give him?

5. _____ healthy people   Twice a year.
   see the doctor?

C Read the sentences. Look at the answers. Write questions with *should.*
Use *How many, What, When,* and *Who.*

1. The doctor should give Al a prescription for the pain.
   Who should the doctor give a prescription to?   To Al.
   What should the doctor give to Al?   A prescription.

2. You should ask the nurse about the medicine tomorrow.
   _____   The medicine.
   _____   The nurse.

3. The children should take two pills every 12 hours.
   _____   Every 12 hours.
   _____   Two.

TIME to TALK

CLASS. **Play this Doctor and Patient game. Half of the class will be patients. The other half will be doctors.**

Patients: Look at the vocabulary on pages 202–203 and choose two problems. Then go sit with a doctor. Explain one problem to the doctor. Ask questions about what you should do. Then go to a new doctor. Explain the second problem and ask questions.

Doctors: Sit with a patient and give advice. Answer his or her questions.

Example:
A: *Doctor, I have a backache. Should I go to the gym?*
B: *No, you shouldn't. You should rest at home.*

Review and Challenge

Grammar

CD 3 TRACK 19 Correct the conversation. There are six mistakes. The first mistake is corrected for you. Then listen and check your answers.

Teri: The baby is sick. What ~~I should~~ _should I_ do?

Jon: You should to call the doctor.

Teri: But it's 9 P.M. The doctor's not in his office.

Jon: What's wrong with the baby?

Teri: He feels hot.

Jon: Did you take his temperature?

Teri: No, I didn't. We should take him to the hospital?

Jon: No, we don't. You should do take his temperature.

Teri: I'm worried.

Jon: You should no worry. He's fine.

Dictation

CD 3 TRACK 20 Listen. You will hear five sentences. Write them on a piece of paper.

Speaking

GROUPS. Find out the meanings of the medical conditions in the box. Ask a classmate or look in the dictionary. What should people with the conditions do? What shouldn't they do?

asthma	diabetes	high blood pressure	high cholesterol

Example:
A: _People with asthma should not have cats._
B: _And they shouldn't smoke . . ._

WRAP-UP. Share your ideas with the class. Do you have the same answers?

Listening

CD 3 TRACK 21 **A** Look at the different kinds of food in the picture. What do you think the listening will be about? Check (✓) the correct answer. Then listen. Was your answer correct?

❏ grocery shopping   ❏ eating healthy food   ❏ cooking for special occasions

CD 3 TRACK 22 **B** Listen again. How much of each food group should people eat a day? Write the correct amounts.

Look
1 ounce = 31.103 grams
8 ounces = 1 cup

1. grains

   _____

2. vegetables

   _____

3. fruit

   _____

4. low-fat milk
   products

   _____

5. meat group

   _____

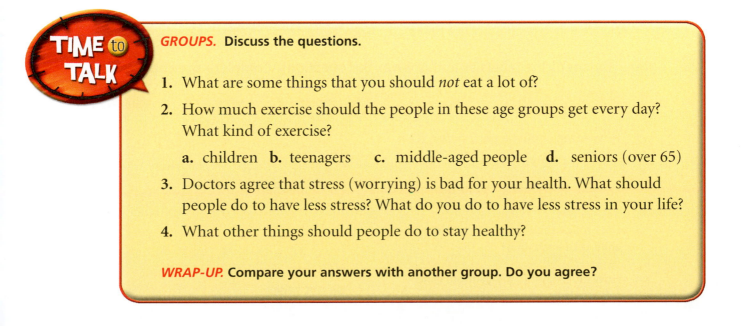

oil, fats, & sweets

SUGAR

Butter

milk group

meat & protein group

vegetable group

fruit group

grains

TIME to TALK

GROUPS. Discuss the questions.

1. What are some things that you should *not* eat a lot of?

2. How much exercise should the people in these age groups get every day? What kind of exercise?
   a. children **b.** teenagers **c.** middle-aged people **d.** seniors (over 65)

3. Doctors agree that stress (worrying) is bad for your health. What should people do to have less stress? What do you do to have less stress in your life?

4. What other things should people do to stay healthy?

WRAP-UP. Compare your answers with another group. Do you agree?

Reading and Writing

Reading

A Read the medicine labels. Which medicine should you *not* give to an 8-year-old child? _____

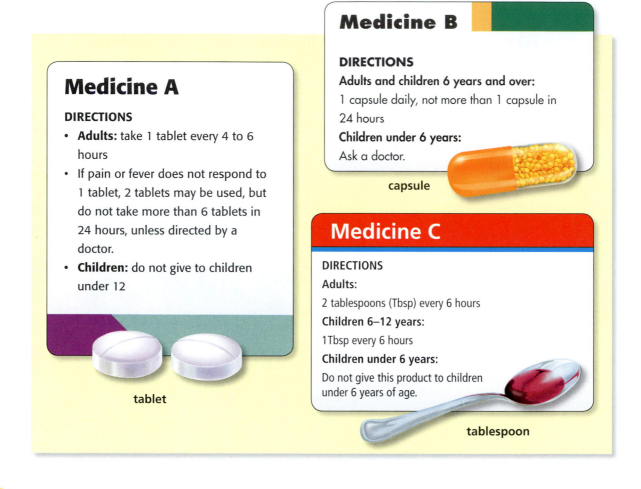

Medicine A

DIRECTIONS

- **Adults:** take 1 tablet every 4 to 6 hours
- If pain or fever does not respond to 1 tablet, 2 tablets may be used, but do not take more than 6 tablets in 24 hours, unless directed by a doctor.
- **Children:** do not give to children under 12

tablet

Medicine B

DIRECTIONS

Adults and children 6 years and over: 1 capsule daily, not more than 1 capsule in 24 hours

Children under 6 years: Ask a doctor.

capsule

Medicine C

DIRECTIONS

Adults:
2 tablespoons (Tbsp) every 6 hours

Children 6–12 years:
1 Tbsp every 6 hours

Children under 6 years:
Do not give this product to children under 6 years of age.

tablespoon

B Read the medicine labels again. Answer the questions. Complete the chart.

	MEDICINE A	MEDICINE B	MEDICINE C
1. How often should a person take it?			
2. How much should an adult take each time?	1 or 2 tablets		
3. How much should an 11-year-old child take each time?			
4. How much should a 6-year-old child take each time?	do not take		

Writing

Read the e-mail. Then write an e-mail to a doctor with some questions about a medical problem. The problem can be real or imaginary. Use Mrs. Lang's e-mail as a model.

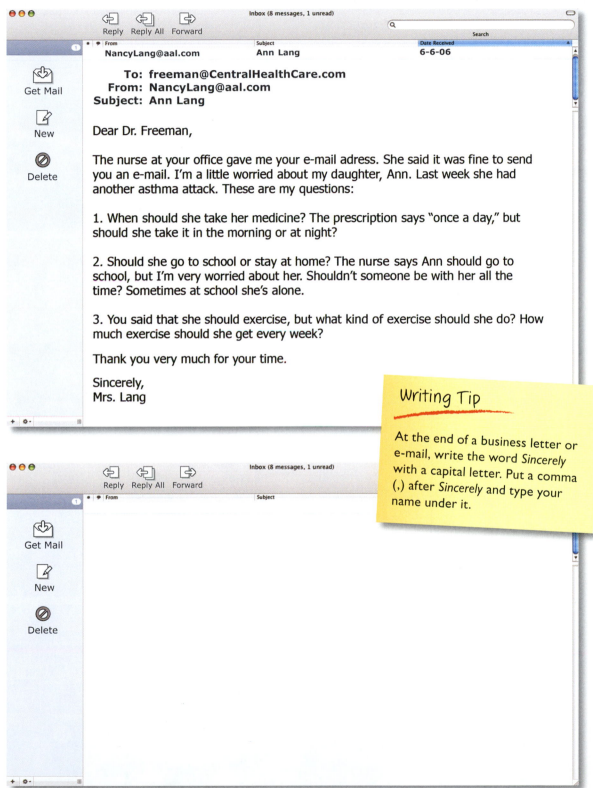

Inbox (8 messages, 1 unread)

Reply   Reply All   Forward   Search

From   Subject   Date Received
NancyLang@aal.com   Ann Lang   6-6-06

Get Mail

New

Delete

To: freeman@CentralHealthCare.com
From: NancyLang@aal.com
Subject: Ann Lang

Dear Dr. Freeman,

The nurse at your office gave me your e-mail adress. She said it was fine to send you an e-mail. I'm a little worried about my daughter, Ann. Last week she had another asthma attack. These are my questions:

1. When should she take her medicine? The prescription says "once a day," but should she take it in the morning or at night?

2. Should she go to school or stay at home? The nurse says Ann should go to school, but I'm very worried about her. Shouldn't someone be with her all the time? Sometimes at school she's alone.

3. You said that she should exercise, but what kind of exercise should she do? How much exercise should she get every week?

Thank you very much for your time.

Sincerely,
Mrs. Lang

Writing Tip

At the end of a business letter or e-mail, write the word *Sincerely* with a capital letter. Put a comma (,) after *Sincerely* and type your name under it.

Inbox (8 messages, 1 unread)

Reply   Reply All   Forward

From   Subject

Get Mail

New

Delete

A Place to Live

Grammar
- Comparative of Adjectives
- Superlative of Adjectives
- Comparative and Superlative

Vocabulary

CD 3 TRACK 23 Read and listen. Then circle the words that describe your home and your neighborhood.

1. low rent
2. close to public transportation
3. public transportation
4. convenient
5. dangerous street
6. ugly
7. pretty view
8. high rent
9. modern
10. safe
11. far from public transportation
12. in the country

Listening

A **24** Listen. Doug is looking for an apartment. Which apartment is he going to visit? Check (✓) the correct answer.

❏ The apartment on Mercer Street
❏ The apartment in Brighton Park
❏ The apartment in the West End
❏ The apartment on Trenton Street

B **25** Read and listen again. Write the missing words. Use the words in the box.

> ~~best~~   cheaper   cheapest   more   than   the most

Miranda: The _____best_____ apartment is on Mercer Street
1.
near the new theater. It's $1,300 a month.

Doug: Wow. That's expensive. How about the other

two apartments? Are they _____ than
2.
that?

Miranda: Yes, they are, but the Mercer Street apartment

is in _____ convenient location.
3.

Doug: But I don't want to spend that much money.

How much is the _____ apartment?
4.

Miranda: It's $400 a month, but it's also the smallest.
And it's the farthest from downtown. It's out
in Brighton Park.

Doug: Oh, that is far. How about the last apartment?

Miranda: It's in a better location _____ the
5.
Brighton Park apartment. It's also larger and

sunnier, and it's in a _____ modern
6.
building.

A Place to Live **215**

Grammar to Communicate 1

COMPARATIVE OF ADJECTIVES

Adjective	Comparative	Rules to Form Comparatives
small	small**er**	With one syllable: Add -er
nice	nice**r**	With one syllable ending in -e: Add -r
pretty	prett**ier**	With two syllables ending in -y: Change the -y to -i, and add -er
modern	**more modern**	With two or three syllables: Add *more* + adjective

Irregular Adjectives

Adjective	Comparative
good	**better**
bad	**worse**
far	**farther**

small   smaller

Look

We often use *than* with comparatives.
His house **is smaller than** her house.
This house **is more modern than** that one.

A Read the chart. Complete the sentences. Write *Home A* and *Home B*.

	SIZE	YEAR BUILT	RENT	DISTANCE TO SUBWAY	LOCATION	NUMBER OF WINDOWS
home A	8 rooms	1960	$1,000	1 mile	on quiet street, near lake and park	15
home B	5 rooms	2000	$900	1/2 mile	on city street, next to stores	5

1. __Home B__ is smaller than __Home A.__

2. _____ is more modern than _____.

3. The rent for _____ is higher.

4. _____ is closer to the subway than _____.

5. _____ is sunnier than _____.

6. _____ is closer to the park than _____.

B Write the comparative form of the adjectives.

1. old   __older__
2. expensive   __more expensive__
3. low   _____
4. noisy   _____
5. close   _____
6. convenient   _____

7. far   _____
8. dark   _____
9. sunny   _____
10. bad   _____
11. safe   _____
12. good   _____

 Unit 18

C Write sentences about Home A and Home B in Exercise A. Use comparatives.

1. <u>Home A is larger than Home B.</u>   5. _____
   (large)   (close to stores)

2. _____   6. _____
   (old)   (expensive)

3. _____   7. _____
   (in a pretty area)   (noisy)

4. _____   8. _____
   (far from the lake)   (convenient)

D **PAIRS.** Look at the pictures on pages 214–215. Talk about Kathy's place and Estelle's place. Use the comparative form of the words in the box.

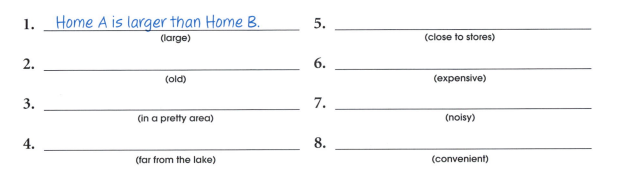

Look

River Street is quiet**er than** Mercer Street.
NOT River Street is ~~more quiet than~~ Mercer Street.

big	convenient	modern	noisy	pretty	quiet	small

Example:
A: *Estelle's place is quieter than Kathy's place.*

TIME to TALK

PAIRS. Talk about five differences between where you live now and your old home. Talk about the apartments or houses, the neighborhoods, and the neighbors. Use the comparative forms of the words in the box.

cheap / expensive	convenient / inconvenient	large / small	quiet / noisy
clean / dirty	friendly / unfriendly	modern / old	safe / dangerous
close / far	good / bad	pretty / ugly	sunny / dark

Example:
A: *My new apartment is more modern than my old apartment. And my new neighborhood is safer than my old neighborhood.*
B: *That's good.*
A: *But my new neighbors are noisier than my old neighbors.*

Grammar to Communicate 2

SUPERLATIVE OF ADJECTIVES

Adjective	Superlative	Rules to Form Superlatives
small	the small**est**	With one syllable: Add -*est*
nice	the nic**est**	With one syllable ending in -*e*: Add -*st*
pretty	the prett**iest**	With two syllables ending in -*y*: Change the -*y* to -*i*, and add -*est*
modern	**the most modern**	With two or three syllables: Add *most* + adjective

Irregular Adjectives

Adjective	Superlative
good	the **best**
bad	the **worst**
far	the **farthest**

small   smaller   smallest

A   Write about the rooms in your house.

1. The biggest room is _____.

2. The smallest room is _____.

3. The sunniest room is _____.

4. The most crowded room is _____.

5. The most comfortable room is _____.

Look

We use *the* with superlatives.
Our house is **the most modern**.
That room is **the sunniest**.
Her room is **the biggest**.

B   Write the superlative form of the words.

1. big — *the biggest*

2. comfortable — *the most comfortable*

3. sunny — _____

4. quiet — _____

5. crowded — _____

6. good — _____

7. dark — _____

8. noisy — _____

9. bad — _____

10. old — _____

11. ugly — _____

12. modern — _____

13. safe — _____

14. expensive — _____

218   Unit 18

C Complete the sentences. Use superlatives.

1. _The smallest_ room is the bathroom.
   (small)
2. _____ room is the living room.
   (noisy)
3. _____ room is the dining room.
   (ugly)
4. _____ room is my bedroom.
   (cold)
5. _____ room is the kitchen.
   (nice)
6. _____ things are in the living room.
   (expensive)
7. _____ chairs are in the kitchen.
   (uncomfortable)

PAIRS. Which sentences above are true about your home? Tell your partner.

D Write sentences. Use the superlative form of the adjectives. Then circle the sentences you agree with.

1. _Orange is the worst color for a living room._
   (orange / bad / color for a living room)
2. _____
   (rugs / dirty / things in a home)
3. _____
   (a closet / important / thing in a bedroom)
4. _____
   (the kitchen / comfortable / room in a house)
5. _____
   (yellow / good / color for a kitchen)

PAIRS. Read the sentences you circled.
Do you and your partner agree?

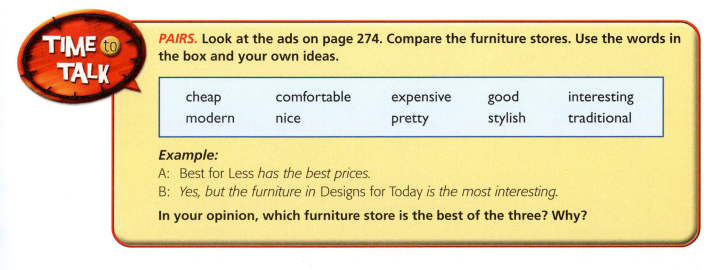

TIME to TALK

PAIRS. Look at the ads on page 274. Compare the furniture stores. Use the words in the box and your own ideas.

| cheap | comfortable | expensive | good | interesting |
| modern | nice | pretty | stylish | traditional |

Example:
A: Best for Less *has the best prices.*
B: Yes, but the furniture in Designs for Today *is the most interesting.*

In your opinion, which furniture store is the best of the three? Why?

Grammar to Communicate 3

COMPARATIVE AND SUPERLATIVE

Adjective	Comparative	Superlative
small	small**er**	the small**est**
nice	nic**er**	the nic**est**
pretty	prett**ier**	the prett**iest**
famous	**more famous**	the **most famous**

Irregular Adjectives		
Adjective	Comparative	Superlative
good	**better**	the **best**
bad	**worse**	the **worst**
far	**farther**	the **farthest**

Rio de Janeiro

A Complete the questions. Use the comparative or the superlative.

1. (better, the best)
    a. Which city has _____*better*_____ weather—Rio de Janeiro or Chicago?
    b. Which city has _____*the best*_____ weather—Toronto, Tokyo, or Honolulu?

2. (smaller, the smallest)
    a. Which country is _____—Haiti, Vietnam, Canada, or Russia?
    b. Which country is _____—Venezuela or China?

3. (more famous, the most famous)
    a. Which city has _____ buildings—Seoul, San Juan, or Paris?
    b. Which city has _____ buildings—Dallas or London?

4. (closer, the closest)
    a. Which country is _____ to your country—Canada or France?
    b. Which country is _____ to your country—China, Italy, or the U.S.?

B Complete the chart.

ADJECTIVE	COMPARATIVE	SUPERLATIVE
1. *bad*	worse	the worst
2. big	*bigger*	the biggest
3. cheap	cheaper	
4. dangerous		the most dangerous
5. expensive	more expensive	

ADJECTIVE	COMPARATIVE	SUPERLATIVE
6.	better	the best
7. high		the highest
8. hot	hotter	
9. nice		the nicest
10.	prettier	the prettiest

 220   Unit 18

C Compare the places. Write sentences with comparatives and superlatives. Write on a piece of paper if you need more room.

> **Look**
>
> Russia, Canada, and China are countries.
> Russia is the biggest **of the three**.

1. _A town is bigger than a village. A city is the biggest of the three._
   a city / a village / a town / (BIG)

2. _____
   the Pacific Ocean / the Atlantic Ocean / the Mediterranean Sea / (LARGE)

3. _____
   a room / an apartment building / a house / (SMALL)

4. _____
   Toronto / Rio de Janeiro / San Diego / (HOT)

D Complete the questions. Use the comparative or superlative form. Add *than* where necessary.

1. Is a home in the city _____ better than _____ a home in the country?
   (good)

2. What is _____ the best _____ thing about a big city?
   (good)

3. What is _____ thing about a big city?
   (bad)

4. Is it _____ to live in a dangerous or an ugly neighborhood?
   (bad)

5. Which neighborhood in your city has _____ apartments?
   (cheap)

6. Which is _____ to you, a neighborhood with cheap
   (important)

   homes or a neighborhood with good schools?

GROUPS. Discuss the questions.

TIME to TALK

GROUPS. Compare the city you live in now with other cities you know well. Talk about five differences. Use the topics in the box and your own ideas.

buses	parks	universities
museums	sports teams	weather

Example:
A: *Chicago has better sports teams than Atlanta.*
B: *Yes, but the weather is nicer in Atlanta.*
C: *Yeah, but Miami's weather is the best, and its sports teams are good, too.*

Miami Heat

Grammar

Find the mistake in each sentence. Circle the letter and correct the mistake.

Chinatown, San Francisco

1. Chinatown is <u>more</u> <u>famouser</u> <u>than</u> Diamond Hill.
              A   Ⓑ   C

   Chinatown is more famous than Diamond Hill.

2. <u>Which</u> neighborhood has the <u>worstest</u> <u>schools</u>?
     A   B   C

   _____

3. <u>Is</u> Dolores Street <u>nicer</u> <u>to</u> Mission Street?
    A   B C

   _____

4. This is <u>the</u> <u>most</u> <u>prettiest</u> neighborhood.
            A B   C

   _____

5. This house is <u>more</u> <u>moderner</u> <u>than</u> that house.
                  A   B   C

   _____

Dictation

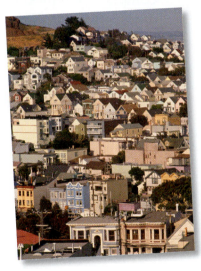

Diamond Hill, San Francisco

26 Listen. You will hear five sentences. Write them on a piece of paper.

Speaking

PAIRS. Wayne, Jerry, and Hiro and Satoko are looking for apartments. Look at the pictures. Then read the apartment ads on page 273. Which apartment is the best for Wayne? For Jerry? For Hiro and Satoko?

Wayne

Jerry and his kids

Hiro, Satoko, and their grandson

Listening

A 🔊 **27** Listen to a radio report about the best cities to live in. Check (✓) the topics the reporter talks about.

❏ clean air and water   ❏ number of jobs

❏ cost of living   ❏ public transportation

❏ friendly people   ❏ restaurants and nightlife

❏ noise and traffic   ❏ safety and crime

❏ number of doctors   ❏ weather

Hong Kong

B 🔊 **28** Listen again. Check (✓) the correct information about the cities.

CITY NAME	CLEAN	EXCITING	EXCELLENT PUBLIC TRANSPORTATION	GOOD WEATHER	SAFE
Hong Kong					
Tokyo					
Vancouver					
Vienna					
Zurich					

TIME to TALK

In your opinion, what is important in a neighborhood or home? What is not important? Look at the list below. Write *1* for the most important, *2* for important, and *3* for less important.

_____ a lot of children in the neighborhood   _____ good jobs

_____ a lot of parks   _____ good public schools

_____ close to family   _____ good public transportation

_____ close to supermarkets and other stores   _____ safety

_____ the cost of living   _____ the weather

_____ friendly people   _____ other? _____

GROUPS. Explain your answers to your classmates.

Example:

A: *The most important things for me are good schools and safety because I have children.*

B: *Good schools aren't important to me. The most important thing for me is good public transportation because I don't have a car.*

A Place to Live **223**

Reading and Writing

Reading

A Read the web page. What is the best title for the page? Check (✓) the correct answer.

❏ Houses for Sale

❏ Buying a Home

❏ Renting a Home

Look

investment = something that you buy because it will be more valuable or useful later

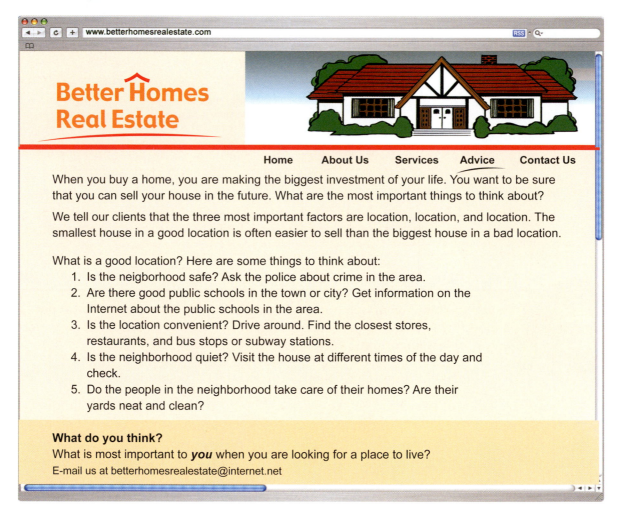

www.betterhomesrealestate.com

Better Homes Real Estate

Home   About Us   Services   Advice   Contact Us

When you buy a home, you are making the biggest investment of your life. You want to be sure that you can sell your house in the future. What are the most important things to think about?

We tell our clients that the three most important factors are location, location, and location. The smallest house in a good location is often easier to sell than the biggest house in a bad location.

What is a good location? Here are some things to think about:
1. Is the neigborhood safe? Ask the police about crime in the area.
2. Are there good public schools in the town or city? Get information on the Internet about the public schools in the area.
3. Is the location convenient? Drive around. Find the closest stores, restaurants, and bus stops or subway stations.
4. Is the neighborhood quiet? Visit the house at different times of the day and check.
5. Do the people in the neighborhood take care of their homes? Are their yards neat and clean?

What do you think?
What is most important to *you* when you are looking for a place to live?
E-mail us at betterhomesrealestate@internet.net

B Read the web page again. For each statement, write *T* (true) or *F* (false).

_____ 1. Houses in good locations are easier to sell than houses in bad locations.

_____ 2. The Internet has information about the best public schools in an area.

_____ 3. It's harder to sell a house in a bad neighborhood than in a safe neighborhood.

_____ 4. A big house is always better than a small house.

_____ 5. Convenience is the most important thing.

Prewriting

Read Cara's e-mail. For Cara, what is most important about a place to live?

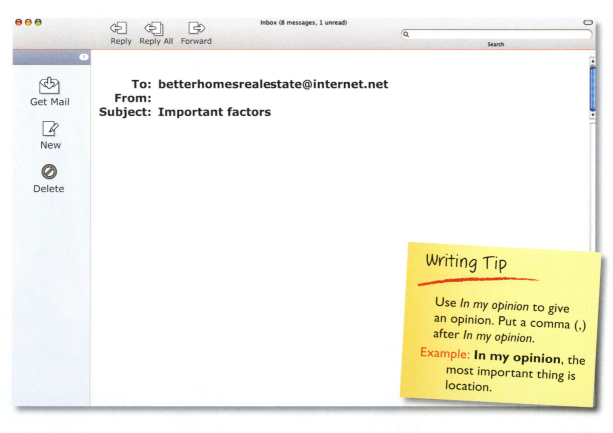

To: betterhomesrealestate@internet.net
From: carap@aal.com
Subject: Important factors

Hello,

    In my opinion, the most important things are safety and convenience. I am a single woman and I live alone, so security is very important to me. Also, I don't have a car, so I need to be close to stores and transportation. Of course, price is important too, but safety and convenience are more important. For me, a more expensive apartment downtown is better than a cheap apartment in an inconvenient location.

Cara

Writing

Write your own e-mail. Write about what is most important to you in a place to live. Use Cara's e-mail as a model.

To: betterhomesrealestate@internet.net
From:
Subject: Important factors

> ## Writing Tip
>
> Use *In my opinion* to give an opinion. Put a comma (,) after *In my opinion*.
>
> **Example:** **In my opinion**, the most important thing is location.

Vocabulary

29 Read and listen. Which changes do you think are in your future? Tell your partner.

1. get a raise
2. get in touch with someone
3. make plans
4. start a business
5. get bad news
6. succeed
7. have a good time

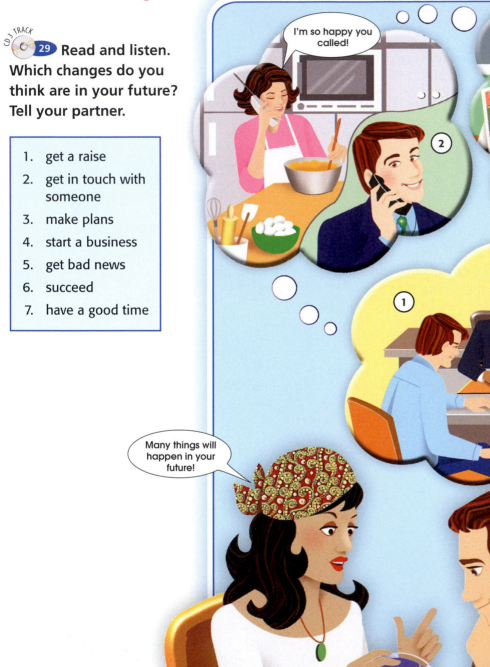

Listening

A   **30** **Listen. Betty is visiting a fortune teller. What does the fortune teller see in Betty's future? Check (✓) the correct answer.**

❏ good things   ❏ bad things   ❏ good and bad things

B   **31** **Read and listen again. Write the missing words. Use the words in the box.**

~~will~~   will it be   won't   won't be   You'll

Betty: So, tell me! What do you see? Will there be any changes in my life?

Fortune teller: Yes, there _____will_____. I see a
1.
handsome, dark man. He will get in touch with you soon.

Betty: That sounds interesting. Will he be tall?

Fortune teller: No, he _____.
2.

Betty: Oh . . . Well, why will he get in touch with me?

Fortune teller: He will have some news for you.

Betty: What kind of news _____? Will
3.
it be good or bad?

Fortune teller: I'm sorry, but it _____
4.
good . . . I also see money.

Betty: Oh, good!

Fortune teller: Hmmmm . . .

Betty: What's the matter?

Fortune teller: Well, you won't *get* money. _____
5.
lose it.

Future Changes   227

Grammar to Communicate 1

WILL: AFFIRMATIVE AND NEGATIVE STATEMENTS

Subject	Will	Verb		Subject	Will + Not	Verb		Contractions		
I You He She It We They	will	make	him happy.	I You He She It We They	will not	make	him happy.	I + will you + will he + will she + will it + will we + will they + will	→ → → → → → →	I'll you'll he'll she'll it'll we'll they'll
There	will	be	good news.	There	will not	be	good news.	will + not	→	won't

A Complete the sentences with a time expression.

Look

go up = ↑
go down = ↓

1. My rent will probably go up ___in two years___.

2. My rent probably won't go down _____.

3. I'll probably buy a new car _____.

4. I probably won't be a student here _____.

5. I'll probably change jobs _____.

6. I probably won't take a vacation _____.

7. I'll probably visit my family _____.

8. I probably won't move to another city _____.

PAIRS. Tell each other your sentences.

B Rewrite the sentences about Mr. and Mrs. Smith's future. Use *won't* and the words in the box. Do not change the meaning of the sentences.

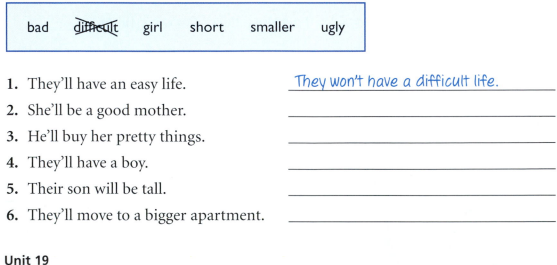

| bad | ~~difficult~~ | girl | short | smaller | ugly |

1. They'll have an easy life.   ___They won't have a difficult life.___

2. She'll be a good mother.   _____

3. He'll buy her pretty things.   _____

4. They'll have a boy.   _____

5. Their son will be tall.   _____

6. They'll move to a bigger apartment.   _____

C Sara is an optimist. She thinks the future will be good. Keith is a pessimist. He thinks the future will be bad. Complete their statements with *will* or *won't*.

Sara

1. I _____*will get*_____ a good job in two years.
      (get)

2. My boss _____ me a raise.
                        (give)

3. It _____ at the beach this weekend.
              (not rain)

4. My new business _____.
                            (not succeed)

5. I _____ a lot of problems in my
          (have)

   classes next year.

Keith

6. My friends and I _____ this summer.
                        (not have fun)

D Write five predictions about events in a few years. Write your predictions on a piece of paper. Use *probably* and *will* or *won't* with the words in the box.

I	my friends	become a U.S. citizen	move to a bigger home
my boss	my husband and I	change jobs	move to a different city
my daughter	my mother	get a raise	retire
my father	my son	get married	start a business
my friend	my wife and I	have a baby	succeed in business

PAIRS. Tell your partner your sentences.

Example:
A: *My husband will probably change jobs in a few years. How about you?*
B: *My girlfriend and I probably won't change jobs. But we'll probably get married in a few years.*

PAIRS. Look at the photos on page 97. Make predictions about the people in the pictures. Talk about what will and won't happen. Make at least five predictions.

Example: (page 97, picture a)
A: *The girl and her mother will stop fighting. She will listen to her mother.*
B: *Her mother will not stay angry with her. They will be nice to each other.*

Grammar to Communicate 2

Will	Subject	Verb			Short Answers					
Will	I you he she it we they	change	a lot in the next ten years?	Yes,	I you he she it we they	will.	No,	I you he she it we they	won't.

Will	There	Be			Short Answers				
Will	there	be	problems in the next ten years?	Yes,	there	will.	No,	there	won't.

A   **What do you think life will be like in 2050? Write short answers.**

1. Will people work five days a week?   <u>Yes, they will. OR No, they won't.</u>

2. Will men and women have the same jobs?   _____

3. Will most people live to 100?   _____

4. Will children go to school 12 months a year?   _____

5. Will there be better public transportation?   _____

6. Will most people get married?   _____

PAIRS. Compare your answers.

B   **Will things be the same in ten years? Write questions.**

1. My boss drives to work every day.   <u>Will he drive to work every day in ten years?</u>

2. My friend eats a lot of fast food.   _____

3. There aren't a lot of good jobs.   _____

4. There's a lot of traffic.   _____

5. College costs a lot of money.   _____

6. My friends pay for everything in cash.   _____

PAIRS. Ask and answer the questions above. Use *probably* or *probably not* in your answers.

Example:
A: *My boss drives to work every day.*
B: *Will your boss drive to work every day in ten years?*
A: *Yes, he probably will. He lives far from the office.*

C Complete the sentences about life in the year 2050. Use *will* or *won't*.

1. People <u>will read</u> OR <u>won't read</u> newspapers.
   (read)

2. People _____ cash in stores.
   (use)

3. People _____ food on the Internet.
   (buy)

4. The price of water _____.
   (go up)

5. The price of computers _____.
   (go down)

6. There _____ computers in every home.
   (be)

PAIRS. Change the statements above to questions. Ask the questions. Answer with *will* or *won't*.

Example:
A: *Will people read newspapers in 2050?*
B: *No, they won't.*

PAIRS. *Someday* means "at some time in the future." Look at the ideas in the box. Will these things happen someday? Ask and answer questions.

> commute to Earth from the moon
> find intelligent life on other planets
> fly to work
> live on the moon
> make friends with computers
> take vacations on the moon

Example:
A: *Will we find intelligent life on other planets someday?*
B: *Yes, I think we will.*

WRAP-UP. What other things will probably happen in the future? Ask and answer questions with *will*.

WILL: INFORMATION QUESTIONS

Wh- word	Will	Subject	Verb	Answers
What	will	I	do?	You'll find a new job.
Who		you	call?	The boss.
How much		he	pay you?	A lot.
When		they	see you?	From 9 to 5 tomorrow.

WILL: QUESTIONS WITH WHAT / WHO AS SUBJECT

Wh- word	Will	Verb		Answers
What	will	happen	to me in the future?	You'll get married.
Who		make	a lot of money?	You will.

A Read the horoscopes and the questions below. Which horoscopes are the questions about? Circle the correct answers.

 Aries (March 21–April 20)
This month will be good for business. You'll make a lot of money.

 Taurus (April 21–May 21)
You'll meet new people this month. They will be important for your future.

 Gemini (May 22–June 21)
This month won't be great, but things will be better next month.

 Cancer (June 22–July 22)
You'll find love this month, but remember: Love is never perfect.

 Leo (July 23–Aug 23)
This month will be a lot of fun. Relax and have a good time!

Virgo (Aug 24–Sept 23)
This month will be exciting and different. You'll learn a lot.

 Libra (Sept 24–Oct 23)
You'll work with other people this month. It won't be easy, but you'll succeed.

 Scorpio (Oct 24–Nov 22)
You'll be busy all month. You'll feel tired, but you'll make other people happy.

 Sagittarius (Nov 23–Dec 21)
This month. You'll want to spend time with your family.

 Capricorn (Dec 22–Jan 20)
A man from the past will get in touch with you. He'll have some good news.

 Aquarius (Jan 21–Feb 18)
You'll want something expensive. Don't do it! You'll need the money.

 Pisces (Feb 19–March 20)
You'll make some people angry. But don't worry. They'll soon forget.

1. What will be better next month?
   a. Aquarius   b. Gemini

2. How much money will he make?
   a. Pisces   b. Aries

3. Where will she meet them?
   a. Taurus   b. Libra

4. Why will it be fun?
   a. Leo   b. Cancer

B Imagine you have these horoscopes. Write questions about the horoscopes. Use *will*.

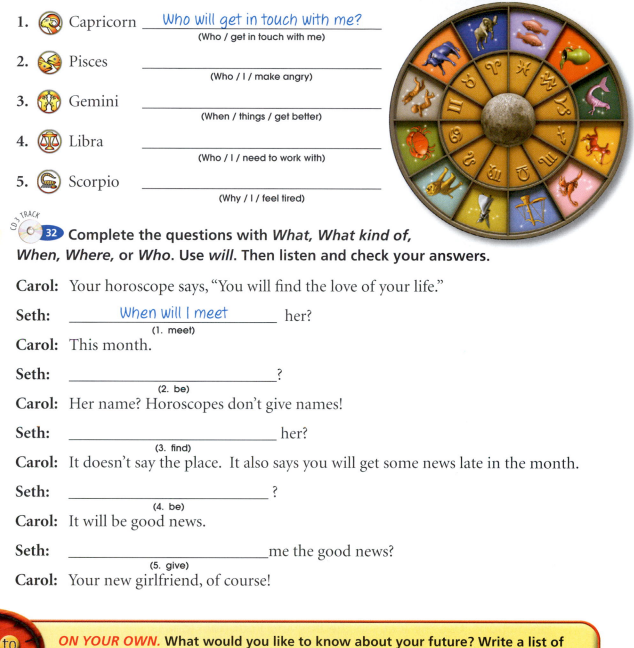

1. Capricorn ___Who will get in touch with me?___
   (Who / get in touch with me)

2. Pisces _____
   (Who / I / make angry)

3. Gemini _____
   (When / things / get better)

4. Libra _____
   (Who / I / need to work with)

5. Scorpio _____
   (Why / I / feel tired)

C CD 3 TRACK 32 Complete the questions with *What, What kind of, When, Where,* or *Who*. Use *will*. Then listen and check your answers.

Carol: Your horoscope says, "You will find the love of your life."

Seth: _____When will I meet_____ her?
        (1. meet)

Carol: This month.

Seth: _____?
        (2. be)

Carol: Her name? Horoscopes don't give names!

Seth: _____ her?
        (3. find)

Carol: It doesn't say the place. It also says you will get some news late in the month.

Seth: _____ ?
        (4. be)

Carol: It will be good news.

Seth: _____me the good news?
        (5. give)

Carol: Your new girlfriend, of course!

TIME to TALK

ON YOUR OWN. What would you like to know about your future? Write a list of questions.

GROUPS. Student A: You are the fortune teller. Answer the questions of the people in your group. Tell them about their future.

Students B, C, D: Ask the fortune teller your questions. Do you like the fortune teller's answers?

Example:

B: *When will I get a raise?*

A: *You won't get a raise this year. You'll probably get a raise next year.*

C: *How many children will I have?*

A: *You'll have three children.*

Review and Challenge

Grammar

33 Find and correct the mistakes in the conversation. There are seven mistakes. The first mistake is corrected for you. Then listen and check your answers.

Paul: Mom, I want to move closer to my job.

Mom: But where ~~you will~~ *will you* live?

Paul: I'll to find an apartment. It won't is hard.

Mom: But who will cook for you?

Paul: I cook.

Mom: Will visit me often?

Paul: Yes, I'll. Every weekend.

Mom: Good. Then I'll make you food for the week, and you will no need to cook.

Dictation

34 Listen. You will hear five sentences. Write them on a piece of paper.

Speaking

PAIRS. Write a list of six predictions about classmates. Give reasons for your predictions. Use the ideas in the box and your own ideas.

buy a house	graduate from college	move to another city
find a good job	have a lot of children	retire at a young age
get a big raise	make a lot of money	start a business someday

Example:
A: *Luz is smart and hardworking. She will probably find a good job.*
B: *I think so, too. And she'll make a lot of money someday.*

Listening

A 🔘 **35** Listen to the radio report. Two reporters are talking about a new way of paying for things. According to Rob Willis, how will people pay for things in the future?

❏ with credit cards   ❏ with phone cards   ❏ with tickets   ❏ with cell phones

B 🔘 **36** Listen again. Why doesn't Carlos Icaza think the new technology will succeed? Check (✓) his reasons.

❏ 1. It will be a big computer.
❏ 2. The price will go down.
❏ 3. It will be too expensive.

❏ 4. People will lose it.
❏ 5. It won't work in a lot of places.

TIME to TALK

GROUPS. Talk about how technology will probably change people's lives in the next 100 years. Write at least one change for each category.

MEDICINE	EDUCATION
find a cure for cancer	get more education from TVs and computers

TRANSPORTATION	ENTERTAINMENT

WRAP-UP. Now share your ideas with the class.

Example:

GROUP A: *We think that medicine will change a lot in 100 years. For example, scientists will probably find a cure for cancer.*

GROUP B: *We think that children won't go to school. They'll get education from TVs and computers.*

Reading and Writing

Reading

A Every year on New Year's Day, many Americans make New Year resolutions. Read Mary's New Year resolutions. Write the number of the paragraph next to the topic. (Be careful. There is one extra topic.)

_____ family   _____ health   _____ work   _____ love life

My New Year Resolutions

1. I won't be late to work, and I won't take any time off. If the kids get sick, my husband will stay home with them. At the end of the year, I will ask my boss for a raise, and he'll give it to me. I won't take "no" for an answer.

2. At home, my husband will help me more with the kids and the housework We'll try to eat dinner together every night. We won't watch as much TV. Instead, we'll read or play games. We'll also go to bed early. That way, we'll all get enough sleep and we won't get sick.

3. Finally, I will lose 20 pounds this year. I'll eat healthy food and exercise every day. I won't eat fast food or sweets. By summertime, I'll look great in a bathing suit.

B Read Mary's resolutions again. Then read the sentences. Write _T_ (true) or _F_ (false).

__T__ **1.** Mary was probably late to work a lot last year.

_____ **2.** Mary probably got a raise last year.

_____ **3.** Mary's husband does not help very much with the children.

_____ **4.** Mary and her family probably got sick a lot last year.

_____ **5.** Mary probably doesn't like fast food and sweets.

Prewriting

What things in your life would you like to change this year? Write a list.

_____

_____

_____

_____

Writing

Write a paragraph about the things in your life that you would like to change in the next year. Use the reading on page 236 as a model.

My New Year Resolutions

_____

_____

_____

_____

_____

_____

_____

_____

_____

_____

_____

_____

_____

Writing Tip

We use the word _instead_ to show different ideas in two sentences.

We won't watch as much TV. We'll read or play games **instead**. (= In the past, we watched TV. Now we will watch less TV.)

Unit 20
Transportation

Vocabulary

CD 3 TRACK **37** Read and listen. What do the words describe? A plane, train, taxi, bus, or subway? Tell your partner.

1. seat belt
2. passenger
3. flight attendant
4. airplane
5. pilot
6. show your ticket
7. one-way ticket
8. get off
9. subway
10. get on
11. reserve
12. reserve in advance
13. train station
14. schedule
15. sold out
16. round trip ticket

 Unit 20

238

Listening

A  **38** Listen. Mrs. Jones is talking to a ticket agent. Complete the sentences. Circle the correct answers.

Look

reserve a ticket in advance = buy a ticket early

1. Mrs. Jones **did** / (**didn't**) reserve seats on the 2:55 train.

2. There **are** / **aren't** any seats on the 2:55 train.

3. The 5:30 train **is** / **isn't** full.

4. Mrs. Jones **is** / **isn't** traveling alone.

5. Mrs. Jones **is** / **isn't** going to wait for the later train.

B **39** Read and listen again. Write the missing words. Use the words in the box.

~~can~~	have to	I'd like	Would	would you like

Ticket agent: _____*Can*_____ I help you, ma'am?
1.

Mrs. Jones: Yes please. _____ to buy two
2.

tickets to New York.

Ticket agent: _____ you like round-trip or
3.

one-way tickets?

Mrs. Jones: Round-trip, please.

Ticket agent: For when?

Mrs. Jones: Excuse me?

Ticket agent: When _____ to travel?
4.

Mrs. Jones: Today. On the next train, the 2:55.

Ticket agent: Sorry, but the 2:55 is sold out.

Mrs. Jones: What do you mean?

Ticket agent: The 2:55 is a reserved train. You

_____ reserve tickets in advance.
5.

Grammar to Communicate ❶

HAVE TO

Subject	Have to		Subject	Has to	
I You We They	**have to**	leave.	He She	**has to**	leave.
			It		stop here.

> **Look**
>
> We use *have to* when we need to do something.

A Which kinds of transportation do the sentences describe? Check (✓) the correct answers.

	Bus	Subway	Plane	Taxi
1. Passengers have to wait on the street.	✓	❏	❏	❏
2. The passenger has to talk to the driver.	❏	❏	❏	❏
3. Passengers have to wait in the station.	❏	❏	❏	❏
4. The driver has to stop at every stop.	❏	❏	❏	❏
5. The driver has to open and close the doors.	❏	❏	❏	❏
6. You have to reserve your seat in advance.	❏	❏	❏	❏

B Rewrite the sentences with *have to* or *has to*.

1. Passengers must wear seat belts.

   <u>Passengers have to wear seat belts.</u>

2. Passengers must pay for their tickets on the plane.

   _____

3. The pilot must wear a uniform.

   _____

4. Flight attendants must take care of the passengers' children.

   _____

5. That man must turn off his cell phone now.

   _____

6. You must pay to watch the movie.

   _____

> **Look**
>
> *Have to* and *must* are similar in meaning. *Have to* is more common in conversation.
> You **have to wait** at the bus stop.
> You **must wait** at the bus stop.

PAIRS. Circle the statements above that are true about traveling by plane. Then compare sentences with your partner. Did you circle the same statements?

C  **40** Complete the conversations with *has to* or *have to*. Then listen and check your answers.

1. **A:** Excuse me? Where does the bus usually stop?

   B: You ___have to___ wait next to that sign.

2. **A:** I need to get off. Is the driver going to stop here?

   B: Yes. The driver _____ stop at every bus stop.

3. **A:** Are you ready?

   B: No, I _____ get some money for the bus.

4. **A:** Excuse me, this woman _____ sit down. She's sick.

   B: Oh, sure. Here—I'll help you.

5. **A:** Sorry, but I _____ run. My bus is coming.

   B: OK, I'll talk to you later.

D Complete the sentences. Circle the correct answers.

1. The driver **has** / (**has to**) have a special license.

2. The driver **has** / **has to** wear a uniform.

3. The driver always **has** / **has to** some money with him.

4. The passengers **have** / **have to** sit in the back seat.

5. The passengers **have** / **have to** pay in cash.

6. The driver **has** / **has to** a good job.

> **Look**
>
> Use *have to* when something is necessary.
>   You **have to** buy a ticket.
> Use *have* + noun for possessions.
>   You **have a ticket**.

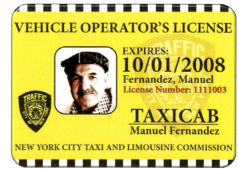

PAIRS. Which sentences above are about taxicabs? Which sentences are about the subway? Which are about both?

TIME to TALK

PAIRS. Imagine that you are going to travel to another country next month. Talk about five things you have to do before you leave.

Example:
A: *I have to buy a plane ticket.*
B: *I have to ask my boss for time off.*

Grammar to Communicate 2

WOULD LIKE

Subject	Would like		Noun	Contractions		
I He We You They	would like	to buy	one ticket.	I'd He'd We'd You'd They'd	like	one ticket, please.
			a ticket, please.			to buy a ticket, please.

Would	Subject	Like		Noun	Answers
Would	you	like	to buy	a one-way ticket?	Yes, please.
				a ticket?	No, thank you.

A Read the sentences. Who are the passengers talking to?
Write *passenger, flight attendant,* or *bus driver.*

1. I'd like a window seat, please.   _flight attendant_

2. I'd like to get off at the next stop.   _____

3. We'd like to change our seats.   _____

4. Would you like my seat?   _____

5. Would you like to read my newspaper?   _____

window seat

B Rewrite the sentences. Use *to + verb.*

1. I'd like a glass of water, please.   _I'd like to drink a glass of water, please._
(drink)

2. I'd like a magazine, please.   _____
(read)

3. I'd like a sandwich, please.   _____
(have)

4. Would you like some music?   _____
(listen to)

5. Would you like my cell phone?   _____
(use)

Now rewrite the sentences. Do not use *to + verb.*

6. I'd like to drink a cup of coffee, please.   _I'd like a cup of coffee, please._

7. I'd like to have a newspaper, please.   _____

8. I'd like to buy three tickets, please.   _____

9. Would you like to eat some fruit?   _____

10. Would you like to have a cup of tea?   _____

C Serge is a flight attendant. Read the list of things passengers on the plane want. Write sentences with *would like*.

> Ms. Amar (31A)—some coffee
>
> Mr. Fong (11B)—something to eat
>
> Mr. and Mrs. Lin (9G-H)—magazines
>
> Mr. Quinn (15B)—watch a movie
>
> Ms. Gomez (22J)—change seats

1. Ms. Amar would like some coffee.

2. _____

3. _____

4. _____

5. _____

PAIRS. What are some things you would like right now in class?

D Sue and Bob are on a train. Bob is in a bad mood. Sue wants to help him. Write Sue's questions. Use *Would you like* and the words in the box.

> an ~~aspirin~~   my jacket   some water   something to eat   something to read   to sit here

1. **Bob:** I have a headache.
   Sue: Would you like an aspirin?

2. **Bob:** I'm bored.
   Sue: _____

3. **Bob:** I'm thirsty.
   Sue: _____

4. **Bob:** I'm hungry.
   Sue: _____

5. **Bob:** I'm cold.
   Sue: _____

6. **Bob:** I don't like my seat.
   Sue: _____

TIME to TALK

PAIRS. Look at the picture. What are the people saying? Write short conversations.

Example:
A: *Would you like to sit down?*
B: *Thank you very much, young man.*

Grammar to Communicate 3

CAN / COULD / WOULD

Can / Could / Would	Subject	Verb		Answers
Can **Could**	**I**	**have**	a one-way ticket, please?	Sure. Sorry, that train is sold out.
Can **Could** **Would**	**you**	**give**	me a one-way ticket, please?	Of course. I'm sorry. We're sold out.

A Match the situations with the requests.

> **Look**
>
> To make requests, use *would, could,* or *can.*
> We often use *please* with polite requests.

_e_ 1. Myra wants to look at a schedule.

_____ 2. Anna's bag is heavy.

_____ 3. Alan's in a taxi. He's cold.

_____ 4. Rick doesn't have a ticket for the bus.

_____ 5. Chris wants some information.

_____ 6. Louisa doesn't like her seat.

_____ 7. The flight attendant thinks two passengers are in the wrong seats.

a. "Could I have a ticket, please?"

b. "Can I ask you a question?"

c. "Would you show me your tickets, please?"

d. "Can I change my seat?"

e. "Could I have a schedule, please?"

f. "Would you help me with my bag, please?"

g. "Can you close the window, please?"

B Change the sentences to requests. Use *please.*

1. Give me two tickets.

_____Can you give me two tickets, please?_____
(can)

2. Open the window.

_____
(would)

3. Sit down.

_____
(could)

4. Wait.

_____
(would)

5. Help me.

_____
(can)

6. Take me to the airport.

_____
(could)

PAIRS. Think of a situation for each request above.

Example:
A: *In number 1, the speaker is in a train station and wants to take a train.*

C CD 3 TRACK **41** **Write requests. Use** *Can, Could,* **or** *Would* **and** *Please.* **Then listen and compare your requests.**

1. You're in a cab and you're hot. The windows aren't open. You are talking to the cab driver.

   A: _Can you open the windows, please?_

   B: It's windy today. I'll turn on the air conditioner.

2. You want to get a round-trip ticket to Chicago. You are talking to a ticket agent.

   A: _____

   B: Sure. That'll be $35.

3. You want to get off at the next stop. You ask the bus driver.

   A: _____

   B: No problem.

4. You need some coffee. You are talking to a flight attendant.

   A: _____

   B: Sure. Here you are.

5. You want to stop at the next street. You are talking to the cab driver.

   A: _____

   B: Okay.

6. You're a flight attendant. A passenger should go back to his seat. You are talking to him.

   A: _____

   B: All right.

7. You're getting in a cab. Your friend is coming. Ask the cab driver to wait.

   A: _____

   B: OK.

TIME to TALK

GROUPS. What requests do people often make in the places in the box? Make a list of three requests for each place.

| at a train station | at a travel agency | at airport customs | at airport security |

WRAP-UP. Tell another group your requests. Can they guess the place?

Example:
A: *Here is my request: Could I reserve a seat on the 9:55 to Philadelphia, please?*
B: *Are you at airport customs?*
A: *No.*
B: *I know. You're at a train station.*

Review and Challenge

Grammar

Find the mistake in each sentence. Circle the letter and correct the mistake.

1. <u>Would</u> you <u>please</u> <u>to</u> sit down?
   A   B   Ⓒ   Correct: _Would you please sit down?_

2. We <u>like</u> <u>to</u> <u>have</u> some water, please.
   A   B   C   Correct: _____

3. The child <u>have</u> <u>to</u> <u>have</u> a ticket.
   A   B   C   Correct: _____

4. <u>Do</u> <u>you</u> like <u>a one-way ticket</u>?
   A   B   C   Correct: _____

5. <u>She</u> would <u>likes</u> a different <u>seat</u>.
   A   B   C   Correct: _____

6. <u>I</u> <u>can</u> <u>use</u> your pen, <u>please</u>?
   A   B   C   Correct: _____

Dictation

CD 3 TRACK 42 Listen. You will hear five sentences. Write them on a piece of paper.

Speaking

PAIRS. **Choose one of the situations and write a conversation. Then perform your conversation for the class.**

Situation 1

Student A: You live in Los Angeles. You have to travel to Las Vegas because your mother is sick. You don't have a lot of money, but you really want to get there quickly. You go to a travel agency.

Student B: You are a travel agent. A customer walks into your office.

Situation 2

Student A: You are at the train station. You have to travel from New York to Washington, D.C. today. This is the first time you are traveling by train.

Student B: You are a ticket agent at Union Station in Washington, D.C. It is a very busy weekend, and many of the reserved trains are sold out. A customer comes up to your window.

Example: (Situation 1)

A: *Hello. I'd like to buy a ticket from Los Angeles to Las Vegas.*

B: *OK. What kind of ticket would you like? . . .*

246   Unit 20

Listening

A **43** **Listen to the conversation. Where are the people? Check (✓) the correct answer.**

❏ on a flight from New York to Las Vegas
❏ on a flight from Los Angeles to Las Vegas
❏ on a flight from Las Vegas to New York
❏ on a flight from Los Angeles to New York

B **44** **Listen again. Match the start of each sentence with the correct endings.**

_____ 1. The woman would like
_____ 2. The man would like
_____ 3. The woman has to
_____ 4. The woman liked
_____ 5. The man has
_____ 6. The woman loves
_____ 7. The man would like to

a. basketball.
b. a newspaper.
c. some water.
d. go to the restroom.
e. Las Vegas.
f. see the woman at the basketball game.
g. two tickets to a basketball game.

TIME to TALK

GROUPS. Imagine that you are on an airplane. Students A, B: You are passengers. Student C: You are a flight attendant. Write a conversation about one of the situations.

Situation 1: The flight is very rough. Some of the passengers are scared.

Situation 2: The passengers are complaining about everything. The flight attendant is polite, but she is losing her patience.

Situation 3: A young couple is traveling with their two sons. The children are behaving very badly. They won't listen to their parents. The other passengers are angry.

WRAP-UP. Now perform your conversation for the class.

Example: (Situation 1)
A: *Mommy! I'm scared, and I have to go to the bathroom!*
B: *Oh, Timmy, can you wait? We have to stay in our seats right now.*

Reading and Writing

Reading

A Read the letter. What is the problem? Check (✓) the correct answer.

❑ The number 12 bus driver does not stop after 11:00 P.M.

❑ Mr. and Mrs. Thomas have to take the number 12 bus every day.

❑ The number 12 bus does not come at the times on the schedule.

Emily O'Toole
Public Transportation Commissioner
City of Boston
20 Harrison Ave.
Roxbury, MA 02119

5 Washington St., Apt. 2A
Roxbury, MA 02119
May 28, 2006

Dear Ms. O' Toole:

   I am writing because I would like to report a problem on the Roxbury bus line. My husband and I do not have a car, so we have to take the number 12 bus every day. My husband has to be at work by 7:00 A.M. I have to take the bus home after work at 11:00 P.M. The number 12 bus schedule says that on weekdays the buses run every 20 minutes from 6:00 A.M. until midnight. However, my husband often has to wait 30 minutes for a bus in the morning. I have the same problem at night.
   We would like your help. A few months ago, we called the transportation hotline to complain, but they didn't do anything. Could you please someone to contact us? Thank you for your attention.

Sincerely,

Thomas

Frances Thomas

B Read the letter again. Answer the questions. Write in complete sentences.

1. Why do Mr. and Mrs. Thomas have to take the bus?

_____

2. What time does Mrs. Thomas get off work?

_____

3. How long do Mr. and Mrs. Thomas usually have to wait for the bus?

_____

4. What did Mrs. Thomas do a few months ago?

_____

Prewriting

GROUPS. Are there problems with the transportation in your city or town? Make a list of things that you would like the city to fix.

1. The city does not take care of the roads.

_____   _____

_____   _____

_____   _____

Writing

Choose a problem from the list your group wrote. Write a letter of complaint to the appropriate city official. Find the name and address in the local phone book. Use the letter on page 248 as a model.

Writing Tip

Indent the beginning of a new paragraph. To indent, leave about 5 spaces blank at the beginning of the paragraph.

Game 5
Units 17-20

PLAYERS | 3 students
MATERIALS | 1 book
1 coin
3 markers

INSTRUCTIONS
▶ Put your markers on the START box.
▶ Student A: Toss the coin. Heads = Move 1 box. Tails = Move 2 boxes.
▶ Make a question about the picture in the box.
▶ Students B, C: Make sure Student's A question is correct. Then Student B answers Students A's question. Student C makes a new question about Student A's picture. Give 1 point for a correct answer or question:

Example: PICTURE 1

Student A: What should Bill do?
Student B: He should take an aspirin.
Student C: How many should he take?

▶ Student B: Now take your turn.
▶ Students: If your answer is not correct, put your marker on the box from your last turn. If you land on another student's box, move your marker to the next box.
▶ Continue taking turns until you get to the FINISH box. The student with the most points wins.

START

1 should / Bill

Tommy

5 should / Tommy / go to school today

Brutus 2 Chico
big / small

3 rent / probably / go up / in six months

4 have to / wear a uniform

Grammar Summaries

Be: Affirmative and Negative Statements

1. Use the verb *be* to make an affirmative statement:
   He is quiet.
2. Use the verb *be* and *not* to make a negative statement:
   He **is not** quiet.
3. *You* is singular (one person) or plural (two or more people).
   Bill, you're quiet.
   Dan and Alice, you're quiet.
4. There are two forms—the full form (*I am*) and the contracted form (*I'm*). The contracted form is more common in conversation.
5. There are two forms of negative contractions. They have the same meaning.
   You're not quiet. = **You aren't** quiet.
6. There is only one negative contraction for *I*:
   I'm not

Be: Yes / No Questions and Short Answers

1. For *yes / no* questions with the verb *be*, change the word order of the subject (*he, she, they*, etc.) and the verb (*am, is, are*).
   They are late.   **Are they** late?
2. There are two negative short answers. They have the same meaning.
   No, it**'s not**.   No, it **isn't**.
3. There is only one negative short answer for *I*:
   No, I'm not.

Regular Count Nouns and Irregular Nouns

1. Add *–s* to change regular singular nouns to plural nouns.
   student ⟶ student**s**
2. Add *–es* to regular nouns that end in *–s*.
   boss ⟶ boss**es**
3. Some plural nouns are irregular. They do not end in *–s* or *–es*.
   child children
4. Look at page 263 for spelling rules for plural nouns. Look at page 264 for pronunciation rules for plural nouns.

Possessive Adjectives

1. Possessive adjectives come before nouns.
   My name is Sylvia.
2. Possessive adjectives do not change forms. Use the same form with singular and plural nouns.
   Her brother is here.
   Her brothers are here.
3. *Your* is singular (one person) or plural (two or more people).
   Your mother is tall, **Lucy.**
   Your mother is tall, **Ken and Lucy.**
4. Be careful! Do not confuse *Its* with *It's*.
   The dog's ears aren't white. **Its** nose is white.
   (**Its**=possessive adjective)
   Don't worry. **It's** friendly.
   (**It's**=It is)

Possessive Nouns

1. Add *'s* after singular nouns.
   My sister**'s** name is Anna.
2. Add *'* after the *–s* ending of regular plural nouns.
   My sisters**'** names are Michele and Janine.
3. Add *'s* after irregular plural nouns.
   The women**'s** names are Meg and Gina.
4. When there are two nouns, add *'s* to the last noun.
   Dan and Sue**'s** last name is Riley.
5. Be careful! The possessive *'s* is different from the contraction *'s* for *is*.
   Dan**'s** last name is Riley. (possessive)
   Dan**'s** late for work today. (contraction)
6. Look at page 264 for pronunciation rules for possessive nouns.

Be: Information Questions

1. In information questions, *is* or *are* comes after the *wh-* word (*who, what*, etc.)
   How old is he?
   Where are your sisters?
2. In conversation, use the contracted form of *is* (*'s*) after the *wh-* word.
   What's your name?   (=What is your name?)
   Who's in the picture?   (=Who is in the picture?)
3. Use *how* + adjective to ask questions.
   How old are you?

A and An with Singular Count Nouns

1. Use *a* before singular nouns that begin with a consonant (*b, c, d, f, g, h, j, k, l, m, n, p, q, r, s, t, v, w, x, y, z*)
   My brother is **a m**echanic.
2. Use *an* before singular nouns that begin with a vowel (*a, e, i, o, u*).
   My sister is **an a**ccountant.
3. Do not use *a* or *an* before plural nouns.
   My brother and sister are engineers.
   NOT My brother and sister ~~an~~ engineers.
4. Use *a* before *u* if the *u* sounds like *you*.
   Paul is **a university** worker.
   [pronounced **you**•niversity]
5. Use *an* before *h* if the *h* is silent.
   Sheila is **an honest** waitress.
   [the *h* is NOT pronounced.]
   Sheila is **a hard-working** waitress.
   [the *h* is pronounced.]

Adjective and Noun Word Order

1. Adjectives describe people and things. Use adjectives after the verb *be* or before a noun.
   The job is **interesting**.
   She's an **excellent** hairdresser.
2. Adjectives do not change form with plural nouns.
   The **waiter** is **careful.** The waiters are careful.
   NOT The waiters are ~~carefuls~~.
3. Use *a* before an adjective that begins with a consonant + a singular noun.
   It is a **good** job.
4. Use *an* before an adjective that begins with a vowel + a singular noun.
   It is **an interesting job**.
5. Do not use *a* or *an* before an adjective alone.
   It **is interesting.** NOT It is ~~an~~ interesting.

A / An / 0 and The

1. Use *the* before singular and plural nouns.
   The **worker** is neat.
   The **workers** are neat.
2. Use *the* when the noun is the only one in that situation.
   Jerry is **the** mechanic at A-1 Garage (=Jerry is the only mechanic at A-1 Garage.)
3. Also use *the* for the second time you talk about something.
   I work at a garage. **The** garage is big.
4. Use *a/an* when the singular noun is one of many. The noun is NOT the only one.
   Jerry is **a** mechanic. (=Jerry is not the only mechanic.)
5. Do NOT use an article when the plural noun is two (or more) of many.
   Jerry and Tom are mechanics. (=Jerry and Tom are not the only mechanics.)

There is / There are: Statements

1. Make sentences with *There is* and singular nouns:
   There is a restaurant near my home.
2. Make sentences with *There are* and plural nouns:
   There are restaurants near my home.
3. There are two forms—the full form (*There is*) and the contracted form (*There's*). *There are* does not have a contracted form.
4. The subject comes after *There is* or *There are*. *There* is NOT the subject.

Some / A lot of / Any

1. Use *some* with plural nouns in affirmative statements. Use *any* with plural nouns in negative statements.
   There **are some** restaurants.
   There **aren't any** stores.
2. Use *a lot of* with plural nouns in affirmative and negative statements.
   There are a **lot of** good restaurants.
   There aren't a lot of cheap stores.
3. Use *a lot of* for large numbers.
   Use *some* for small numbers.
   Use *any* for zero in negative statements.
   There are **a lot of** people here. (50 people)
   There are **some** people here. (5 people)
   There aren't **any** people here. (0 people)
4. We can use plural nouns without *some* or *any*.
   There are expensive stores on 5th Avenue in New York.
5. We can use *no* instead of *not any*.
   There are **no** restaurants near here.
6. Be careful! The pronunciation of *there, their*, and *they're* is the same. The meaning is different.
   There is a good restaurant near here.
   They're in the restaurant. (**they are**)
   Their table is ready. (His and her table)
   The restaurant isn't here. It's over **there**. (a specific place)

Is there / Are there

1. In questions with *Is there*, use *a* or *an*.
   Is there a bank near here?
   Is there an office building near here?
2. In questions with *Are there*, use *any* or *a lot of*.
   Are there any banks near here?
   Are there a lot of stores here?
3. Use *there is* or *there are* to talk about something the first time. Use *it* or *they* the second time.
   A: Is there a big store near here?
   B: Yes, **there is. It** is expensive.
   A: Are there restaurants near here?
   B: Yes, **there** are. **They**'re on Main Street.

Count and Noncount Nouns

1. Count nouns are singular (1 apple) or plural (2 apples.) We can count them.
2. Use *a* or *an* with singular count nouns in affirmative and negative statements.
   > There is **a** banana in the bag.
   > There isn't **an** orange in the bag.
3. We can not count noncount nouns. They do not have plural forms. Do not add *–s* or *–es*.
   > The **fruit** is good.
   > NOT ~~The fruits are good~~ .
4. Use the singular form of the verb (*is*, for example) with noncount nouns.
   > There is some meat on the table.
   > NOT ~~There are some meat on the table~~ .
5. Use *How much* to ask about the price of both count and noncount nouns.
   > **How much** is the fruit?   Three **dollars**.

Quantifiers: *Some / A little / A lot of / A few / Any*

1. We can use full forms (*there is not /there are not*), but we usually use contractions in conversation.
   > **There aren't** any oranges.
2. Use *some* with noncount nouns and plural nouns in affirmative statements.
   > There **is some** milk.   There **are some** eggs.
3. Use *any* with noncount nouns and plural nouns in negative statements.
   > There **isn't any** milk.   There **aren't any** eggs.
4. Use *a little* with noncount nouns. Use *a few* with plural count nouns.
   > There is **a little** sugar.   There are **a few** cookies.
5. Use *a lot of* in affirmative and negative statements, with both noncount nouns and plural count nouns.
   > There **is a lot** of rice.   There aren't **a lot of** oranges.
6. We can use noncount and plural nouns alone.
   > There **is sugar** in the cookies.
7. We can use *no* instead of *not any*.
   > There **is no** salt in the soup.
   > There **isn't any** salt in the soup.
8. When we talk about a specific amount of food, we use words for containers or weight.
   > There are **two bottles** of soda.

Count and Noncount Nouns: *Yes / No* Questions

1. Use *Is there a / an* with singular count nouns in *yes / no* questions.
   > Is there **a** banana in the bag?
2. Use *Are there any* with noncount nouns and plural nouns in *yes / no* questions.
   > **Are there any** eggs?
3. Use *How much* with noncount nouns. Use *How many* with plural count nouns.
   > **How much** milk is there?
   > **How many** bottles of milk are there?

Present Progressive: Statements

1. For the present progressive, use the simple present of the verb *be* and a verb + *-ing*.
   > I **am** talk**ing**.
   > Linda **is** talk**ing**.
   > Mike and Lee **are** talk**ing**.
2. Use the present progressive to talk about activities happening now.
   > The children are in bed. They **are sleeping**.
3. With the present progressive, we understand that the time is now or right now. We can say *now* or *right now*, but it is not necessary.
   > I'm **writing right now**. OR I'm **writing**.
4. There are two forms—the full form and the contracted form. The contracted form is more common in conversation.
   > I **am eating**.   (Full form)
   > I'm **eating**.   (Contracted form)
5. There are two forms of negative contractions. The meaning is the same.
   > **You're not** sleeping. = **You aren't** sleeping.
   > **He's not** sleeping.   = **He isn't** sleeping.
   > **They're not** sleeping. = **They aren't** sleeping.
6. There is only one negative contraction for *I*.
   > I'm **not** running.
7. Look at page 262 for spelling rules for the present progressive.

Present Progressive: *Yes / No* Questions

1. To make a *yes / no* question, change the word order of the subject and the verb.
   > **They are** eating.   **Are they** eating?
2. There are two negative short answers. They have the same meaning.
   > Are they eating?   No, they**'re not**. OR
   >   No, they **aren't**.
3. There is only one negative short answer for *I*.
   > Are you running?   **No, I'm not.**

Present Progressive: Information Questions

1. In information questions, *is* or *are* comes after the *wh-* word (*what, where,* etc.)
   > **What** is **Chris** doing?
2. In conversation, the contracted form is common after the *wh-* word.
   > **What's** she eating? (=What is she eating?)
3. Look at the difference in these questions.
   > **Who's** Mary talking to?
   > (Conversation and informal writing)
   > **To whom** is Mary talking?
   > (Formal English)

Imperatives

1. To make an affirmative imperative, use the base form of the verb. To make a negative imperative, use *don't* + the base form of the verb.

   Wait for me.   (Affirmative)
   Don't wait for me.   (Negative)

2. *You* is the subject of imperative, but we do not usually say *you* in the sentence.

   Please close the door.
   NOT ~~Please you~~ close the door.

3. Use *please* to be polite. Put *please* at the beginning or end of the sentence.

   Please don't talk.
   Don't talk, please.

Prepositions

1. Many sentences have prepositions. A preposition always has an object. The object is a noun or pronoun.

   Listen   **to**   your **mother**.
         preposition   noun (object)

2. Some prepositions give location.

   Put the wastebasket **in** the room.
                        behind the door.
                        under the desk.

3. Some prepositions come after verbs or adjectives.

   Look at these sentences.   (Verb + preposition)
   Be **nice to** your sister.   (Adjective + preposition)

Object Pronouns

1. Use an object pronoun in place of a noun after a verb or preposition.

   Wait for **him**.   (Object pronoun)
            the bus.   (Noun)
            Mr. Chiu.   (Noun)

2. *You* is an object pronoun and a subject pronoun.

   I'm listening to **you**.
   You aren't listening to me.

This / That / These / Those

1. Use *this* and *that* for singular nouns. Use *these* and *those* for plural nouns.

2. Use *this* and *these* for things near you. Use *that* and *those* for things not near you.

3. Use *this / that / these / those* before a noun.

   This camera is nice.
   (This + noun + verb)

4. You can use *this / that / these / those* as a pronoun.

   This is my camera.
   (This + verb)

Possessive Adjectives and Pronouns

1. Use a possessive adjective before a noun. Do not use a possessive pronoun before a noun.

   My shoes are clean.
   NOT ~~Mine~~ shoes are clean.

2. Possessive pronouns do not change forms. Use the same form to refer to singular and plural nouns.

   The pen is **mine**.
   The pens are **mine**.
   NOT ~~The pens are mines~~.

3. *His* is both a possessive adjective and a possessive pronoun.

   His hair is black.
   (possessive adjective, describes hair)
   His is blond.
   (possessive pronoun, replaces *his hair*.)

Simple Present: *Have*

1. Use *have* or *has* to talk about possessions.

   I **have** a car. (The car is my possession.)

2. Use *have* with *I, you, we*, and *they*.

   I **have** a new car.
   My wife and I have a new car.
   You have a new laptop.
   They have a new computer.

3. Use *has* with the third person singular (*he, she, it*).

   Mr. Robinson has a new computer.
   She has a new cell phone.

Simple Present: Affirmative Statements

1. Use the simple present to talk about everyday activities and things that happen again and again.

   My brother **works** on Tuesday.
   (=This is his routine.)
   I **eat** ice cream after dinner.
   (=This is my habit.)

2. *You* is singular (one person) or plural (two or more people).

   Bill, you sleep a lot.
   Dan and Alice, you sleep a lot.

3. The third person singular (*he, she, it*) of *have* is *has*.

   I **have** a cup of coffee.
   He **has** a cup of coffee.

4. Look at page 264 for information about the pronunciation of the third person singular *-s-* or *-es* (*he, she, it*).

Simple Present: Spelling Rules

1. For the third person singular (*he, she, it*) of the simple present, add *–s* or *–es* to the base form of the verb. Look at page 263 for more spelling rules.

   He cook**s** every day.
   She wash**es** her hair in the morning.

Simple Present: Negative Statements

1. With *I, you, we,* and *they,* use *do not* + the base form of the verb in negative statements.

   We do not stay up late on weekends.

   With *he, she,* and *it,* use *does not* + the base form of the verb in negative statements.

   She does not stay up late on weekends.

2. Use *don't* + verb or *doesn't* + verb for negative statements in conversation.

   I **don't** sleep a lot.
   He **doesn't** sleep a lot.

3. When you have one subject and two negative verbs in the simple present, you can connect the verbs with *or*. Do not repeat *don't* or *doesn't* after *or*.

   They **don't cook** or **wash** the dishes in the evening.
   NOT ~~They don't cook or don't wash the dishes in the evening.~~

Frequency Adverbs with the Simple Present

1. Use frequency adverbs to say how often people do things or how often something happens.

   I **never** pay for things with a credit card.
   (=0% of the time)
   The store **always** opens at 9 o'clock.
   (=100% of the time)

2. Use frequency adverbs *before* the base form of the verb.

   I **often buy** things at the mall.
   I **don't often buy** things at the mall.
   Do you often buy things at the mall?

3. Use frequency adverbs *after* the verb *be*.

   The store **is usually** busy on the weekend.

4. We also put *sometimes* at the beginning or end of sentences.

   We **sometimes** go to that store.
   Sometimes we go to that store.
   We go to that store **sometimes**.

Simple Present: *Yes / No* Questions

1. To make a *yes / no* question, add *do* or *does* before the subject and the base form of the verb.

   They spend a lot of money.
   Do they spend a lot of money?
   He spends a lot of money.
   Does he spend a lot of money?

2. When you use *does* in a *yes / no* question, do not use *–s* or *–es* at the end of the base form of the verb.

   Does it **close** at 6 o'clock?
   No, it closes at 6:30.
   NOT ~~Does it closes at 6 o'clock?~~

3. Use *do* or *does* in short answers.

   Do you have a new car?
   Yes, we **do**. OR No, we **don't**.
   Does she have a new car?
   Yes, she **does**. OR No, she **doesn't**.

4. Remember: For questions with the verb *be*, use *is, am,* or *are* in short answers.

   Is the store big?
   Yes, it **is**. OR No, it **isn't**.

Simple Present: Information Questions

1. In information questions, *does* or *do* comes after the *wh-* word (*what, how much,* etc.)

   What does the store **sell**?
   How much do the shoes **cost**?

2. When you use *does* in an information question, do not use *–s* or *–es* at the end of the base form of the verb.

   How much does it cost?
   NOT How much does it ~~costs~~?

3. We can also use *do / does* with the expression *What kind of* + noun.

   What kind of car **do** you want?

Direct and Indirect Objects

1. Some verbs have direct and indirect objects. The verbs *buy, get, give, make,* and *send* have both direct and indirect objects.
2. When a sentence has a direct and indirect object, the objects can come in either order.

   I send **cards to many people**.

   (direct object + preposition + indirect object)

   I send **many people cards**.

   (indirect object + direct object).
3. When the indirect object is a pronoun (*me, him, her, them,* etc.) put the direct object after the pronoun.

   I send **them cards.**

   (indirect object pronoun) (direct object)

Simple Present: Information Questions

1. In information questions, *does* or *do* comes after the *wh-* word (*how, why,* etc.)

   How do you **celebrate** your birthday?
   Why does she **give** him candy?
2. When you use *does* in an information question, do not use *–s* or *–es* at the end of the base form of the verb.

   When **does** the party **start?**
   NOT When does the party starts?

Who as Subject and Object

1. When *who* is the subject of the question, use verb + *-s* after *who.*

   Who   cooks the food?
   (subject) (verb)
2. When *who* is the object of the question, add *do* or *does* before the subject.

   Who do you invite? My friends.
   (object) (subject)
3. In formal English, use *whom* for a question about an object. Use *who* for informal questions.

   Whom do people invite to a wedding? (formal)
   Who do people invite to a wedding?(informal)
4. When a verb has a preposition, put the preposition at the end of the question in conversation.

   Who do you **give** flowers **to?**
   I **give** flowers **to** my girlfriend.
   Who does he **buy** gifts **for?**
   He **buys** gifts **for many** people.
5. In formal English, do not use prepositions at the end of questions. Put the preposition before *whom.*

   To whom do people give gifts? (formal)
   Who do people give gifts **to?** (informal)

Simple Present and Present Progressive

1. Use the simple present to talk about routines, schedules, and general facts.

   My brother **works** everyday. (routine)
   The store **closes** at 9:00. (schedule)
   A lot of women in the U.S. **work**. (general fact)
2. Use the present progressive to talk about activities happening now or these days:

   I **am reading** right **now.**
   We **are studying** English **these days**.

Stative Verbs

1. Stative verbs do not describe actions. Some common stative verbs are: *be, have, know, like, need, understand, want, hear, see.* (See page 265 for a list of more stative verbs.)
2. Use the simple present with stative verbs. Do not use the present progressive.

   This book **costs** a lot.
   NOT This book is costing a lot.
3. Some stative verbs can also be used as action verbs, but with different meanings. When they are used as action verbs, they can be used in the present progressive or simple present.

   have=stative verb meaning possession
   I **have** a car now. (possession)
   NOT I'm having a car now.

   have=action verb meaning eat
   I'm **having** dinner now. (action)
   I **have** dinner at 6:00 every night. (habit)

Like / Need / Want + Infinitive

1. If you use a verb after *need, want,* or *like,* use the infinitive form of the verb.
   (Infinitive=*to* + the base form of the verb)

   I need **to get** a job.
   He doesn't want **to work** part-time.
   She likes **to work** in the morning.
2. Don't forget! You can also use a noun or pronoun after *need, want* and *like.*

   I need a **job.** I need **it** now.
   She wants two **eggs.** She wants **them** now.
   He likes his **boss.** He likes **her** a lot.

Simple Past of *Be*: Statements
1. *Was* is the past of *am* and *is*. *Were* is the past of *are*.
   I **was** here yesterday.   I **am** here today.
   You **were** late yesterday.   You **are** late today.
2. *There was* is the past of *there is*. *There were* is the past of *there are*.
   There **was** a line yesterday.
   There **were** a lot of cars yesterday.
3. *Was not* is the past of *am not* and *is not*. *Were not* is the past of *are not*.
   The weather **was not** bad yesterday.
   The weather **is not** bad today.
   We **were not** busy yesterday.
   We **are not** busy today.
4. There are two negative forms—the full form (*I was*) and the contracted form (*I wasn't*). The contracted form is more common in conversations. There are no contracted forms for the affirmative (*was, were*).
5. *There wasn't* is the past of *there isn't*. *There weren't* is the past of *there aren't*.
   There wasn't a lot of food. There weren't any lines.
6. Past time expressions can go at the beginning or at the end of a sentence.
   Last night I was at home.
   I was at home **last night**.

Simple Past of *Be*: Yes / No Questions
1. To make a *yes / no* question with the past of *be*, change the word order of the subject (*he, she, they,* etc.) and the verb (*was / were*).
   They were on vacation last week.
   Were they on vacation last week?
2. To make a *yes / no* question with the past of *there was* or *there were*, change the word order of the two words.
   There was a test in class yesterday.
   Was there a test in class yesterday?
3. Look at the different short answers.
   Was the food good?
   Yes, **it** was. OR No, **it** wasn't.
   Was there a lot of food?
   Yes, **there** was. OR No, **there** wasn't.

Simple Past of *Be*: Information Questions
1. In information questions, *was* or *were* come after the *wh-* word (*how, where,* etc.)
   How was the party?
   Where were the children?
2. Be careful! Questions with *who* have two forms.
   Who was at the party?
   My friends were at the party.
   Who were you with at the party?
   I was with my friends.

Simple Past: Regular Verbs
1. For the simple past, add *–ed* to the base form of the verb.
   I cook**ed** yesterday evening.
   I cook every evening.
2. If the verb ends in *–e*, add *–d*.
   The stores **close** at 6:00 P.M. every day.
   The stores **closed** at 6:00 P.M. yesterday.
3. If the verb ends in a consonant + *-y*, change the *–y* to *–i*. Then add *–ed*.
   They study every day.
   They stud**ied** yesterday.
4. If the verb ends in consonant + vowel + consonant, double the consonant. Then add *–ed*.
   We stop at 5 P.M. every day.
   We sto**pped** at 5 P.M. yesterday.
5. Look at page 262 for more spelling rules. Look at page 264 for pronunciation rules for the *–ed* ending of regular past tense verbs.

Simple Past: Irregular Verbs
1. Many verbs are irregular. The simple past of these verbs do not have *–ed* at the end. Here are some common irregular past tense verbs.
   do → **did**   eat → **ate**
   go → **went**   have → **had**
2. Look at page 265 for a list of irregular past forms of verbs.

Simple Past: Negative Statements
1. For the negative past form of verbs, use *did not* + the base form of the verb.
   I **did not watch** TV last Sunday.
   I **watched** TV last Monday.
   I **did not eat** dinner at 6 o'clock.
   I **ate** dinner at 8 o'clock.
2. Use *didn't* + the base form of the verb for negative statements in conversation.
   I **didn't watch** TV last Sunday.
   I **didn't eat** dinner at 6 o'clock.
3. Do not use the *–ed* ending or the irregular past form in negative sentences.
   He **didn't work** yesterday.
   NOT He didn't worked yesterday.
   I **didn't take** the bus yesterday.
   NOT I didn't took the bus yesterday.
4. The affirmative and negative forms of the past are the same for all persons (*I, you, he, she, it, we, they*).
   She walk**ed** to the office yesterday.
   She walks to the office every day.
   They didn't have breakfast yesterday.
   They don't have breakfast every day.
5. Be careful! The past of *be* is *was / wasn't* and *were / weren't*. Do not use *didn't* with the past of *be*.
   I **wasn't** at home last night.
   NOT I didn't be at home last night.

Simple Past: *Yes / No* Questions

1. To make a *yes / no* question, add *did* before the subject and use the base form of the verb.
    > **They got** married in 1998.
    > **Did they** get married in 1998?
    > **She retired** in 2004.
    > **Did she retire** in 2004?
2. When you use *did* in a *yes / no* question, do not use *–ed* at the end of the base form of the verb.
    > Did it close last year?
    > NOT Did it ~~closed~~ last year?
3. Use *did* in short answers.
    > Did you meet a long time ago?
    > Yes, we **did**. OR No, we **didn't**.
4. For questions with the verb *be*, do not use *did*. Use *was* or *were*.
    > **Was** he married for a long time?
    > Yes, he **was**. OR No, he **wasn't**.

Simple Past: Information Questions

1. In information questions, *did* comes after the *wh-* word (*what, how much*, etc.)
    > **Where did** you **live**?
    > **Why did** he **live** in Miami?
2. When you use *did* in an information question, do not use *–ed* at the end of the base form of the verb.
    > When **did** they **move**?
    > NOT ~~When did they moved?~~
3. When *who* or *what* is the subject of a question, do not use *did* in the question. Use the past form of the verb.
    > Who   got   married?
    > (Subject) (Verb)
    > What   happened?
    > (Subject) (Verb)

How long ago / How long

1. Use *ago* after an expression of time—for example, *two months ago* or *five days ago. Ago* tells us "when before now."
    > She graduated **two months ago.**
    > (=two months before now)
    > They visited us **five days ago.**
    > (=five days before now)
2. Use *for* before an expression of time—for example, *for two months* or *for five days*.
    > He lived there **for two months.**
    > (=from October 10th to December 10th)
    > They stayed here **for five days**.
    > (=from Friday to Wednesday.)
3. Use *how long ago* to ask when an event happened.
    > **How long ago** did you get married?
    > (=when before now)
    > Five years ago.
4. Use *how long* to ask about the period of time.
    > **How long** were they married?
    > (=how many years)
    > For five years.

Future with *Be going to*: Statements

1. Use *be going to* + verb to talk about the future. Use *am, is,* or *are* before *going to*.
    > I **am going to leave** at 8 tomorrow.
    > Linda **is going to meet** me tomorrow afternoon.
    > Mike and Lee **are going to play** cards with us tomorrow night.
2. Always use the base form of the verb after *be going to*.
    > The store **is going to close.**
    > NOT ~~The store is going to closing~~.
3. Here are some common future time expressions:

later	this week
soon	this month
today	this year
this morning	next week
this afternoon	next month
this evening	next year
tomorrow	in one week
tomorrow morning	in two months

4. Sometimes people use *this morning* and *this afternoon* to talk about the past. For example, at 7 o'clock in the evening, someone says:
    > I went to the store this morning.
    > I went to the library this afternoon.
5. People often say *gonna* for *going to*. We do not write *gonna*.

Future with *Be going to*: *Yes / No* Questions

1. To make a *yes / no* question, change the word order of the subject and the verb *be*.
    > **They are** going to stay home.
    > **Are they** going to stay home?
2. There are two negative short answers. They have the same meaning.
    > Are they going to eat out?
    > No, they**'re not**. OR No, they **aren't.**

Be going to: Information Questions

1. In information questions, *am, is,* or *are* comes after the *wh-* word (*what, where,* etc.)
    > **What is Chris** going to do?
    > **Where are you** going to wait?
2. In conversation, the contracted form is common after the *wh-* word.
    > **What's** she going to wear?
    > (=What is she going to wear?)
    > **Where's** he going to work?
    > (=Where is he going to work?)
3. When *who* or *what* is the subject of the question, do not use *he, she, it*, etc., in the question.
    > **Who** is going to come?
    > (Subject)

Should: Affirmative and Negative Statements

1. Use *should* and *should not* to give advice and express opinions.
2. Use the base form of the verb after *should* or *should not*.

   You **should take** the medicine right now.
   You **should not forget**.
3. Use *shouldn't* + the base form of the verb for negative statements in conversation.

   You **shouldn't go** to work.
   The baby **shouldn't go** out in the sun.
4. The affirmative and negative forms are the same for all persons (*I, you, he, she, it, we, they*).

   I **should call** the doctor.
   She **should call** the doctor.
   We **shouldn't eat** cake.
   They **shouldn't eat** cake.
5. Use *should* to talk about the present and the future.

   You should put a band-aid on the cut **right now.**
   You should stay in bed all day **tomorrow.**

Should: Yes / No Questions

1. To make a *yes / no* question, put *should* before the subject and use the base form of the verb.

   We should eat more fish.
   Should we eat more fish?
   She should exercise every day.
   Should she exercise every day?
2. Use *should* in short answers.

   Should I ask the pharmacist?
   Yes, you **should**. OR No, you **shouldn't**.
3. Use *or* in questions with two possible answers.

   Should I take two **or** three pills?
   You should take two pills.
   Should I stay home **or** go to work?
   You should stay home.

Should: Information Questions

1. In information questions, *should* comes after the *wh*-word (*what, how much*, etc.)

   Where should I go?
   How often should he **take** the medicine?
2. Use *which* to ask questions about a choice. There is usually a noun after *which*.

   Which cough syrup should I buy?
   (There are five kinds of cough syrup.)
   Which hospital should we go to?
   (There are 10 hospitals in the city.)
3. Be careful! Questions with *who* have two forms.

   Who should take the medicine?
   (subject)
   Who should I call?
   (object)

Comparative of Adjectives

1. Use the comparative to compare two people, places, or things.

   Tim's car is **cheaper than** Jan's car.
   Houses are **more expensive than** apartments.
2. Use *-er* with adjectives that have one syllable.

   small → small**er**   cheap → cheap**er**
3. Use *-er* with two-syllable adjectives that end in *-y*. (Change the *-y* to *-i*.)

   prett**ier** [pret·ty]   dirt**ier** [dir·ty]
   1   2   1   2   1   2   1   2
4. We usually use *more* with two-syllable adjectives and adjectives with three or more syllables.

   more modern   [mod·ern]
                          1   2
   more beautiful [beau·ti·ful]
                        1   2 3
5. The comparative forms of *good, bad*, and *far* are irregular.

   good → **better**   bad → **worse**
   far → **farther**

Superlative of Adjectives

1. Use the superlative to compare three or more people, places, or things.

   We looked at five cars. The Honda Civic was **the cheapest**.
   There are three apartments for rent. The one on 1st Street is the **most expensive**.
2. Use *the* + *-est* with adjectives that have one syllable.

   small → **the smallest** / cheap → **the cheapest**
3. Use *the* + *-est* with two-syllable adjectives that end in *-y*. (Change the *-y* to *-i*.)

   the prettiest [pret·ty]   **the dirt**iest [dir·ty]
4. We usually use *the most* with two-syllable adjectives and adjectives that have three or more syllables.

   the most modern   [mod·ern]
   the most beautiful   [beau·ti·ful]
5. The superlative forms of *good, bad*, and *far* are irregular.

   good → **the best**   bad → **the worst**
   far → **the farthest**

Comparative and Superlative

1. Use the comparative to compare two people, places, or things. Use the superlative to compare three or more people, places, or things.

   Tim's car is **nicer than** Jan's car.
   We looked at five apartments.
   The apartment on Park Avenue was **the nicest**.
2. There are a few exceptions to the rules for forming the comparative and superlative. Here are some examples:

   more bored   the most bored
   quieter   the quietest
   simpler   the simplest
3. Look at page 263 for spelling rules with comparative and superlative forms.

Will: **Affirmative and Negative Statements**
1. Use *will* + verb to make predictions about the future. (You think something will happen, but you aren't sure.)
      Things **will be** more expensive next year.
2. Use the base form of the verb after *will*. For the negative of *will*, use *will not* and the base form of the verb.
      Tony and Rosa **will get** married.
      They **will not have** children.
3. Use the contraction *'ll* or *won't* + base form of the verb in conversation.
      You'll get a raise.
      You **won't lose** your job.
4. The affirmative and negative forms are the same for all persons (*I, you, he, she, it, we, they*).
      She **will meet** new people.
      They **won't be** from here.
5. We often use *probably* when we make predictions. Be careful! The word order is different with *will* and *won't*.
      He **will probably go** to the game.
      He **probably won't go** to the game.
6. We can also use *be going to* to make predictions about the future.
      He **is going to find** a good job.
7. Do not use *will* for plans about the future. Use *be going to* for future plans.
      We **are going to buy** a new car next year.

Will: **Yes / No Questions**
1. To make a *yes / no* question, put *will* before the subject and use the base form of the verb.
      They will need money.
      Will they need money?
2. We use *will* or *won't* in short answers.
      Will she get a raise?
      Yes, she **will**. OR No, she **won't**.

Will: **Information Questions**
1. In information questions, *will* comes after the *wh-* word (*what, where,* etc.)
      What will Chris buy?
      Where will you go?
2. When *who* or *what* is the subject of the question, do not use *he, she, it*, etc., in the question.
      Who will go to the bank? Jane will.
      (Subject)

Have to
1. Use *have to* or *has to* + infinitive form of the verb to talk about necessity.
      I **have to leave**. (=It is necessary for me to leave.)
2. Use *have to* with *I, you, we,* and *they*.
      I **have to** go.
      They **have to** buy round-trip tickets.
3. Use *has to* with the third person singular (*he, she, it*).
      He **has to** wait for the next train.
      The bus **has to** stop.
4. We also use *must* to talk about necessity, but *have to* is more common in conversation.
      You **must sit** in seat 4B.

Would like
1. *Would like* is a polite way of saying *want*.
      We would like some coffee, please.
2. Use the contraction *'d* + verb in conversation.
      I'd like a seat near the window.
3. *Would like* is the same for all persons (*I, you, he, she, it, we, they*).
      They**'d like** some tea.
      She**'d like** a different seat.
4. Use a noun or an infinitive after *would like*.
      I'd like **a sandwich.**
      I'd like **to have** a sandwich.
5. *Would you like . . .* is a polite way of asking people if they want something.
      A: **Would you like** to sit down?
      B: No, thank you. I'm fine.
6. Be careful! Don't confuse *would like* and *like*. *Would like* means *want*. *Like* means *enjoy*.
      Would you like (=Do you want) some tea?
      Do you like (=Do you enjoy) tea?

Can / Could / Would
1. There are several ways to make polite requests:
      Can you close the window, please?
      Can/Could I have two tickets, please?
      Could you close the window, please?
      Would you close the window, please?
2. *Can, could,* and *would* in polite requests are similar in meaning, but *could* and *would* are a little more polite.
3. Use *please* to be more polite. Put *please* at the end of the question or before the verb.
      Would you show me your ticket, **please**?
      Would you **please** show me your ticket?
4. There are many different answers to polite requests. *Sure* and *Of course* are common answers for *yes*. For *no*, we often say *Sorry* (or *I'm sorry*) and give a reason.
      A: Could you move your bag, please?
      B: Sure.
      A: Can you give me a dollar for the bus?
      B: I'm sorry, but I don't have any money.

Charts

Spelling Rules: Present Progressive

1. Add *–ing* to the base form of the verb. rain ⟶ rain**ing**

2. If a verb ends in *–e*, drop *–e* and add *–ing*. smoke ⟶ smok**ing**

3. If a verb ends in *–ie*, change *–ie* to *–y* and add *–ing*. die ⟶ d**ying**

4. If a verb is one syllable and ends in consonant + vowel + consonant (CVC), double the final consonant and add *–ing*. stop ⟶ stopp**ing**

5. Do not double the consonant if it is *w, x*, or *y*. Simply add *–ing*.
snow ⟶ snow**ing**
fix ⟶ fix**ing**
play ⟶ play**ing**

6. If the word has two or more syllables and ends in consonant + vowel + consonant (CVC), double the final consonant only if it is stressed.
permit ⟶ permitt**ing**
visit ⟶ visit**ing**

Spelling Rules: Simple Past of Regular Verbs

1. Add *–ed* to the base form of the verb. rain ⟶ rain**ed**

2. If a verb ends in *–e*, add *–d*. smoke ⟶ smok**ed**

3. If a verb ends in *–ie*, add *–d*. die ⟶ di**ed**

4. If the verb is one syllable and ends in consonant + vowel + consonant (CVC), double the final consonant and add *–ed*. stop ⟶ stopp**ed**

5. Do not double the consonant if it is *w, x*, or *y*. Simply add *–ed*.
snow ⟶ snow**ed**
fix ⟶ fix**ed**
play ⟶ play**ed**

6. If the word has two or more syllables and ends in consonant + vowel + consonant (CVC), double the final consonant only if it is stressed. Then add *–ed*.
permit ⟶ permitt**ed**
visit ⟶ visit**ed**

Spelling Rules for Plural Nouns

1. Add –*es* to words that end in –*ch*, –*s*, –*sh*, –*ss*, –*x*, or –*z*.	watch ⟶	watch**es**
	bus ⟶	bus**es**
	dish ⟶	dish**es**
	pass ⟶	pass**es**
	box ⟶	box**es**
2. Add –*es* to words that end in –*o*.	potato ⟶	potato**es**
3. If the word ends in consonant + –*y*, change –*y* to –*i* and add –*es*.	country ⟶	countr**ies**
4. Add –*s* to words that end in vowel + –*y*.	day ⟶	day**s**

Simple Present: Third Person Singular Spelling Rules

1. Add –*es* to words that end in –*ch*, –*s*, –*sh*, –*ss*, –*x*, or –*z*.	teach ⟶	teach**es**
	wash ⟶	wash**es**
	miss ⟶	miss**es**
	fix ⟶	fix**es**
	fizz ⟶	fizz**es**
2. Add –*es* to words that ends in –*o*.	do ⟶	do**es**
3. If the word ends in consonant + –*y*, change –*y* to –*i* and add –*es*.	cry ⟶	cr**ies**
4. Add –*s* to words that end in vowel + –*y*.	play ⟶	play**s**

Comparative Form of Adjectives

1. If the word ends in 1 vowel + 1 consonant, double the consonant and add –*er*.	thin ⟶	thinn**er**
2. If the word ends in –*y*, change –*y* to –*i* and add –*er*.	pretty ⟶	prett**ier**
3. If the word ends in –*e*, add –*r*.	nice ⟶	nic**er**

Superlative Form of Adjectives

1. If the word ends in 1 vowel + 1 consonant, double the consonant and add –*est*.	thin ⟶	thinn**est**
2. If the word ends in –*y*, change –*y* to –*i* and add –*est*.	pretty ⟶	prett**iest**
3. If the word ends in –*e*, add –*est*.	nice ⟶	nic**est**

Pronunciation Rules

1. If the word ends in a vowel sound or
   /b/, /d/, /g/, /l/, /m/, /n/, /ŋ/, /ɹ/, /θ/, /v/ or /w/,

   it is pronounced /z/.
   gives   onions   Tom's

2. If the word ends in /f/, /h/, /k/, /p/, /t/ or /ð/,

   it is pronounced /s/.
   walks   maps   Matt's

3. If the word ends in /tʃ/, /dʒ/, /s/, /ʃ/, /z/ or /ʒ/,

   it is pronounced /ɪz/.
   sneezes   watches   Nash's

4. If the base form ends in a vowel sound or /b/, /dʒ/, /g/
   /l/, /m/, /ŋ/, /ɹ/, /θ/, /v/, /w/, /z/, or /ʒ/,

   it is pronounced /d/.
   snowed   mailed

5. If the base forms ends in /tʃ/, /f/, /h/, /k/, /p/ or /s/,

   it is pronounced /t/,
   /ʃ/, or /ð/
   stopped   laughed

6. If the base form ends in /d/ or /t/,

   it is pronounced /ɪd/.
   needed   wanted

Telling Time

It's 5:10.
It's ten past five.
It's ten after five.

It's 6:30.
It's half past six.

It's 10:15.
It's a quarter past ten.

It's 9:50.
It's ten to ten.

It's 8:45.
It's a quarter to nine.

It's 11:00 in the morning.
It's 11 A.M.

It's 12:00 during the day.
It's 12 P.M. It's noon.

It's 11:00 at night.
It's 11 P.M.

It's 12:00 at night.
It's 12 A.M. It's midnight.

GO + VERB + –ING

go bowling	go hiking	go sailing
go camping	go horseback riding	go shopping
go dancing	go hunting	go skating
go fishing	go jogging	go skiing
go golfing	go running	go swimming

IRREGULAR VERBS

Base form	Simple Past	Base form	Simple Past
be	was	make	made
become	became	meet	met
buy	bought	pay	paid
catch	caught	put	put
come	came	read	read
cost	cost	ride	rode
cry	cried	ring	rang
cut	cut	run	ran
do	did	say	said
drink	drank	see	saw
drive	drove	sell	sold
eat	ate	send	sent
feel	felt	shine	shone
find	found	sit	sat
fly	flew	sleep	slept
forget	forgot	speak	spoke
get	got	spend	spent
give	gave	stand	stood
go	went	steal	stole
have	had	swim	swam
hear	heard	take	took
hit	hit	teach	taught
hold	held	think	thought
hurt	hurt	try	tried
know	knew	wake	woke
leave	left	wear	wore
lose	lost	win	won
		write	wrote

COMMON STATIVE VERBS

Senses	Possession	Likes	Needs	Mental States	Measurement	Description
feel	belong	hate	need	agree	cost	be
hear	have	like	want	believe	weigh	look
see	own	love		forget		seem
smell				know		
sound				remember		
taste				think		
				understand		

Partner Activities

From Time to Talk, PAGE 33

1. waiter

2. hairdresser

3. engineer

4. accountant

5. Mónica

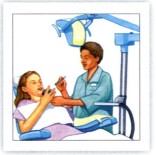

6. Lynn

7. Julio

8. Michael

9. Pete

10. Lili

11. Ali

12. Nicole

From Review and Challenge, Speaking, PAGE 34

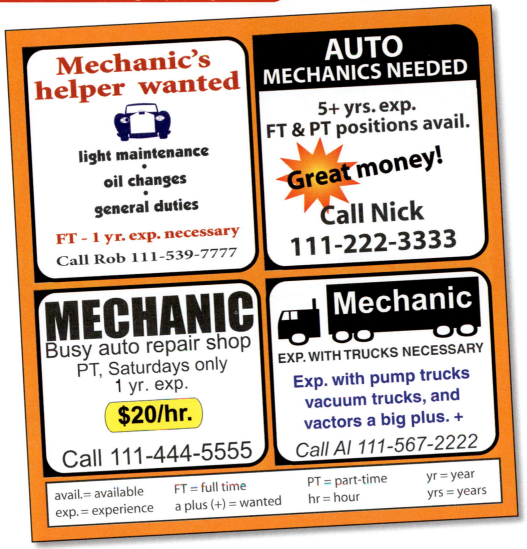

Mechanic's helper wanted

- light maintenance
- oil changes
- general duties

FT – 1 yr. exp. necessary

Call Rob 111-539-7777

AUTO MECHANICS NEEDED

5+ yrs. exp.
FT & PT positions avail.

Great money!

Call Nick
111-222-3333

MECHANIC
Busy auto repair shop
PT, Saturdays only
1 yr. exp.

$20/hr.

Call 111-444-5555

Mechanic

EXP. WITH TRUCKS NECESSARY

Exp. with pump trucks
vacuum trucks, and
vactors a big plus. +

Call Al 111-567-2222

avail. = available	FT = full time	PT = part-time	yr = year
exp. = experience	a plus (+) = wanted	hr = hour	yrs = years

From Time to Talk, PAGE 55

ACE Supermarket

SUPER SAVINGS ON FRUIT AND VEGETABLES!

Apples $1.75 lb.

Bananas $2.50 lb.

Potatoes 59¢ lb.

Spinach $3.00 lb.

Lettuce $2.00 lb.

From Time to Talk, PAGE 55

Deluxe supermarket

GREAT PRICES ON FRUIT AND VEGETABLES

fruit and vegetables

apples $1.85 lb.

potatoes 69¢ lb.

spinach $3.50 lb.

bananas $2.50 lb.

lettuce $2.50 lb.

From Speaking, PAGE 60

Lou's Food to Go

Menu

Chicken Soup.............$3.00	Hamburger............$5.00	Coffee..........$1.00
Cheese Sandwich.......$3.00	Cheeseburger........$5.50	Tea...............$1.00
Fried eggs on toast....$5.50	Pizza...................$3.50/slice	Soda.............$1.50

From Time to Talk, PAGE 71

Partner Activities 269

From Time to Talk, PAGE 81

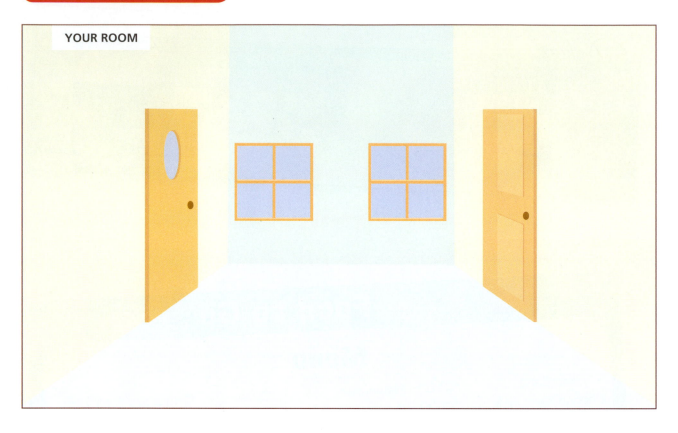

YOUR ROOM

From Time to Talk, PAGE 159

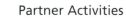

From Time to Talk, PAGE 71

From Time to Talk, PAGE 184

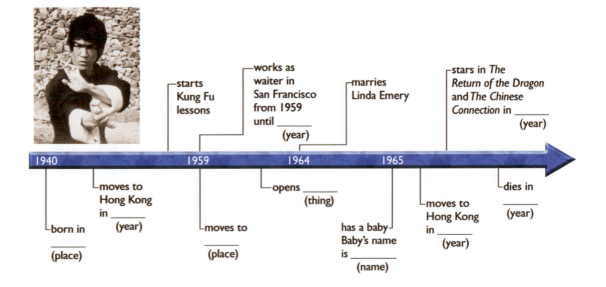

From Time to Talk, PAGE 81

YOUR CLASSMATE'S ROOM

From Speaking, PAGE 159

moves to
San Francisco

works from
1959 to 1961
as a _____
(job)

moves to
_____
(place)

stars in
two movies:
_____
_____

| 1941 | 1953 | 1959 | 1964 | 1971 | 1972 | 1973 |

moves to
_____
(place)

starts
_____
lessons

opens
Kung Fu
Institute
in Seattle
in _____
(year)

marries
_____
(name)

has a baby
boy, Brandon,
in _____
(year)

dies

born in
San Francisco
in _____
(year)

Apartments

2 BR. Great loc. near pub. trans., supermarket, & park.

No pets or smoking. $800 incl. util.

Studio in new bldg. Best loc. downtown, near shops, restaurants, clubs.

$750. Pking extra $150. pets OK.

Cute 3 BR house in quiet, friendly neighborhood 15 miles from city. Lrg. yard and 2-car garage.

$800, all util. incl. Pets OK.

Lrg. 3 BR. Great bldg., central loc. near hospitals and universities.

$1000 incl. 1 pking space.

bldg. = building
lrg. = large
pub. trans. = public transportation

BR = bedroom
loc. = location
util. = utilities (heat, hot water, electricity)

incl. = including or included
pking = parking

From Time to Talk, PAGE 219

	Designs for Today	American Homes	Best for Less
Sofa	$3,000	$900	$400
Lamp	$1,500	$175	$55
Rug	$5,000	$350	$75

From Speaking, PAGE 60

Sheila's
soups, salads, and sandwiches

Soups
Tomato soup	$5.00
Chicken soup	$5.00
Fish soup	$5.50

Salads
Egg salad	$5.50
Chicken salad	$6.00
Potato salad	$5.50
Mixed salad	$5.00
Fruit salad	$5.50

Sandwiches
Cheese sandwich	$6.00
Egg salad sandwich	$6.50
Chicken salad sandwich	$6.50
Hamburger	$7.00
Cheeseburger	$8.00

1. Martin

2. Meg

3. Marina

4. John

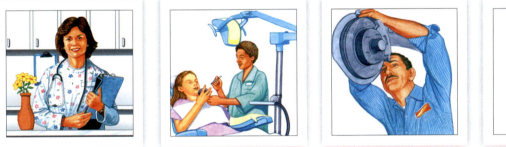

5. nurse

6. dentist

7. mechanic

8. electrician

9. Pete

10. Lili

11. Ali

12. Nicole

Audioscript

Unit 1: People

Listening, A and B, page 3

Ava:	Patty isn't here. Where is she?
Mia:	She's with her new boyfriend.
Ava:	Her new boyfriend?
Mia:	Yeah. His name's Álvaro.
Ava:	Álvaro? Is he American?
Mia:	No, he's not. He's Mexican.
Ava:	Is he good-looking?
Mia:	He's OK. He's tall. He isn't thin, but he isn't heavy. He's average weight.
Ava:	Are he and Patty students in the same class?
Mia:	No, they're not. They're neighbors. And he's a doctor, not a student.
Ava:	A doctor? Is he old?
Mia:	No, he's not old. He's about 35.
Ava:	35? But Patty's only 22.
Mia:	So? 35 isn't old!

Grammar to Communicate 2, C, page 7

Lara:	Are you a student in this class?
Bob:	No, I'm the teacher.
Lara:	Oh, are you Professor Michaelson?
Bob:	Yes, I am. Are you in English 101?
Lara:	Yes, I am.
Bob:	Then you're in my class. Welcome.

Grammar to Communicate 3, B, page 8

1. Are your classmates noisy?
2. Are most actors rich?
3. Are most actresses beautiful?
4. Are your parents young?
5. Are your friends smart?
6. Are the classes small at your school?

Review and Challenge

Grammar, page 10

Juan:	Hello. I'm Juan Montero.
Nicole:	Hi. My name is Nicole Summers
Juan:	Are you from Miami?
Nicole:	Yes, I am. My boyfriend is from here, too.
Juan:	My girlfriend and I are not from here. We're from Caracas, Venezuela.
Nicole:	Is Caracas nice?
Juan:	Very nice. The people are friendly.

Dictation, page 10

1. I'm late.
2. Are they here now?
3. Are they men or women?
4. She isn't short.
5. He's tall and handsome.

Listening, A and B, page 11

Reporter:	Good Morning. This is Amy Warren reporting for WKBC. Today's topic is happiness. What are the secrets of happy people? A new study says that one secret is marriage. 38 percent of married women and 42 percent of married men say they are very happy. But only 22 percent of single people are happy. A second secret is age. 65 percent of people who are 50 say they are happy, but only 52 percent of 20-year-olds are happy. Isn't that interesting? So, what is the secret to a happy life? Let's ask some people on the street. Hello, sir? I'm a reporter for WKBC News. May I ask you a question?
Man 1:	Okay . . .
Reporter:	What is the secret to a happy life?
Man 1:	Hmmm . . . Oh, I know—good health and the love of a good woman.
Reporter:	How about you? Are you happy?
Man 2:	Yes, I am.
Reporter:	What's your secret?
Man 2:	Well, I'm an easygoing guy. Life is short, so I try to have fun.
Reporter:	Excuse me, ma'am?
Woman:	I don't have time! I'm late for work!
Reporter:	Oh well, she's probably not a good person to ask! For WKBC, this is Amy Warren . . .

Unit 2: Families

Listening, A and B, page 15

Mark:	Is this your family?
Elena:	Yes, it is.
Mark:	Wow, your family is big! Is she your mother?
Elena:	Yeah. She's my mom.
Mark:	She's beautiful—like you!
Elena:	Thank you!
Mark:	Who are they? Are they your brothers?
Elena:	No, they're my father's brothers—my uncles.
Mark:	Really? How old are they?
Elena:	Eduardo is 10, and Felipe is 12.
Mark:	Wow . . . Your uncles are children!
Elena:	That's right!

Grammar to Communicate 1, C, page 17

Stan: Hi. I'm your new neighbor. My name is Stan Sims.

Betty: It's nice to meet you, Stan. I'm Betty.

Stan: Nice to meet you, too. Um … are you Josh's mother?

Betty: No, Ann and Jim Parr are his parents. Their apartment is next door.

Stan: Oh. Well, he's very noisy! His music is always so loud.

Betty: Um … that's our daughter's music. Is it loud? Sorry!

Stan: Oh! Um . . that's OK . . . It is nice music. Is she a music student?

Betty: Yes, she is! We're very proud of her.

Grammar to Communicate 3, C, page 21

1. **A:** Where are your parents from?
   B: My parents are from South Korea.
2. **A:** How is your family?
   B: My family's fine, thanks.
3. **A:** How old are you?
   B: I'm 19.
4. **A:** Who's Nina?
   B: Nina is my aunt—my mother's sister.
5. **A:** Where are the children?
   B: The children are at my mother's house.
6. **A:** How tall is your brother?
   B: My brother is six feet tall.
7. **A:** What are your uncles' names?
   B: My uncles' names are Greg and Norman.

Review and Challenge

Grammar, page 22

Andrea: This is a nice picture. Who's in it?

Leona: Oh, that's my son, Paul. And here's a picture of his children—my two grandsons and my granddaughter.

Andrea: What are their names?

Leona: The boys' names are Bill and Tommy. Their sister's name is Alicia.

Andrea: They're cute! How old is Alicia?

Leona: Oh, she's 7 years old. And here she is in a picture with her mother.

Andrea: Oh, so that's your daughter-in-law. She's pretty.

Leona: Yes, she is.

Dictation, page 22

1. Is she your mother?
2. No, she's my mother-in-law.
3. How old are they?
4. Who is he?
5. They're my mother's brothers.

Listening, A and B, page 23

Reporter: Good afternoon. This is Carla Espinoza for

World Beat. This week, our topic is family life around the world. Today, let's look at two families, from two very different parts of the world: Italy and Saudi Arabia. Silvia Bertolino is from an Italian family. She is 10 years old. Her father is 42 and her mother is 37. Silvia's family is like many Italian families today. In Italy, the age of marriage for most women is about 27. For men, it's a little older—about 30. Like many Italian children these days, Silvia is an only child—she has no brothers or sisters. Silvia is close to both her parents. Saleh Al-Ahmed is from Saudi Arabia. He is one of ten children. In Saudi Arabia, many family members live together in one large house. In Saleh's house, for example, there are 14 people: Saleh, his parents, his father's parents, three of Saleh's seven sisters, his two married brothers, his brothers' wives, and their two children. Saleh's four married sisters live in their own houses with their husbands, children, and in-laws. In Saudi Arabia, married women usually live with their in-laws. That's all for today. Tomorrow, we'll talk about Brazil and Mexico.

Unit 3: Jobs

Listening, A and B, page 27

Bill: Hey, Nick, what's up? How are you?

Nick: I'm great. I have a new job.

Bill: Really?

Nick: Yeah, I'm a cook at Rico's on First Street.

Bill: Oh, my friend Andy is a cook there too.

Nick: Oh yeah, Andy…he's the breakfast cook. I'm the lunch cook.

Bill: So, how is it?

Nick: Well, it isn't an easy job, but it's interesting. The restaurant is always busy.

Bill: Is the pay good?

Nick: It's not bad. And the boss is a nice guy. How about you? Are you still in school?

Bill: No, I'm an electrician now.

Nick: An electrician! Good for you!

Bill: Yeah, it's great. Anyway, I have to get going— I'm late for work! I'll see you later—Oh, and say hi to Andy for me!

Nick: I will. Take it easy!

Bill: You too.

Review and Challenge

Dictation, page 34

1. She's a good dentist.
2. Are you the doctor?
3. The mechanics are fast.
4. It isn't an interesting job.
5. They're messy cooks.

Man: Good morning, Stage Restaurant.

Gabriella: Hello. I'm calling about the job in Sunday's Newspaper . . . for a waitress?

Man: Just a minute, please. I'll get the manager.

Tommy: Hello? This is Tommy. So . . . are you an experienced waitress?

Gabriella: Yes, I am.

Tommy: How much experience?

Gabriella: One year at McDonald's and one year as the morning waitress at Bob's Diner in Brooklyn.

Tommy: Oh, Bob's Diner. It's a very busy place . . . lots of customers. Are you fast?

Gabriella: Yes, I think so. And I'm very organized.

Tommy: Good. Are you available on weekends?

Gabriella: I'm available on Saturdays, but not on Sundays.

Tommy: Are you available in the morning?

Gabriella: Yes, I am.

Tommy: Okay, I need a waitress Wednesdays to Saturdays, from 5:00 to 11:00 A.M. Are you interested?

Gabriella: Yes, I am.

Tommy: Can you come in today for an interview?

Gabriella: What time?

Tommy: 3:00. Ask for me—Tom Jackson.

Gabriella: Tom Jackson. Great! Thank you very much.

Tommy: Oh, wait a minute. What's your name?

Gabriella: Oh, I'm sorry. I'm Gabriella Campozano.

Tommy: Okay, Gabriella, so we'll see you at 3:00.

Gabriella: Okay, thanks a lot. Goodbye.

Tommy: 'Bye.

Unit 4: Places

Listening, A and B, page 39

Pedro: Hi, Natasha! How are you? How's your new apartment?

Natasha: It's great! And it's in a wonderful neighborhood.

Pedro: Really?

Natasha: There are some nice stores and cafés, and there's a new movie theater on the next street.

Pedro: It sounds nice. Are there any good restaurants?

Natasha: Yes. There's a good restaurant near my apartment building. It's expensive, but the food is excellent. There are also some cheap restaurants in the neighborhood.

Pedro: Is there a supermarket near your apartment?

Natasha: No, there isn't a supermarket, but there's a big outdoor market.

Pedro: And is there a nice park?

Natasha: There aren't any parks, but there's a beautiful beach.

Pedro: Wow. You're lucky! My apartment is nice, but there aren't any restaurants in my neighborhood, and there isn't a beach! Hey— are there any apartments for rent in your building?

Natasha: I'm not sure, but I'll ask.

Pedro: Thanks.

Review and Challenge

Grammar, page 46

A: I'm from Pittsburgh. It's a great city. There are a lot of stores and beautiful houses.

B: Are there any good restaurants?

A: Oh, yes. There are some Italian and Chinese restaurants in my neighborhood. And they're cheap, too.

B: Is there an art museum in Pittsburgh?

A: Yes. There are three.

B: Is there a new airport?

A: No, there isn't. But our airport is nice.

B: So Pittsburgh is a small city.

A: Yes, it is. But it's really nice.

Dictation, page 46

1. Is there a movie theater near your apartment?
2. There are some expensive stores in the mall.
3. Are there any cheap restaurants?
4. There aren't any supermarkets.
5. There's an apartment building near my house.

Listening, A and B, page 47

Woman 1: Shopping for food is so different here in the United States!

Woman 2: Really? How?

Woman 1: Well, in the United States, there are big supermarkets, but in Colombia, there are a lot of small food stores. For example, in my neighborhood, there's a bakery with delicious bread. There is also an outdoor market with wonderful fruit and vegetables.

Woman 2: Are there any big supermarkets in Colombia?

Woman 1: Yes, of course there are some big supermarkets. But small stores and outdoor food markets are more popular than supermarkets.

Woman 2: But what about price? In the United States, the food in small stores is usually expensive.

Woman 1: Really? That's interesting. In Colombia, big supermarkets are expensive. The food in small stores and outdoor markets is cheap.

Unit 5: Food and Drink

René: Look at these oranges-- $1.89 a pound! That's crazy! Fruit in the United States is so expensive! In Haiti, the fruit is delicious, and it's very cheap.

Lynn: How much are oranges in Haiti?

René: Oh, an orange is just a few cents—maybe 25 cents a pound.

Lynn: That is cheap! Is everything there so cheap?

René: Well, some food is. Vegetables are really cheap…and rice is too, but meat is expensive. And fruit is really cheap. Hmm…There aren't any tomatoes.

Worker: There are a few tomatoes over there, next to the bananas.

René: Oh, great. Thanks. Hmm, is there any spinach?

Worker: It's right here. How much do you need?

René: Just a little. One package is fine.

Lynn: Wow, these tomatoes are expensive—$5.00 a pound!

René: $5.00 a pound? How many are there in a pound?

Worker: A few—about 3 or 4.

René: Forget it!! At that price, I don't need any . . .

Grammar to Communicate 1, D, page 55

1. **Man:** How much are the bananas?
   Woman: They're $1.79.
2. **Man:** How much is the milk?
   Woman: It's $1.89.
3. **Man:** How much is the juice?
   Woman: It's $3.06.
4. **Man:** How much is the rice?
   Woman: It's $2.89.
5. **Woman:** How much are the potatoes?
   Man: They're $1.99.
6. **Woman:** How much are the eggs?
   Man: They're $1.79.
7. **Woman:** How much is the candy?
   Man: It's $2.50.
8. **Woman:** How much is the coffee?
   Man: It's $3.49.
9. **Woman:** How much are the oranges?
   Man: They're $2.00.

Grammar to Communicate 3, A, page 58

1. **Woman 1:** Is there any coffee?
   Woman 2: Yes, there is.
2. **Woman 1:** Are there any eggs?
   Woman 2: No, there aren't.
3. **Woman 1:** Is there any tea?
   Woman 2: Yes, there is.
4. **Woman 1:** Are there any cookies?
   Woman 2: Yes, there are.
5. **Man 1:** Are there any nuts?
   Man 2: No, there aren't.
6. **Man 1:** Is there any sugar?
   Man 2: Yes, there is.
7. **Man 1:** Is there any candy?
   Man 2: No, there isn't.
8. **Man 1:** Is there any juice?
   Man 2: No, there isn't.

Review and Challenge

Grammar, page 60

A: How many potatoes are there?

B: There aren't any potatoes, but there are a few tomatoes.

A: Is there any fruit?

B: There's a little.

A: Is there any beef?

B: No, there isn't any beef.

A: Okay. And how much soda is there?

Dictation, page 60

1. There's an onion in the bag.
2. Is there any meat?
3. There's a little ice cream.
4. How many apples are there?
5. There isn't any candy here.

Listening, A and B, page 61

Sarah: Alice, is that you?

Alice: Yes? Oh, hi, Sarah! How are you?

Sarah: Fine . . . I'm fine. I'm surprised to see you here. Don't you usually shop at Joe's?

Alice: Yes, but I'm not happy with Joe's.

Sarah: Really? Why?

Alice: Well, it isn't very clean. There are never any shopping carts, there are long lines, and the workers aren't helpful.

Sarah: Well, the workers are very nice at Sam's. And it's very clean. But it's expensive. The prices are good at Joe's, right?

Alice: Yes, but they're still too expensive.

Sarah: But Sam's isn't very convenient for you. Your new apartment isn't near here, is it?

Alice: You're right. That is a problem. I'm still not sure what to do . . .

Unit 6: Physical Exercise

Listening, A and B, page 65

Maria: Hello, Jenny? It's Maria! How are you doing?

Jenny: Oh hi, Maria! I'm great. How are you? How's college?

Maria: Oh, it's okay. Is Mom there?

Jenny: No, she isn't. She's at the health club.

Maria: At the health club? What's she doing there?

Jenny: She's swimming.

Maria: What? Mom's swimming!

Jenny: Yeah.

Maria: Well, is Dad at home?

Jenny: No, he isn't. He's out too.

Maria: What's he doing?

Jenny: He's out riding his bike.

Maria: What??? Dad is riding a bike!

Jenny: Yup.

Maria: Amazing…Well, is Bob at home?

Jenny: Nope.

Maria: Wait, let me think . . . he's running.

Jenny: No, he's playing tennis.

Maria: Bob? Playing tennis? Are you kidding? It's Sunday afternoon, and he and Dad aren't watching a soccer game on TV?

Jenny: It's true!!!! Everyone's out exercising.

Maria: What's going on there? Are you all going exercise crazy?

Jenny: Everybody except me.

Maria: Why? What are you doing?

Jenny: I'm talking to you!

Grammar to Communicate 3, C, page 71

Alice: Hi? Jean? This is Alice. Is Rita there?

Jean: No, she's not.

Alice: What's she doing?

Jean: She's playing tennis with Sue.

Alice: How about Tom? Is he at home?

Jean: No, he's not.

Alice: What's he doing?

Jean: He's playing soccer.

Alice: Who's he playing with?

Jean: With Phil and some other friends.

Alice: Where are they playing?

Jean: At Sandy Field.

Alice: Sandy Field? Why are they playing at Sandy Field?

Jean: Because another team is playing at Bradley Field today.

Alice: What are you eating?

Jean: Me? I'm eating an apple…And why are you asking so many questions today?

Review and Challenge

Grammar, page 72

Mike: Hi, Tina. It's me, Mike. What are you doing?

Tina: I'm reading a book.

Mike: Where are you?

Tina: At the health club.

Mike: Why are you reading a book at the health club?

Tina: I'm sitting in the café. I'm waiting for Sara.

Mike: Is she exercising?

Tina: No, she's not. She's taking a shower. Oh, she's coming now.

Sara: Hi, Tina!...Who are you talking to?

Tina: I'm talking to Mike.

Dictation, page 72

1. What are they doing?
2. They're playing soccer.
3. Are they playing in a park?
4. No, they're not.
5. She's not watching a game.

Listening, A and B, page 73

Billy: Good morning. This is Billy Jackson, here at the Summer Olympics. First, let's see how the marathoners are doing. Hello, Fatima?

Fatima: Good morning, Billy! Well, no surprises here today. We're 30 minutes into the race, and so far the Brazilian, Roberto Moto, is winning. But two brothers from Kenya, Kamau Ngugi and Yoni Ngugi, are running close behind him.

Billy: Thank you, Fatima. Now, down to the tennis courts . . . Hello, Pam? Is anything happening there today?

Pam: Hi, Billy. There aren't any matches today, but the Canadian player Christie Daniels is practicing on center court—in the rain.

Billy: That's why she's a winner! Thanks, Pam . . . Now, let's see how things are going at the swimming pool . . . Jerry? What's happening there?

Jerry: Well, the women's 100-meter race is tomorrow, so the swimmers are practicing for that. A group of women are swimming in the pool right now.

Billy: Who's looking good?

Jerry: Well, Yuko Kamata from Japan is swimming really well.

Billy: Thanks, Jerry . . . Now, back to the marathon . . .

Unit 7: Do's and Don'ts

Listening, A and B, page 77

Mother: Matthew, what are you doing?

Matthew: I'm doing my homework.

Mother: Really? Then why is the TV on? You aren't doing your homework! You're watching TV! Turn it off right now!

Matthew: But I am doing my homework...

Mother: So where is it?

Matthew: Here.

Mother: OK, now listen to me. First, finish your homework. Do it right now, and don't be careless. Then, clean your room. Make your bed and put your clothes in the closet. Don't put them under your bed, like last time.

Matthew: Yes, Mom.

Mother: Oh, and one more thing. Don't touch the telephone!

Matthew: But Sylvia is waiting for me to call!

Mother: Well, too bad. Call her tomorrow. And don't eat potato chips! We're having dinner in an hour!

Grammar to Communicate 3, C, page 83

Ana: What exercises are you doing?

Tomás: B and C.

Ana: Are they difficult?

Tomás: I'm not sure. I'm starting them now. Sit down and help me.

Ana: Okay. Hmm. They are difficult.

Tomás: David's a good student. Ask him for help.

Ana: He's not in class today.

Tomás: Then ask her.

Ana: Who?

Tomás: Safira. She's your friend, right?

Ana: Yes, she is. Hey, Safira! Help us with Exercises B and C.

Safira: I'm busy!

Review and Challenge

Dictation, page 84

1. Don't put your shoes in the closet.
2. Listen to them.
3. Wait for me.
4. Please put the bike behind the door.
5. Please don't turn on the TV.

Listening, A and B, page 85

CONVERSATION 1

Man: Stop! Put your hands on your head. Stay where you are. Don't move.

CONVERSATION 2

Woman: Open your mouth and say ahhhhhhhh.

Man: Ahhhhhhhh.

Woman: Good. Now, look at the light. Don't close your eyes.

CONVERSATION 3

Man: Okay, go ahead and rinse.

Man: Okay?

Woman: Mmm-hmm.

Man: Okay, so sit back and open your mouth. Not so wide—close it a little, please. Perfect! You're doing great! We're almost finished.

CONVERSATION 4

Man: Watch out! There's a car coming.

Woman: Oh, thank you.

CONVERSATION 5

Woman: We are approaching Dulles International Airport. Please put your bags under your seat.

CONVERSATION 6

Announcer: Flight #243 is now boarding at Gate 27.

Man: Have a great trip!

Woman: Write to me!

Man: You too! And call me when you get there.

Unit 8: Possessions

Listening, A and B, page 89

Sammi: What's that in your hand?

Bob: This is a camera.

Sammi: Really? But it's the size of a credit card!

Bob: I know. Isn't it cool? My brother has one, and it takes great pictures.

Sammi: Amazing…Excuse me, ma'am, what are those, over there, on the wall?

Saleswoman: Oh, those are speakers.

Sammi: They're so small!

Saleswoman: Yes, but the sound is excellent. Listen to this…

Bob: Wow! Those are great!

Sammi: Hey. What's this?

Saleswoman: That's mine. It's not for sale.

Bob: But what is it?

Saleswoman: It's a radio. We have other radios over there.

Sammi: Amazing…it's so thin—like a piece of paper! Is this yours too?

Saleswoman: No, it isn't. Phil, is this cell phone yours?

Phil: No, it's not mine.

Bob: Hey, that cell phone is mine. And those keys are mine too.

Sammi: These? Here you are. And are these your sunglasses?

Grammar to Communicate 1, C, page 91

1. **A:** What's this?
   B: It's a wallet.
2. **A:** What are these?
   B: They're rings.
3. **A:** What's that?
   B: It's a backpack.
4. **A:** What are those?
   B: They're sunglasses.
5. **A:** What are these?
   B: They're earrings.
6. **A:** What's that?
   B: It's a radio.

Grammar to Communicate 1, D, page 91

1. That is a nice ring.
2. Those are beautiful earrings.
3. That is a nice watch.
4. Those are beautiful sunglasses.

Grammar to Communicate 2, C, page 93

1. **A:** Are these glasses yours?
   B: Yes, they are.
2. **A:** Are these Nicole's glasses?
   B: No. Hers are different.
3. **A:** Hello. I'm Ming Lee and this is my wife, Chiao-lun.
   B: It's nice to meet you.
4. **A:** My name is Ed. What's yours?
   B: Hi, Ed. I'm Stella.
5. **A:** Is that the children's dog?
   B: No. Theirs is black.
6. **A:** Is that a picture of you and Chris?
   B: Yes. And that's our home.
7. **A:** Who's the woman with Ari?
   B: That's his wife.
8. **A:** Is Ari's home in Boston?
   B: No. His is in Cambridge. His brother's is in Boston.

Grammar to Communicate 2, D, page 93

1. **A:** Here's your book.
   B: That's not mine.
2. **A:** Bill and Sue, your dogs are nice.
   B: Those dogs aren't ours.
3. **A:** Are those our records?
   B: No, these are yours.
4. **A:** Is Anna's cell phone black?
   B: No, hers is blue.
5. **A:** They can't find their keys.
   B: Are those keys on the table theirs?
6. **A:** Is that his car in front of the house?
   B: No, his is at home.

Review and Challenge

Grammar, page 96

Carrie: Are these your earrings?
Nadia: Yes, they are. And these are my rings.
Carrie: They're nice. And is that your cell phone over there on the table?
Nadia: No, this is my cell phone.
Carrie: Maybe it's Ann's phone. She has a red phone.
Nadia: No, it's not hers. Her phone is in her bag.

Dictation, page 96

1. This is a camera.
2. Is this radio yours?
3. We have a new computer.
4. My sister has a great stereo.
5. Those are mine.

Listening, A and B, page 97

CONVERSATION 1
Man: Here you go.
Woman: Wait a minute. This is hers, not mine. I ordered fish.
Man: Oh, sorry about that. Here you go. Can I get you anything else right now?

CONVERSATION 2
Man 1: Excuse me, I'm with airport security. Is that your briefcase over there?
Man 2: Where? No, it's not. This is mine, right here.
Man 1: Excuse me, miss, is this yours?
Woman: That? No, sorry, it isn't.
Man 3: Excuse me, sir, is there a problem?
Man 1: Is this yours?
Man 3: That's my briefcase, yes. What's the problem?

CONVERSATION 3
Woman: Are these yours?
Man: No, they're Jamie's.
Woman: Jamie!!
Jamie: Yeah? What's wrong?
Woman: What are your sneakers doing in the middle of the living room?
Jamie: Those aren't mine.
Woman: Well then whose are they? And why are they in the middle of the living room?

CONVERSATION 4
Policeman: Is this your car?
Woman: Yes. Why?
Policeman: It's in a no parking zone.
Woman: No, it isn't. Look at that sign. It says no parking except on Sundays.
Policeman: Today's Saturday.

| Woman: | Oh…well look at all those cars over there. Are you going to give them tickets too? |
| Policeman: | No, theirs are on the right side of the street. Yours is the only car on the left side. |

Unit 9: Routines

Listening, A and B, page 103

Taka:	Hey, Monique, you come from France, right?
Monique:	Yes, why?
Taka:	It says here that in France, most workers have a two-hour break for lunch. Is that true?
Monique:	Well, it depends on the job, but in general, it's true. Many people in France have lunch at home. My mother, my sister, and I eat lunch together every day. But my father works in another city, so he doesn't eat with us.
Taka:	Really? That's interesting. In Japan, we only have an hour for lunch, so we don't have time to go home. I think I like the French way!
Monique:	I do too, but there is one problem. We start work at 8:30, but because we have a break for lunch from 12-2:00, we work until 6:00. In Japan, you only work until 5:00 right?
Taka:	No, we don't! Many people go to work at 8:00 in the morning and finish at 6:00 or even later. My father has his own business. He works 12 hours a day or more. On weekdays, he leaves the house at 7:00, and gets home at 10:00 at night, so he doesn't eat lunch or dinner with us.
Monique:	Business owners in France work long days too. But most of the French work five days a week. They have weekends off, except people who work in banks and shops. They work on Saturday, so they don't work on Sunday or Monday.

Grammar to Communicate 2, B, page 106

1. My daughter brushes her hair all the time.
2. My mother reads the newspaper.
3. My friend Sam drinks coffee.
4. My sister takes the bus to work.
5. My uncle washes his car once a week.

Review and Challenge

Grammar, page 110

| Woman: | My roommates and I don't have the same routines. Julia gets up late, at around 10:00 A.M. Katie and I get up early. Katie has class at 8:00 A.M., and I start work at 9:00 A.M. Julia doesn't work. She just takes two classes in the afternoon. She's lucky because she finishes early. Then she goes out with friends. She doesn't study very much, and she doesn't cook. Katie and I study and go to work every day. Julia's life is pretty good! |

Dictation, page 110

1. I don't eat with my family.
2. My mother works from 9 to 4.
3. My brother has lunch at home.
4. My father doesn't finish late.
5. My children leave the house early.

Listening, A and B, page 111

| Reporter: | Good morning. This is Claire Goodwin reporting. Today we are looking at the way that people around the world spend—and don't spend—their time. The information in this report comes from a study by the Roper Center for Public Opinion Research. Let's start with sleep, work and food. First, sleep—something that we all need. On average, the typical adult sleeps 7.4 hours a day. People from Japan don't sleep much—only 6.7 hours a day. People from South Africa sleep the most—7.9 hours. How about work? The average adult works 9.6 hours a day, but workers in Argentina and Turkey work 9.8 hours a day on average. And what about housework? It depends on whether you are a man or a woman. Worldwide, only 15% of men do housework every day, but in South Africa the percentage is 29%. In Turkey and Egypt, the number of men who do housework every day or most days is low, only 6% in Turkey and 4% in Egypt. Finally, let's discuss food and eating. 79% of people around the world eat at home with their family every day or almost every day. And who cooks? Mostly women—only 21 % of men worldwide cook every day. In Egypt, the typical man doesn't cook much. Only 2% of Egyptian men say that they cook every day or most days. |

Unit 10: Shopping

Listening, A and B, page 115

Martin:	Honey? Do you have your credit card?
Veronica:	Yes, I do. But where's yours?
Martin:	At home.
Veronica:	You never have your credit card with you!
Martin:	That's why I don't spend a lot of money.
Veronica:	You don't, but I do! So, what do you want this time?
Martin:	Great Buy has DVD players on sale. They're 25% off.
Veronica:	Do we need a DVD player?
Martin:	Well, movies are all on DVD these days.
Veronica:	But we never watch movies.

Martin:	That's because we don't have a DVD player.
Veronica:	Okay, so what kind is it?
Martin:	It's a Sovy.
Veronica:	And how much does it cost?
Martin:	$199.
Veronica:	Forget it! That's a lot of money.
Martin:	You always say that.
Veronica:	And you always want to spend a lot of money!

Grammar to Communicate 1, C, page 117

1. I am always friendly.
2. The store sometimes has sales.
3. I am never late for work.
4. The store always opens at 9:00.
5. The customers are usually nice.
6. I love my job. It is never boring.
7. The customers often ask me questions.

Grammar to Communicate 3, C, page 121

1. **A:** I like the T-shirt in the catalog.
   B: How much does it cost?
   A: It's $15.66 including tax.
2. **A:** You have a big car, right?
   B: No, I don't.
   A: What kind of car do you have?
   B: I have a very small car.
3. **A:** Julie doesn't like gold earrings.
   B: What kind of earrings does she like?
   A: Silver.
4. **A:** Marks and Lit Brothers are good stores.
   B: What do they sell?
   A: Clothes, jewelry, umbrellas, handbags—a lot of different things.
5. **A:** My daughter goes to the mall a lot.
   B: How often does she go?
   A: Every weekend.

Review and Challenge

Dictation, page 122

1. She never shops at that store.
2. What kind of camera do you want?
3. How much does this DVD cost?
4. Does the customer want the jacket?
5. Do you and your friend often go to the mall?

Listening, A and B, page 123

CONVERSATION 1

Man:	What kind of TV are you looking for—a regular or a flat screen?
Woman:	How much does the flat screen TV cost?
Man:	It's usually $499, but it's on sale this week for only $299. And the price includes the sales tax.

| Woman: | Wow! That's a great price for a flat screen, but it's still too expensive for me. |

CONVERSATION 2

Man:	What do you want for your birthday? Do you like any of the rings?
Woman:	I like all of them, but they're so expensive.
Man:	Don't worry about that. It's your birthday!
Woman:	Oh, honey. You're so sweet, but we don't have enough money to buy things like this. Anyway, I don't need a new ring.

CONVERSATION 3

Woman:	Paper or plastic?
Man:	Excuse me?
Woman:	What kind of bag do you want?
Man:	I'm sorry?
Woman:	Do you want a paper bag or a plastic one?
Man:	Oh, paper please.

CONVERSATION 4

Man:	Where are the tomatoes?
Woman:	I'm sorry, we don't have any today.
Man:	But you always have tomatoes!

Unit 11: Holidays and Special Occasions

Listening, A and B, page 127

Julie:	Hey, Petra. What's wrong? You don't look very happy.
Petra:	Oh, this weekend is my first birthday alone— my family and friends aren't here. I really miss them.
Julie:	Oh, that's hard. So . . . how do you usually celebrate your birthday?
Petra:	Well, my friends send me cards, and all of my relatives call me.
Julie:	Do you have a party?
Petra:	Oh, yes. We always have a big party.
Julie:	Who do you invite?
Petra:	My friends, my parents' friends, my sisters' friends, and my relatives.
Julie:	Wow. You need a big place for a party like that. Where do you usually have it?
Petra:	Oh, we have a big house.
Julie:	And who makes the food for all those people?
Petra:	My mother, my sisters, and I make almost everything. My grandmother makes the birthday cake.
Julie:	Do all of the people at the party give you gifts?
Petra:	I get some gifts and a lot of flowers and chocolates.
Julie:	And what do you want this year?
Petra:	I want to celebrate my birthday with my family and friends!

Grammar to Communicate 2, B, page 130

1. **Ted:** We celebrate Mother's Day to show that we love our mothers.
   Lia: Why do you celebrate Father's Day?
   Ted: To show that we love our fathers, of course!
2. **Ted:** We celebrate Mother's Day on the second Sunday in May.
   Lia: When do you celebrate Father's Day?
   Ted: On the third Sunday in June.
3. **Ted:** We celebrate Mother's Day in different ways. Most people send cards.
   Lia: How do you celebrate Father's Day?
   Ted: We send cards on Father's Day, too.
4. **Ted:** Mothers often get flowers.
   Lia: What do fathers get?
   Ted: Fathers often get ties.

Review and Challenge

Dictation, page 134

1. I send my friends cards.
2. When do you give presents?
3. Who pays for the party?
4. Who does your family visit on the holiday?
5. Children give flowers to their teachers.

Listening, A and B, page 135

Reporter: Good afternoon. This is Carla Espinoza for World Beat. This week, our topic is gift-giving around the world. In every country, people give gifts on special occasions. But gift-giving customs are different in different countries. Before you give someone from another country a gift, you need to learn about that country's customs. Here are some questions to ask: What kinds of gifts do people usually give in that country? What kinds of gifts do they never give? When do they give gifts? Why do they give them? Who do they give them to? What do you do when someone gives you a gift? Here are some interesting facts. People in China and Japan always use two hands when they give or receive a gift. But in Egypt and most Middle Eastern countries, you give and receive gifts only with your right hand. In most countries, people wrap gifts in paper. However, the color of the paper is very important. In many parts of Asia, white is not a good color for gift wrapping, because people there wear white when someone dies. In Brazil, the color purple has the same meaning, so Brazilians hardly ever wrap gifts in purple paper. And in both South America and Asia, people never give knives to their friends because a knife means the end of the friendship. That's all for today. Tomorrow, we'll talk about the gifts people give and get on New Year's Day.

Unit 12: At work

Listening, A and B, page 139

Doris: Excuse me, Mr. Yu?
Mr. Yu: Yes, Doris? Please, come in. So, what are you doing here today? You don't usually work on Mondays, do you?
Doris: No, I'm working for Liz today. She's visiting her mom in the hospital.
Mr. Yu: Oh, that's right. How is her mother doing?
Doris: She's doing very well.
Mr. Yu: Oh, that's good. So, what's up?
Doris: Well, my husband has a new job, and he works on Tuesdays now, too. And we don't have day care on Tuesdays.
Mr. Yu: So… are you asking me for Tuesdays off?
Doris: Oh no, I need to work 40 hours a week. We need the money. If possible, I want to work Saturdays.
Mr. Yu: Hmmm…I don't know right now. It's quiet then.

Grammar to Communicate 1, C, page 141

Tim: Hi, Dana. This is Tim. What's up? What are you doing?
Dana: I'm eating lunch.
Tim: Really? But it's only 11:00. Do you have lunch this early every day?
Dana: Yeah, usually. I start work early, at 7:00, so I'm always hungry at this time. And my boss goes out around 11:00, so it's always quiet. What are you doing right now?
Tim: I'm driving. I'm going to a movie.
Dana: A movie? But it's Monday! Why aren't you at work?
Tim: I have the first Monday of every month off.

Review and Challenge

Grammar, page 146

Caroline: Are you waiting for me?
Bill: Yes, I am. I need to talk to you.
Caroline: Why do you need to talk to me?
Bill: It's about Jake. Is he here today?
Caroline: Yes. He's cleaning up right now. Why?
Bill: He wants more hours, but we don't need extra workers right now.
Caroline: So tell him.
Bill: But he has a new baby. He needs the money now.
Caroline: Mason doesn't want to work on Saturdays. Maybe Jake wants to work then.
Bill: That's a good idea.

1. Why are you wearing a suit?
2. I'm going to an interview.
3. Do you want to get a new job?
4. I do housework every day.
5. My co-worker needs a day off.

Listening, A and B, page 147

Man:	Hello, Mrs. Pineiro? Please, come in and sit down.
Mrs. Pineiro:	Thank you.
Man:	So, you need a job.
Mrs. Pineiro:	Yes, that's right.
Man:	Are you looking for a part-time job or a full-time job?
Mrs. Pineiro:	A part-time job. I need to be home by 2:00 in the afternoon, when my kids come home from school.
Man:	I understand. Do you have any work experience?
Mrs. Pineiro:	Well, not really. I'm a homemaker. Sometimes I take care of my neighbor's children.
Man:	Hmmm…Do you have a high school diploma?
Mrs. Pineiro:	Yes, I do.
Man:	Great. And do you have a driver's license?
Mrs. Pineiro:	No, I don't. Is that a problem?
Man:	Well, for some jobs, you need to know how to drive.
Mrs. Pineiro:	Oh.
Man:	I'm looking at a list of available jobs, and I don't see anything…oh, wait a minute. Little Friends is looking for a daycare worker—and the hours are perfect—Monday to Friday from 8:00 to 12:00.
Mrs. Pineiro:	Oh, Little Friends is in my neighborhood.
Man:	Let's see—they want someone with a high school diploma—that's no problem. And it says you need to love children—I don't think that's a problem, right?
Mrs. Pineiro:	No, of course not! I love kids.
Man:	Hmmm…
Mrs. Pineiro:	What's wrong?
Man:	Well, they want someone with experience.
Mrs. Pineiro:	But I have a lot of experience with children! I have my own kids, and I come from a big family.

Man:	Okay, okay. You're right. That is experience. I'm writing all of the information on this form . . . OK, take this to office 255, and speak with Mrs. Anderson. She'll schedule an interview for you.
Mrs. Pineiro:	Thank you so much!
Man:	You're welcome—and good luck.
Mrs. Pineiro:	Thank you!

Unit 13: Feelings and Opinions

Listening, A and B, page 153

Man:	So, Angel, where were you last week?
Angel:	I was in Miami for my mother-in-law's 80th birthday.
Man:	Oh, so your wife has relatives in Miami.
Angel:	Yeah, her whole family is there, but we never have the time or the money to visit them. This was our first visit.
Man:	I love Miami. How was the weather?
Angel:	It was wonderful. And my mother-in-law's house is only about ten minutes from the beach. We were there every day from 9:00 to 4:00. The water was really warm.
Man:	Great. How much were the airline tickets? Were they expensive?
Angel:	No, they weren't. They were only $159 from New York.
Man:	Wow, that's cheap! Were your kids with you?
Angel:	Of course! It was spring vacation, so they were off all week.
Man:	Oh, that's right. And how were the beaches? Were they crowded?
Angel:	Yes, they were. There were people everywhere.
Man:	Yeah, Miami is always crowded on school vacation weeks.

Grammar to Communicate 3, C, page 159

Matt:	How was your day yesterday?
Bob:	It was really good.
Matt:	Where were you?
Bob:	I was at the beach.
Matt:	But it was Thursday. Why were you at the beach on Thursday?
Bob:	Thursday's my day off.
Matt:	Who was with you?
Bob:	My girlfriend and her mother.
Matt:	Her mother? Why was her mother with you?
Bob:	Her mother likes the beach.
Matt:	Oh…OK. How was the beach?

Bob: It was very nice. There weren't many people, and it was a beautiful day.

Matt: How was the water?

Bob: It was pretty cold. The water is always cold around here.

Review and Challenge

Grammar, page 160

Greg: I miss my old apartment. It was really nice.

Pearl: Where was it?

Greg: On Cherry Street in Overbrook.

Pearl: Was it big?

Greg: No, it wasn't. There were five rooms, but they were small.

Pearl: Were there a lot of stores in the neighborhood?

Greg: No, there weren't. They were all far away.

Pearl: So what was nice about the apartment?

Dictation, page 160

1. Were there a lot of people at the party?
2. I was in a bad mood yesterday.
3. My family and I weren't at home last Sunday.
4. Was the restaurant clean?
5. How was your day off?

Listening, A and B, page 161

CONVERSATION 1

Woman: So, how was it?

Man: It was terrible. I was late because of the bad weather. The manager was really angry with me. And her questions were pretty difficult.

Woman: Oh, no. That's really too bad.

Man: Yeah…

CONVERSATION 2

Man: So, how was it?

Woman: It was pretty bad. It was really long and boring. And there were a lot of people in the theater and they were very noisy. A man behind me was on his cell phone the whole time!

Man: Wow, that's rude!

Woman: It sure is!

CONVERSATION 3

Woman: How was it?

Man: It was okay. I was really worried about it at first, but it was pretty easy.

Woman: Was it long?

Man: Not really. It was only two pages.

Woman: How many questions were there?

Man: About 25.

CONVERSATION 4

Man: I'm sorry I wasn't there last night. I was sick.

Woman: I'm sorry you weren't there, too. It was a really great game.

Man: How was your son?

Woman: He was wonderful! I think he was scared at first, but he was fine after about ten minutes. I was really happy for him.

Man: How was the other team? Were they good?

Woman: Yes, they were, but our team was better!

Unit 14: Fact or Fiction?

Listening, A and B, page 165

Steve: You'll never believe what happened yesterday on Canal Street.

Marie: Oh, Steve. Is this one of your strange but true stories?

Steve: But this really happened. I promise!

Marie: OK, go ahead. I'm listening.

Steve: Well, the police don't know how, but a gorilla got out of the city zoo.

Marie: A gorilla?

Steve: Yeah, you heard me —a gorilla. First he ran into the park. Then he ran across Canal Street. All the people in their cars stopped and watched him. Then he walked to the bus stop and stood next to it. The people all screamed, but the gorilla didn't move. He just stood there.

Marie: Oh, please!

Steve: Really! Look. It's in the paper. A policeman took a picture of it.

Marie: Wow! That's really strange. Where is he now? Is he back in the zoo?

Steve: Yes, the police caught him and took him back.

Grammar to Communicate 1, B, page 166

1. I invited friends home last month.
2. I exercised the day before yesterday.
3. I washed my hair last night.
4. I started dinner at 6:00 last night.
5. I cooked yesterday morning.
6. I called my friend yesterday.
7. I watched TV yesterday afternoon.

Review and Challenge

Dictation, page 172

1. I heard an interesting story yesterday.
2. I didn't watch TV last night.
3. They didn't go to class last week.
4. We arrived late and missed the bus.
5. She didn't do her homework.

Reporter: Good morning, this is Peter Williams, with this week's strange but true news stories. First, from California and Florida, we have two great excuse stories. Do you need a day off from work? Well, here's an idea: The President of the United States visited a town in California. A woman from the town didn't go to work that day because she wanted to meet the President. But she didn't want to have a problem with her boss, so she wrote an excuse note. Then she asked the President to sign it. "He did, but he laughed first," she said. Hmmm... What do you think—Did her boss laugh when he read the note? And here's one for our young listeners: In Florida, a police officer stopped a car because there was something strange about the driver—he was only 7 years old! The boy's excuse? He didn't want to be late for school, so he took the family car. I'm Peter Williams, for this week's strange but true . . .

Unit 15: Life Stages

Listening, A and B, page 177

Jean: Hey, Paul! How are you? So what's new?

Paul: Umm . . . Where do I start? Well, first…I got married last year.

Jean: Really?

Paul: Yeah. I finally did it.

Jean: That's wonderful! Who's the lucky woman? Do I know her?

Paul: Yes, you do. You met her at Doug's wedding two summers ago. Her name's Patricia Cooper.

Jean: Oh yeah . . . Patricia. I remember her! So how long ago did you get married?

Paul: A year ago. We had a small wedding—just our relatives and a few friends.

Jean: Well, congratulations!

Paul: Thanks, but that's not all. We had a baby last month.

Jean: A baby? That was fast! What did you have—a girl or a boy?

Paul: A boy—Jason.

Jean: Oh that's great! . . . Where are you living? Did you keep your old apartment?

Paul: No, we bought a house in Malden. It needs work, but it didn't cost a lot.

Jean: Wow, that's a big change. How long did you live in Boston?

Paul: For 15 years. I miss the city, but life is really different with a wife and a baby. That's enough about me. What's up with you?

Jean: Well, I have some news too. I became a citizen in March.

Paul: Oh, that's great! And fast, too. How long ago did you come here?

Jean: I came to the United States 8 years ago.

Paul: And are you still at the same job?

Jean: No, I left that job three months ago. I got a new job at International Hotels. The money's great, and I'm a manager now.

Paul: Good for you.

Review and Challenge

Grammar, page 184

Meg: How long ago did you come to the United States?

Aida: I came here 15 years ago. My first home was in Los Angeles.

Meg: How long did you live there?

Aida: I was there for two years.

Meg: Did you work there?

Aida: No, I didn't. I took classes.

Meg: When did you move here?

Aida: Three years ago.

Dictation, page 184

1. How long ago did you get the car?
2. How long did your grandmother live?
3. We didn't visit my parents two weeks ago.
4. We waited for five hours.
5. Did you know your grandparents?

Listening, Exercise A and B, page 185

Reporter: Good afternoon, and welcome to this week's program. I'm here today with Mariela Lopez. Her new book is about the life of artist Frida Kahlo. Welcome, Ms. Lopez.

Mariela: Thank you.

Reporter: So, tell us about Frida Kahlo. Who was she, and why did you write a book about her?

Mariela: Frida Kahlo was a great Mexican painter. She was married to another great Mexican painter, Diego Rivera. I wrote about Ms. Kahlo because I love her paintings. I wanted to know more about her life.

Reporter: And what did you learn?

Mariela: Well, like many famous artists, Frida Kahlo had an interesting but very difficult life.

Reporter: Why do you say "difficult"? What happened to her?

Mariela: When Frida was 18 years old, she was in a terrible bus accident. The experience changed her life. She started to paint at that time.

Reporter: What kind of paintings did she do?

Mariela: It isn't easy to describe her paintings. They're very different from other artists' paintings. A lot of them are about the accident and her feelings about it.

Reporter:	And how did she meet Diego Rivera?
Mariela:	They met when Rivera did a painting at her high school.
Reporter:	When did they get married?
Mariela:	When Frida was 20.
Reporter:	And how long were they married?
Mariela:	Well, they were married twice.
Reporter:	Twice? How did that happen?
Mariela:	They got married for the first time in 1929. Then in 1939, they got divorced. They remarried in 1940. Frida died in 1954, so they were married for 24 years.
Reporter:	We need to take a short break, but we'll be right back with more about the life and art of Frida Kahlo.

Unit 16: Looking Ahead

Listening, A and B, page 189

Amir:	Mom, Sunil invited me to go to a soccer game with him in San Jose this weekend. Can I go?
Mom:	San Jose? That's pretty far away. Are you going to take the bus?
Amir:	No, Sunil's going to drive.
Mom:	Sunil? Does he have his driver's license?
Amir:	Of course!
Mom:	But he doesn't have a car. Whose car is he going to use?
Amir:	His mother's going to give him her car for the weekend.
Mom:	The weekend? Are you going to stay the whole weekend? When are you going to leave?
Amir:	Sunil's going to pick me up after school on Friday.
Mom:	On Friday? When are you going to do your homework?
Amir:	On Sunday night.
Mom:	What time are you going to be home on Sunday?
Amir:	Don't worry. We're not going to be late. We're going to leave San Jose in the morning.
Mom:	And where are you going to stay?
Amir:	With Sunil's uncle. He lives there.
Mom:	What's his name? Do I know him?
Amir:	Yes, Mom, you met him at Sunil's birthday party. His name is Rupesh.
Mom:	Oh, Rupesh. All right, I guess it's okay. But I want Rupesh's telephone number, please. And make sure you call me when you get there.
Amir:	Of course. Thanks, Mom. You're the best. Oh, and just one more thing…
Mom:	Don't even ask! I'm not going to give you any money.
Amir:	Ah, Mom, come on…

Review and Challenge

Grammar, page 196

Steve:	Are you going to go out tonight?
Ted:	No, I'm going to stay at home. My brother is going to come over. We're going to play cards. Do you want to come?
Steve:	No. I don't like cards.
Ted:	Are you sure? Jan and Kate are going to come over too.
Steve:	Do you mean Jan Richards? Is she going to be at your place tonight? Um…What time is the game going to start?
Ted:	Why? Are you going to come? But you don't like cards!

Dictation, page 196

1. What are you going to do this Saturday?
2. Is it going to rain tomorrow?
3. I'm not going to stay home.
4. We're going to have people over next week.
5. When is he going to come?

Listening, A and B, page 197

Natalie:	And here's Chet Kraft with the 5-day forecast. Good morning, Chet.
Chet:	Good morning, Natalie.
Natalie:	So, Chet, what do you think?? Is this beautiful weather going to stay around for the weekend?
Chet:	Well, Natalie, I'm going to give you the good news first. Today is going to be a beautiful day. There's going to be a lot of sunshine and it's going to be warm. And for the rest of your week? Not so great. Tomorrow morning it's going to be cloudy, windy, and cool. In the afternoon it's going to rain. And I'm afraid it's going to rain again on Friday.
Natalie:	Oh, Chet! Please give us some good news for the weekend!
Chet:	Well, Natalie, I think you and our listeners are going to be happy—On Saturday, it's going to be perfect beach weather sunny, no clouds, and in the 80s. It's going to be a little humid, but the water temperature is going to be perfect for swimming—about 75 degrees.
Natalie:	And what about Sunday? Are we going to have good picnic weather?
Chet:	Well, it's a little early to say, but it looks like some cool, rainy weather is going to come in from Canada late Saturday evening. So, this is my advice. If you are going to go to a picnic on Sunday, wear a sweater, and take your umbrella.

Natalie: Thanks, Chet. That was Chet Kraft, with the morning weather update. Tune in at 10:00 for more on the weekend weather.

Unit 17: Health

Listening, A and B, page 203

Glenda: Abby, yoo hooo! Where is my perfect grandson and his beautiful mother?

Abby: We're out here!

Glenda: What are you doing outside? The baby shouldn't be out! He's only a month old!

Abby: The doctor said the fresh air is good for him. And it's warm out.

Glenda: Don't get angry, Abby. I'm just thinking about my grandson's health.

Abby: I know, I'm sorry . . . So, where should we go for lunch?

Glenda: Go? Oh, I don't think we should go out for lunch.

Abby: Why not?

Glenda: Well, the baby shouldn't be around a lot of people. What if someone has a cold and coughs on him?

Abby: But that's crazy!

Glenda: Really? I don't agree. Should we call the doctor and ask?

Abby: No, we shouldn't! He told me it was OK.

Glenda: Who told you? Dr. Mendez? Why should we believe him? He's just a kid!

Abby: Dr. Mendez is 30 years old, and he's a great doctor. Now, what about lunch? Should we go to the Museum Café or Jake's Barbecue?

Review and Challenge

Grammar, page 210

Teri: The baby is sick. What should I do?

Jon: You should call the doctor.

Teri: But it's 9 P.M. The doctor's not in his office.

Jon: What's wrong with the baby?

Teri: He feels hot.

Jon: Did you take his temperature?

Teri: No, I didn't. Should we take him to the hospital?

Jon: No, we shouldn't. You should take his temperature.

Teri: I'm worried.

Jon: You shouldn't worry. He's fine.

Dictation, page 210

1. Should I go to the hospital?
2. You shouldn't take that medicine.
3. Which doctor should I call?
4. You should stay in bed.
5. What should I ask the pharmacist?

Listening, A and B, page 211

Reporter: This is Leslie Lu with the weekly health report. Of course, everyone wants to be healthy. But how? What should you eat? What shouldn't you eat? Here is some advice from the U.S. government. There are 5 important food groups. You should eat different things from each group every day. What are the groups? Grains, for example bread, cereal, rice, or pasta; vegetables; fruit; and milk products, for example, milk, cheese and yogurt. The last group is the meat group, but the name is confusing because it includes not just meat, but chicken, fish, nuts and beans too. How much should you eat every day? Well, first, let's talk about grains. Most adults should eat six ounces of whole grains, which is about 6 slices of bread, or 3 cups of rice. And think brown, not white: brown rice, not white rice, and so on. And vegetables? You should eat about 2 and ½ cups a day. That's, say, three carrots, a few leaves of spinach, and a little broccoli. Choose vegetables in dark, bright colors—for example, dark green vegetables such as spinach and orange vegetables such as carrots. And fruit? You should eat about 2 cups of fruit every day. That's two apples, for example. Try to eat fruit of many different colors—for example, a green apple, some blueberries, and an orange. What about milk? You should have about 3 cups of low-fat or fat-free milk products every day. You shouldn't drink whole milk or eat a lot of cheese because it has a lot of fat. Finally, you should eat about 5 and 1/2 ounces a day from the meat group, including meat, chicken, beans, fish, or nuts. For example, you can eat a piece of chicken, some beans, and about ten nuts. But be careful—you shouldn't eat a lot of red meat. Of course, every person is different. For more information about your age and weight group, call or write to the U.S. Department of Agriculture at . . .

Unit 18: A Place to Live

Listening, A and B, page 215

Miranda: Hello, Morgan Realty. This is Miranda.

Doug: Hi. I'm looking for a one-bedroom apartment, and I saw your ad in Sunday's paper.

Miranda: Which neighborhoods are you interested in?

Doug: Well, I don't have a car, so I need to be close to public transportation.

Miranda: Hmmm . . . Let me see. OK, I have three apartments near public transportation. The best apartment is on Mercer Street near the new theater. It's $1,300 a month.

Doug: Wow. That's expensive. How about the other two apartments? Are they cheaper than that?

Miranda:	Yes, they are, but the Mercer Street apartment is in the most convenient location.
Doug:	But I don't want to spend that much money. How much is the cheapest apartment?
Miranda:	It's $400 a month, but it's also the smallest. And it's the farthest from downtown. It's out in Brighton Park.
Doug:	Oh, that is far. How about the last apartment?
Miranda:	It's in a better location than the Brighton Park apartment. It's also larger and sunnier, and it's in a more modern building.
Doug:	How much is it?
Miranda:	It's $500 a month—oh, but wait a minute. That's with utilities, so it's really cheaper than the Brighton Park apartment.
Doug:	And where is it?
Miranda:	It's on Trenton Street, next to the post office.
Doug:	That sounds perfect. When can I see it?
Miranda:	Well, first you need to come to the office and fill out a rental application form . . .

Review and Challenge

Dictation, page 222

1. Which house is the cheapest?
2. The most comfortable chair is in the living room.
3. The bedroom is larger than the kitchen.
4. This apartment is more convenient than my apartment.
5. Is your home closer to the mall than my home?

Listening, A and B, page 223

Reporter: Good afternoon, this is Dolores Oakes reporting for World Beat. Today we are going to talk about the best cities in the world to live in. But first, what do we mean by "the best"? Of course, different people are looking for different things. In fact it is not possible to say that one city is better than another, or that one city is the best of all. Remember that as we look at what some famous magazines, newspapers, and websites are saying. Three cities are on many 10-best lists: Vienna, Austria; Zurich, Switzerland; and Vancouver, Canada. What makes these cities special? Well, they are generally safe cities. They are safer than other cities with the same number of people. They are also cleaner, and they have better public transportation than many other cities of the same size. They are also "healthy" cities—they have excellent doctors and hospitals, and clean air and water. Finally, their weather is rarely very hot or very cold. In Asia, Tokyo and Hong Kong are often on the 10 best lists. Why? Well, Tokyo has better public transportation than almost any other city in the world. In addition, it is perhaps the safest large city in the world, with a lower crime rate than other large cities. As for Hong Kong, many people think it is the most exciting city in Asia, with the best restaurants and nightlife. Many people say that Hong Kong has the best of both East and West. But before you pack your suitcase and buy your tickets to one of these cities, you should know one thing: They are all very expensive to live in. So for many of us, they are not the best, or even a good choice. Next week, we'll look at which cities are on the list of the 10 worst places to live, and why.

Unit 19: Future Changes

Listening, A and B, page 227

Betty:	So, tell me! What do you see? Will there be any changes in my life?
Woman:	Yes, there will. I see a handsome, dark man. He will get in touch with you soon.
Betty:	That sounds interesting. Will he be tall?
Woman:	No, he won't.
Betty:	Oh… Well, why will he get in touch with me?
Woman:	He will have some news for you.
Betty:	What kind of news will it be? Will it be good or bad?
Woman:	I'm sorry, but it won't be good …I also see money.
Betty:	Oh, good!
Woman:	Hmmmm…
Betty:	What's the matter?
Woman:	Well, you won't get money. You'll lose it.
Betty:	Really? How much will I lose? How will I lose it?
Woman:	I'm not sure, but it will be a lot of money.
Betty:	Oh no! I'm starting a new business, and I need every penny. Can you see anything about that? Will I succeed?
Woman:	Let me see…Uh oh…
Betty:	What? What do you see?
Woman:	I'm sorry, but it looks like there will be some problems. Wait a minute! Where are you going?
Betty:	I'm going to find a different fortune teller—one who can see some good news!

Grammar to Communicate 3, C, page 233

Carol:	Your horoscope says, "You will find the love of your life."
Seth:	When will I meet her?
Carol:	This month.
Seth:	What will her name be?
Carol:	Her name? Horoscopes don't give names!
Seth:	Where will I find her?
Carol:	It doesn't say the place. It also says you will get some news late in the month.

Seth:	What kind of news will it be?
Carol:	It will be good news.
Seth:	Who will give me the good news?
Carol:	Your new girlfriend, of course!

Review and Challenge

Grammar, page 234

Paul:	Mom, I want to move closer to my job.
Mom:	But where will you live?
Paul:	I'll find an apartment. It won't be hard.
Mom:	But who will cook for you?
Paul:	I'll cook.
Mom:	Will you visit me often?
Paul:	Yes, I will. Every weekend.
Mom:	Good. Then I'll make you food for the week, and you won't need to cook.

Dictation, page 234

1. You'll have a good time.
2. They'll get in touch with you next month.
3. She won't live alone.
4. Will prices go down?
5. When will I get a raise?

Listening, A and B, page 235

Carlos:	Good afternoon. This is Carlos Icaza with today's technology update. Reporter Rob Willis is at the Technology Fair in Tokyo, Japan. So, Rob, what new products will we see in the stores next year?
Rob:	Well, cell phones are really hot this year.
Carlos:	Cell phones? But they're old news!
Rob:	Not these cell phones. I think that very soon these cell phones will replace credit cards, bank cards, and even cash.
Carlos:	Really? How will that happen?
Rob:	Well, these cell phones are not just phones. They're also very small computers.
Carlos:	So?
Rob:	When you're in a store or restaurant, you will just hold your cell phone up to a special machine. The machine will get in touch with your bank or credit card company. If you have the money or credit in your account, you'll be able to buy anything that you want.
Carlos:	But what will happen if you lose your cell phone, or if someone steals it?
Rob:	You'll call the bank or credit card company and cancel it. You won't lose more than $50.
Carlos:	But wait a minute. You'll only be able to buy things with your cell phone in stores and

restaurants with those special machines. That won't be very convenient.

Rob:	That's true right now, but the machines will be everywhere in a year or two.
Carlos:	And how much will a cell phone like that cost?
Rob:	They won't be cheap at first—maybe $500 or so—but the prices will go down.
Carlos:	What? At $500, nobody will buy them! I don't think this idea will ever succeed.
Rob:	Well, talk to me in a year or so, and we'll see who was right.

Unit 20: Transportation

Listening, A and B, page 239

Ticket Agent:	Can I help you, Ma'am?
Mrs. Jones:	Yes, please. I'd like to buy two tickets to New York.
Ticket Agent:	Would you like round-trip or one-way tickets?
Mrs. Jones:	Round-trip, please.
Ticket Agent:	For when?
Mrs. Jones:	Excuse me?
Ticket Agent:	When would you like to travel?
Mrs. Jones:	Today. On the next train, the 2:55.
Ticket Agent:	Sorry, but the 2:55 is sold out.
Mrs. Jones:	What do you mean?
Ticket Agent:	The 2:55 is a reserved train. You have to reserve tickets in advance.
Mrs. Jones:	But we have to be in New York tonight! My son has to go to an important job interview. Could you please look again?
Ticket Agent:	Sorry, Ma'am. There are no seats on the 2:55. But there is a train at 5:30. It gets into New York at 9:30.
Mrs. Jones:	But that's three hours from now. What are we going to do here in the train station for three hours?
Man:	Lady, can you hurry up? I'm going to miss my train!
Ticket Agent:	Ma'am, do you want tickets for the 5:30 or not?
Mrs. Jones:	All right, give me two.
Ticket Agent:	That'll be one hundred and twenty dollars.

Grammar to Communicate 1, C, page 241

1. A: Excuse me? Where does the bus usually stop?
   B: You have to wait next to that sign.
2. A: I need to get off. Is the driver going to stop here?
   B: Yes. The driver has to stop at every bus stop.
3. A: Are you ready?
   B: No, I have to get some money for the bus.
4. A: Excuse me, this woman has to sit down. She's sick.

B: Oh, sure. Here—I'll help you.

5. A: Sorry, but I have to run. My bus is coming.

   B: OK, I'll talk to you later.

Grammar to Communicate 3, C, page 245

1. A: Can you open the windows, please?

   B: It's windy today. I'll turn on the air conditioner.

2. A: Could I have a round-trip ticket to Chicago, please?

   B: Sure. That'll be $35.

3. A: Can I get off at the next stop, please?

   B: No problem.

4. A: Could I have some coffee, please?

   B: Sure. Here you are.

5. A: Would you stop at the next street, please?

   B: Okay.

6. A: Would you go back to your seat, please?

   B: All right.

7. A: Could you wait a minute, please?

   B: OK.

Review and Challenge

Dictation, page 246

1. Could you open the window, please?

2. Would you like to sit here?

3. He has to get off now.

4. You have to turn off your cell phone.

5. I'd like a seat near the door, please.

Listening, A and B, page 247

Airline attendant: Would you like a newspaper or magazine?

Veronica: Could you give me a newspaper, please?

Airline attendant: Here you go . . . And for you, sir?

Tom: No, thank you . . . but I would like a bottle of water, if you don't mind.

Airline attendant: Of course, but can you wait a few minutes? We have to finish with the magazines first. Some passengers don't have any magazines yet.

Tom: Oh, that's fine. Thanks.

Veronica: Excuse me. I'm sorry to bother you, but I have to go to the restroom.

Tom: No problem.

Airline attendant: Here's your water, sir.

Tom: That was fast! Thank you very much.

Airline attendant: You're welcome.

Veronica: Excuse me again…Sorry!

Tom: Don't worry about it. Would you like a piece of gum?

Veronica: Sure, thanks.

Tom: So, are you from Las Vegas?

Veronica: Oh, no. I'm from New York. I was on vacation.

Tom: Was this your first visit to Las Vegas?

Veronica: Yes, it was.

Tom: And how did you like it?

Veronica: I loved it. Are you from Las Vegas?

Tom: No, I'm not. I'm from Los Angeles, but I'm in Las Vegas a lot. I'm Tom Lewis, by the way.

Veronica: Nice to meet you, Tom. I'm Veronica Lane. Are you going to New York on business?

Tom: Yes, I am. I have to meet a client there. I'll just be in town for a few days.

Veronica: Oh.

Tom: But I travel to New York often. My best friend lives there. In fact, I have two tickets to a basketball game tomorrow night, and we're going to go.

Veronica: Really? I love basketball! Which game?

Tom: The Knicks game at Madison Square Garden.

Veronica: I'm going to that game too! With my sister. Maybe we'll see you there!

Tom: Great!! I'd really like that . . .

Index

LIFESKILLS

Business and Employment

Consumer Education

Environment and World

Government and Community

Health and Nutrition

Interpersonal Communication

People